MICROTECHNOLOGY
THE M6809

COMPUTER SCIENCE TEXTS

COMPUTER SCIENCE TEXTS

Microtechnology
The M6809

P. J. THEWLIS
BSc, PhD, MBCS
School of Mathematics, Computing and Statistics,
Leicester Polytechnic

BLACKWELL SCIENTIFIC PUBLICATIONS
OXFORD LONDON EDINBURGH
BOSTON PALO ALTO MELBOURNE

Editorial ofices:
Osney Mead, Oxford, OX2 0EL
8 John Street, London, WC1N 2ES
23 Ainslie Place, Edinburgh, EH3 6AJ
52 Beacon Street, Boston
Massachusetts 02108, USA
744 Cowper Street, Palo Alto
California 94301, USA
107 Barry Street, Carlton
Victoria 3053, Australia

First published 1985

Phototypesetting and illustrations by
Gecko Ltd, Bicester
Printed and bound in Great Britain
at the Alden Press, Oxford

Distributed in North America by
Computer Science Press Inc.,
11 Taff Court, Rockville,
Maryland 20850, USA

British Library
Cataloguing in Publication Data

Thewlis, P.J.
Microtechnology: the M6809. —
(Computer science texts)
1. Motorola 6809 (Computer)
I. Title II. Series
001.64′04 QA76.8.M67

ISBN 0–632–01315–X

Contents

Introduction

The aim of this book is to provide the reader with a concise text describing microprocessor architecture, microcomputer design, interfacing and assembly language programming. It is intended both as a text that accompanies a lecture course for computer science and information technology students, and as a handbook for the qualified engineer who either wants to update his knowledge to include microcomputer technology, or who needs specialist and detailed information on Motorola 6809 systems.

Each section starts with a general description of the topic being covered, followed by a more detailed coverage of the M6809. The internal structure and bus configuration of an 8-bit processor are described in Chapter 1, followed by an introduction to machine code instruction sets, assemblers and assembly language programming in Chapters 2 and 3. The design of single board microcomputers is then developed through the chapters on memory systems and interfacing, and expanded to cover real-time control applications in Chapter 6.

Simple assembly language programs, illustrating the main application areas for low-level programming, are developed throughout the chapters on interfacing, real-time applications and systems' monitors. These provide examples of the driver routines, control programs and systems' firmware for the hardware given in the corresponding circuit diagrams.

The book assumes no more than a basic knowledge of computer architecture such as can be obtained from the author's *From Logic to Computers* although readers with no knowledge of electronics should read Appendix 2, 'Electrical Principles', before Chapter 6, 'Real-Time Applications'.

The author would like to give special thanks to Syntel Microsystems for providing detailed technical data on their hardware and software products, to Ferranti, Hitachi and Motorola Semiconductors for permission to incorporate information from their publications, and to colleagues Peter Messer and Ian Marshall for their support and encouragement. (Motorola reserves the right to make any changes to any products herein to improve reliability, function or design. Motorola does not assume any liability arising out of the application or use of any product or circuit described herein. No licence is conveyed under patent rights in any form.)

Chapter 1

Microprocessors and Buses

1.1 INTRODUCTION

The basic structure of any microcomputer consists of a processor connected to various support devices by three buses (series of wires), the address bus, the data bus and the control bus (Fig. 1.1).

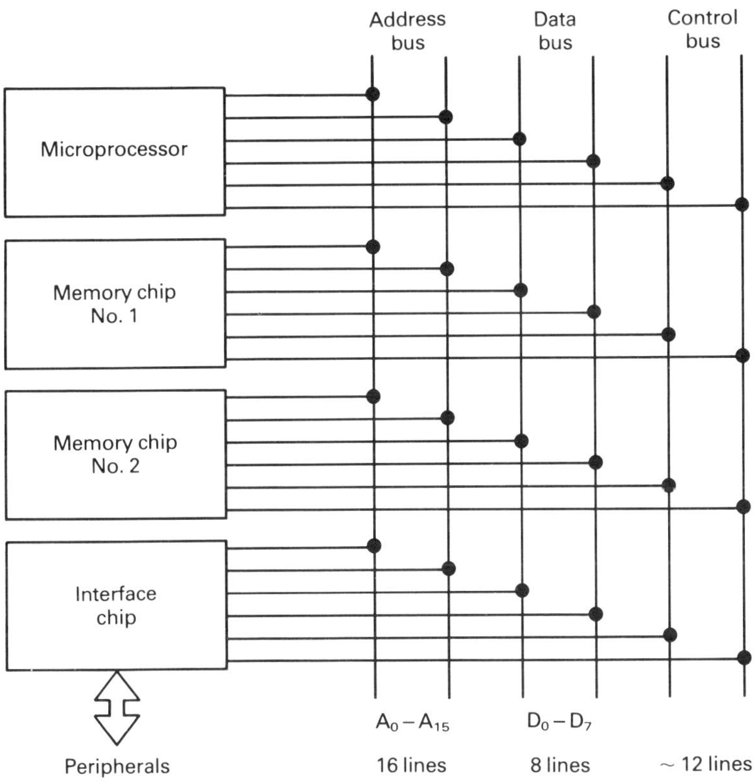

Fig. 1.1. Bus structure for an 8-bit microcomputer.

Machine code instructions operate on data held in registers within the processor, or transfer data in parallel between the registers and the support devices using the bus lines. This chapter describes a typical register set and explains the functions of the various bus lines. The

Motorola 6809 microprocessor is used as a typical example of both register sets and bus structures.

1.2 REGISTERS

Registers are the key to a central processor's architecture; the characteristics and performance of the processor being determined to a large extent by the number, length and functions of its registers. Figure 1.2 shows a typical register set for a small computer. It should be noted that a register may have its output directed to one of a number of internal buses by means of separate output enable signals.

The program counter (PC) contains the address in memory of the next instruction. An instruction cycle starts by placing the contents of the program counter onto the address bus and initiating a memory read (using the read/write control bus line) in order to get the next instruction from memory.

On a word-based system, the processor then increments the program counter so that the next instruction cycle will fetch the next instruction. On a byte-based system, where instructions may occupy more than one byte of memory, the program counter must be incremented each time a byte is read, and several cycles may be needed to read an instruction.

The instruction, which is read into the temporary buffer register (B), is then transferred to the instruction register (I), which holds that instruction until it is decoded and executed. Some processors have two instruction registers, enabling them to obtain the next instruction whilst executing the current one, a technique known as pipelining.

An accumulator (A register) is the main temporary storage or working register within the central processing unit (CPU). It is used by the programmer to hold current data or intermediate results on which the program is operating. Most processors have several accumulators.

The arithmetic and logical unit is the hardware which, as its name implies, performs both arithmetic and logical operations on data presented to it from either the temporary register (R) or the internal arithmetic bus, or both. Typically it can add the contents of a memory location which has just been read into the buffer register (B) to the accumulator (A) by:

1 transferring the contents of the accumulator to the temporary register (R),

2 gating the contents of the buffer register (B) onto the internal parallel arithmetic bus,

3 performing the addition,

4 returning the result to the accumulator via the common bus.

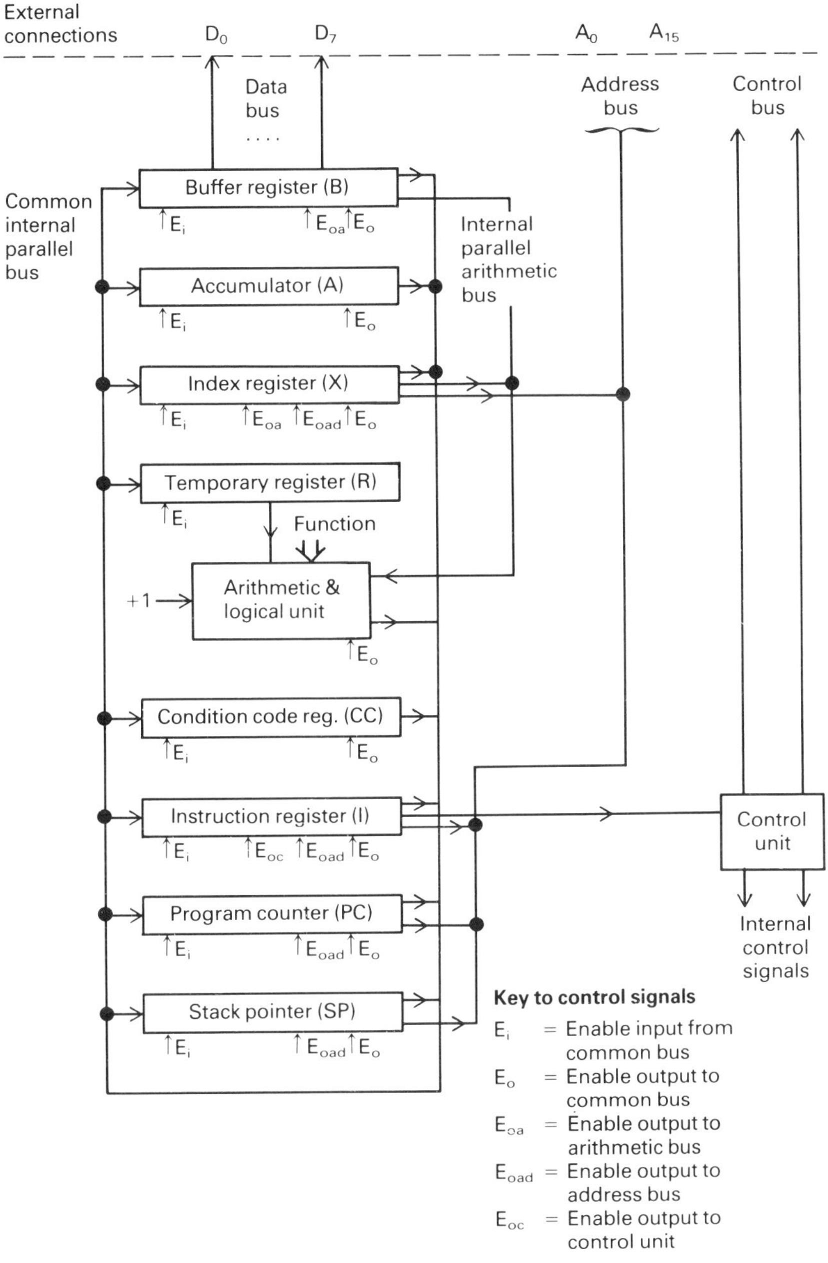

Fig. 1.2. Schematic diagram for a simple 8-bit computer.

One of the results of operations performed by the processor may be to set flags. For example the addition of two numbers may result in overflow (the result being too large to store within the register length of the machine), and this event can be recorded by a single bit (a flag) being set in the condition code register. Typical of the flags in condition code registers are:

1 Overflow—a 1 indicating that the last operation resulted in two's complement overflow.

2 Carry—a 1 indicating that the last operation generated a carry from the most significant bit.

3 Zero—a 1 indicating that the result of the last operation was zero.

4 Sign—a 1 indicating that the most significant bit of the result of the last operation was 1, i.e. the result was a negative two's complement number.

5 Half Carry—a 1 indicating that the last operation resulted in a carry from the lower half of the byte to the upper half of the byte (from the least significant nibble to the most significant nibble).

6 Inhibit Interrupts—a 1 inhibiting interrupts, i.e. preventing external events from interrupting the program currently being executed.

These flags form the basis of all decision-making within a computer system, but the number and type of flags vary from computer to computer.

The index register is used during memory addressing. There are various methods that the programmer can use to specify the address in memory of the data on which an instruction is to operate. One of these methods is indexed addressing, in which the contents of the index register are added to the address specified in the instruction to give the effective address (the true address of the data). Some addressing modes automatically increment or decrement this register, a function known as auto-increment or auto-decrement. Many central processors have more than one index register.

Computers use stacks to handle data in an organized way. A stack is a Last In First Out queue (LIFO), held in memory. Items are added to the top of the stack by a Push operation and removed from it by a Pull or Pop operation.

A computer's stack is often implemented in Random Access Memory (RAM) and it would be very wasteful of processor time to move the entire contents of the stack during each Push or Pull operation as depicted in Fig. 1.3. To overcome this problem a register called the stack pointer is used. This register contains the address of the top of the stack, and the stack is allowed to grow downwards in memory (Fig. 1.4). Note: on some processors the stack pointer points to the first free location in the stack, rather than the last value pushed onto it.

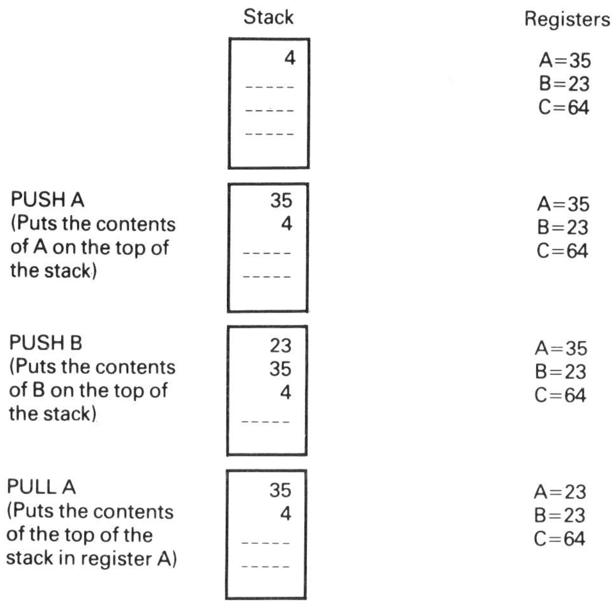

Fig. 1.3. A Last In First Out queue (LIFO).

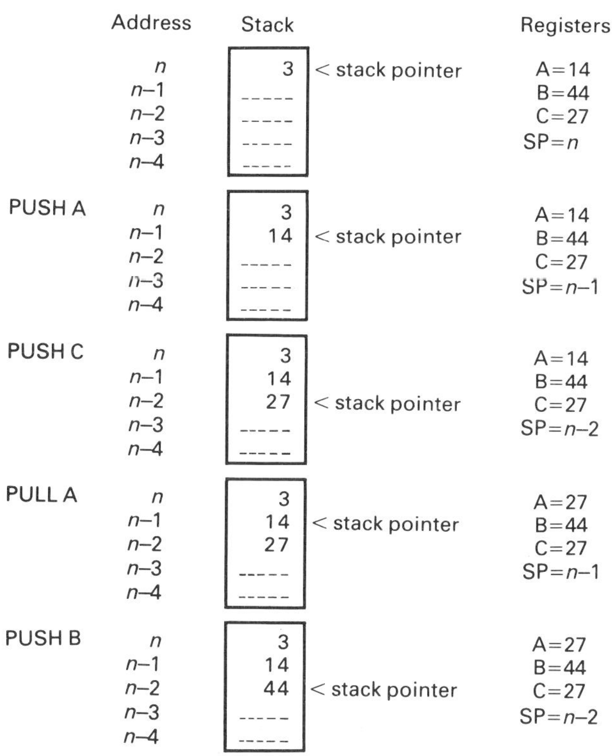

Fig. 1.4. A stack.

Typical uses of the stack are:

1 to store the contents of registers, thus allowing the registers to be used for some other purpose,

2 for parameter passing between programs and subroutines,

3 for holding subroutine return addresses for use with return from subroutine instructions (see Chapter 2).

Note that some implementations allow stacks to grow upwards, by incrementing the stack pointer during a Push operation rather than by decrementing it.

1.3 THE M6809 REGISTERS

Figures 1.5 and 1.6 show the hardware configuration and the programmer's model for the M6809 processor chip.

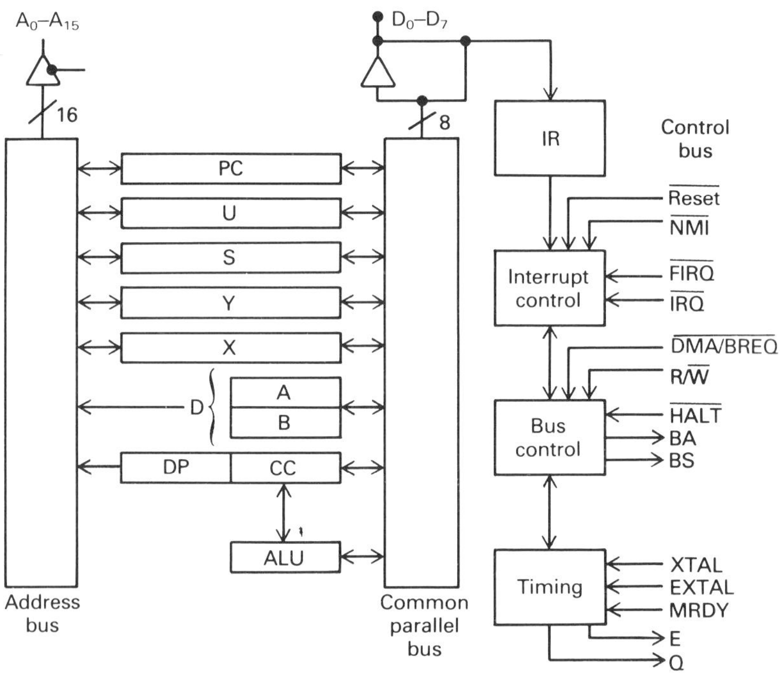

Fig. 1.5. Hardware configuration of the M6809.

The internal structure of this chip is similar to the general one given in Fig. 1.2, although the layout shown in Fig. 1.5 also details the external bus connections, which are described fully in Section 1.9.

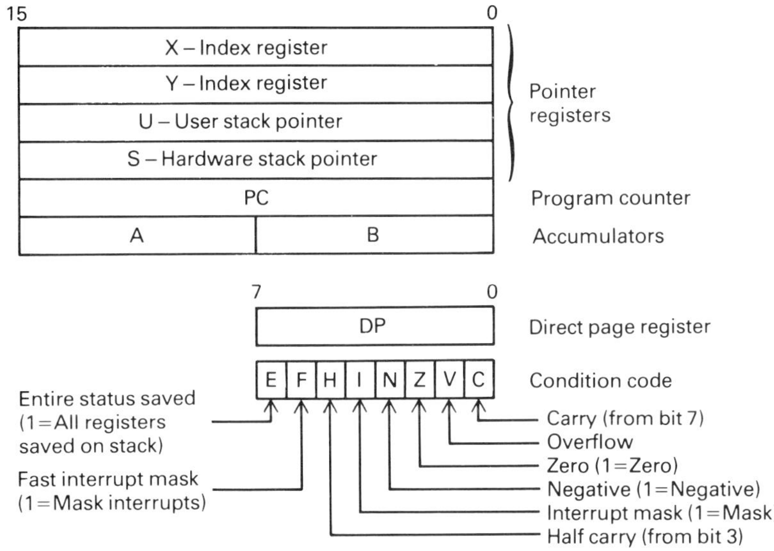

Fig. 1.6. The M6809 programmer's model.

The programmer's model shown in Fig. 1.6 specifies the register set and flags available to the programmer and provides a simplified model for use during program design.

Accumulators (A&B)

These are general-purpose registers which can be used separately or may be combined when they are referred to as D.

Typical instructions are given in Fig. 1.7.

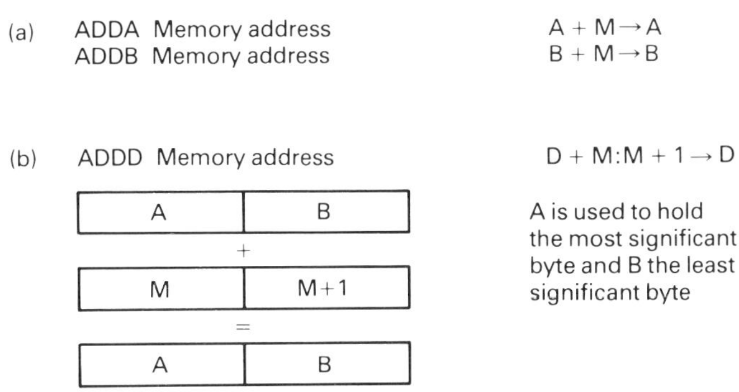

Fig. 1.7 (a) Typical instructions, or (b) when accumulators are combined.

Index registers (X&Y)

The 16-bit address held in either of these registers takes part in the calculation of the effective address. During some instructions, the contents of the specified index register may be automatically incremented or decremented. All of the pointer registers may be used as index registers.

Hardware stack pointer (S)

The hardware stack pointer is used automatically by the processor during subroutine calls and interrupts. The hardware stack pointer points to the top of the system stack. The stack grows downwards so the first register pushed onto the stack will end up at the highest address and the first register pulled will come from the lowest address.

User stack pointer (U)

The user stack pointer is controlled exclusively by the programmer thus allowing parameters to be passed to and from subroutines.

Program counter (PC)

The program counter points at the address of the next instruction to be executed by the processor.

Condition code register (CC)

The condition code register contains eight flags which define the state of the processor at any time.

Direct page register (DP)

The contents of this eight bit register appear on the higher address line A_8 to A_{15} during direct addressing, thus allowing direct addressing to be used at any place in memory (64K bytes).

1.4 MICROPROCESSOR BUS CONNECTIONS

In any microcomputer system, the microprocessor chip is connected to its support devices by the data, address and control buses. On an 8-bit microcomputer the data bus is, by definition, 8 lines wide, whilst on a 16-bit system it is 16 lines wide. The width of the address bus determines the number of bytes that can be addressed. An 8-bit microprocessor will typically have 16 address lines giving it an addressing capability of 64K bytes (Fig. 1.8).

Most 8-bit microprocessors are manufactured in 40-pin Dual In Line (DIL) packages and the remaining 16 pins are used for power supplies and control signals. The following sections describe some of the functions that dictate the use of these pins and Section 1.9 describes in detail the pin connections for the M6809 processor chip.

1.5 POWER SUPPLIES

Most modern microprocessors need only a single 5 volt power supply and a ground connection. If the processor chip includes serial interface circuitry then +12 volt and −12 volt supplies will also be needed (see Chapter 5).

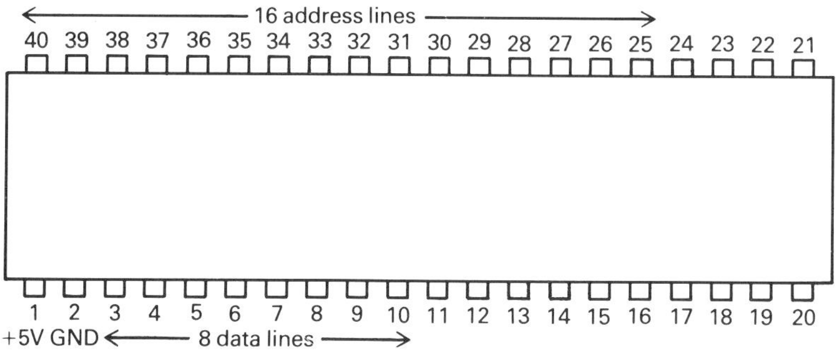

Fig. 1.8. An 8-bit microprocessor chip.

1.6 CLOCK SIGNALS

Operations within a microprocessor are controlled by a clock signal usually designated ϕ. This signal oscillates between two levels (0 and 1) giving two states and two edges on which to initiate operations within the microprocessor (Fig. 1.9).

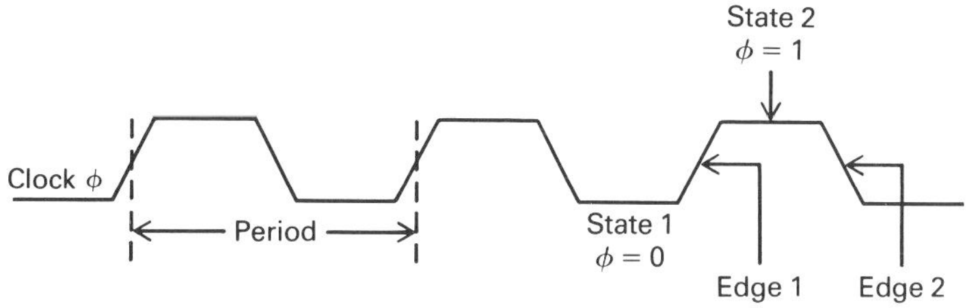

Fig. 1.9. A single-phase clock.

On more complex microprocessors the clock may consist of a more complex interaction of signals. Figure 1.10 shows a dual-phase clock which generates four edges and three different states on which to initiate operations.

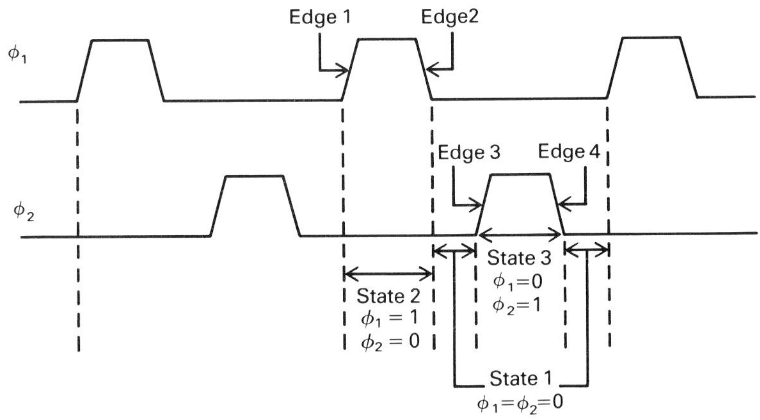

Fig. 1.10. A dual-phase clock.

Some support devices in a microcomputer system require synchronization with the processor, and this is achieved by supplying them with the processor clock signal, or a signal derived from it.

The circuitry that generates the clock signal bases its frequency on the resonant frequency of a crystal. Early microprocessors used external circuitry to generate the clock signal for both the processor and synchronous support devices (Fig. 1.11).

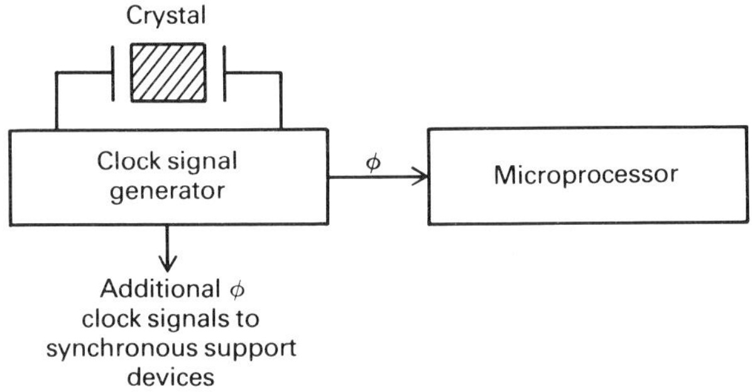

Fig. 1.11. External clock signal generator.

More recent processors have used on-chip logic, the crystal being connected across two processor pins. A further pin has then to be used as an output clock signal for any synchronous support devices (Fig. 1.12).

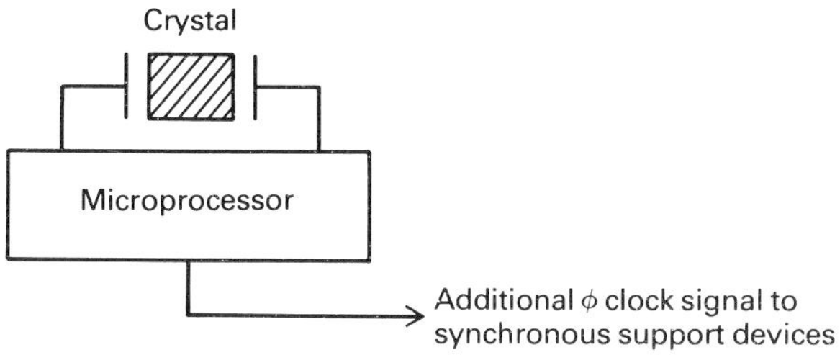

Fig. 1.12. On-chip clock logic.

A microprocessor that generates its own clock signal will usually give the option of inputting an external clock to allow two or more microprocessors in one logic system to be driven by the same clock (i.e. in phase) (Fig. 1.13).

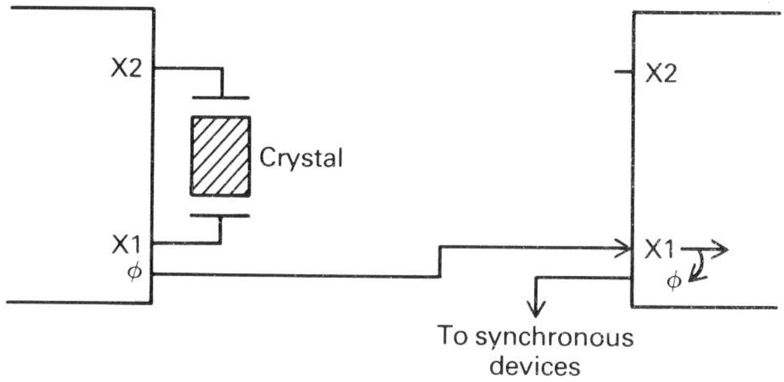

Fig. 1.13. Clock signals on a multi-microprocessor system.

The pin connections for an 8-bit microprocessor with on-chip clock logic is shown in Fig. 1.14.

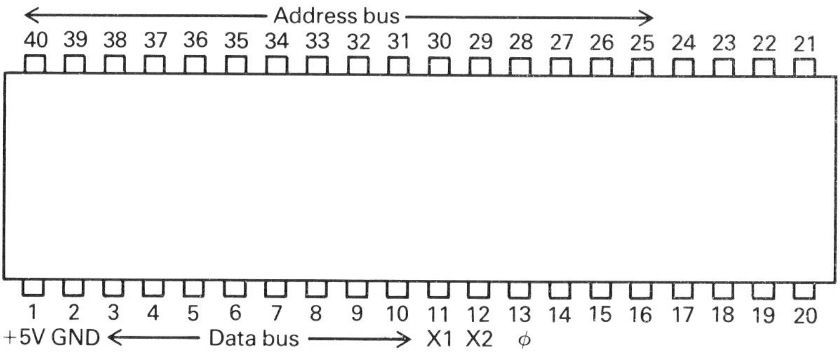

Fig. 1.14. An 8-bit microprocessor with on-chip clock logic.

1.7 MEMORY TRANSFERS

There are various types of memory chips, all of which are connected to the microprocessor via the data, address and control buses.

Random Access Memory (RAM) chips, which can have data both read from and written to them, require the processor to have a control bus line (R/W) to signal the direction of the transfer. The speed of response of memory chips varies from manufacturer to manufacturer. To enable slow memories to be used, a control bus line (MRDY or WAIT) is often provided to allow a memory chip either to stretch the processor's clock cycle or add further cycles, thus increasing its data access time (Fig. 1.15).

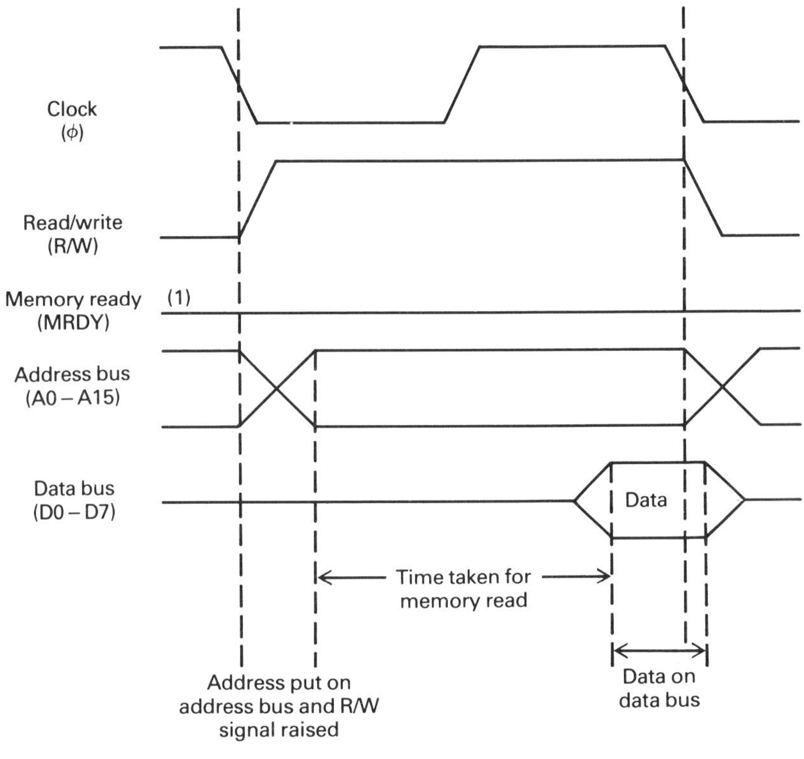

Fig. 1.15. A memory read.

Figure 1.16 shows the timing diagram for a memory read in which the MRDY signal is used to stretch the processor's clock cycle.

The pin connections for the 8-bit microprocessor including the control signals for memory transfers are shown in Fig. 1.17.

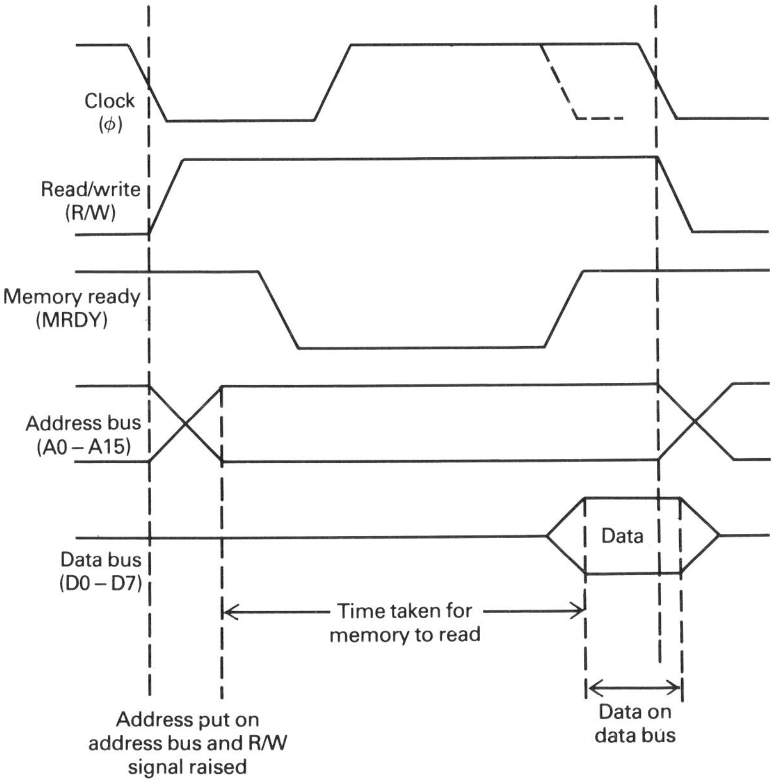

Fig. 1.16. Memory read using MRDY to stretch the clock signal.

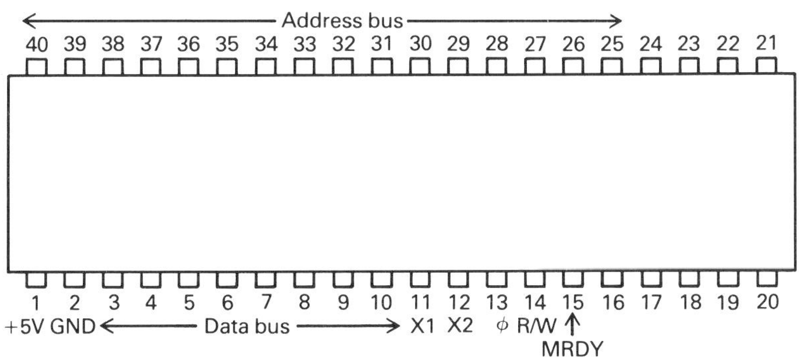

Fig. 1.17. An 8-bit microprocessor with memory timing signals.

1.8 INPUT/OUTPUT

There are three basic types of input/output systems:

1 polling
2 interrupt
3 direct memory access

In all three methods the peripheral is connected to the processor's address, data and control buses by means of an interface (input/output port). This handles either serial or parallel data transfers to or from the peripheral depending on the type of device being driven. The major differences between the three methods are in the way that the processor determines if an input/output transfer is to take place and in the way in which those transfers are controlled.

Polling

In polling or programmed input/output, all transfers to and from the interface are performed under software control. The interface contains a control or status register, one bit of which acts as a status flag. This indicates that the interface is available either to receive data from the processor for output to the peripheral, or that it has data input from the peripheral ready for transfer to the processor. The status or device-ready flags in each of the interfaces on the system are periodically checked by software, or polled, to see if a peripheral requires servicing.

```
Polling Routine: Entered periodically
    begin
        if A requesting then call service routine for
                                    device A
        if B requesting then call service routine for
                                    device B
        if C requesting then call service routine for
                                    device C
    end
```

Fig. 1.18. Polling routine.

The sequence in which the devices are polled determines their priority. In the example shown in Fig. 1.18, if device A is requesting it will always be dealt with before either device B or device C.

Polling requires minimal hardware but at the expense of using processor time to check the interfaces periodically. It is also slow, since all ports have to be checked whether or not they are in use, and many ports may be inspected before the one that actually requires servicing is tested.

Interrupts

In interrupt-driven input/output (Fig. 1.19), the device-ready flag in the interface status or control register is connected to a pin on the chip. This pin is then connected via a control bus line to an interrupt pin on the processor. The processor checks for interrupts at the end of each instruction, and if one is present services it, or if not, executes the next instruction in the current program.

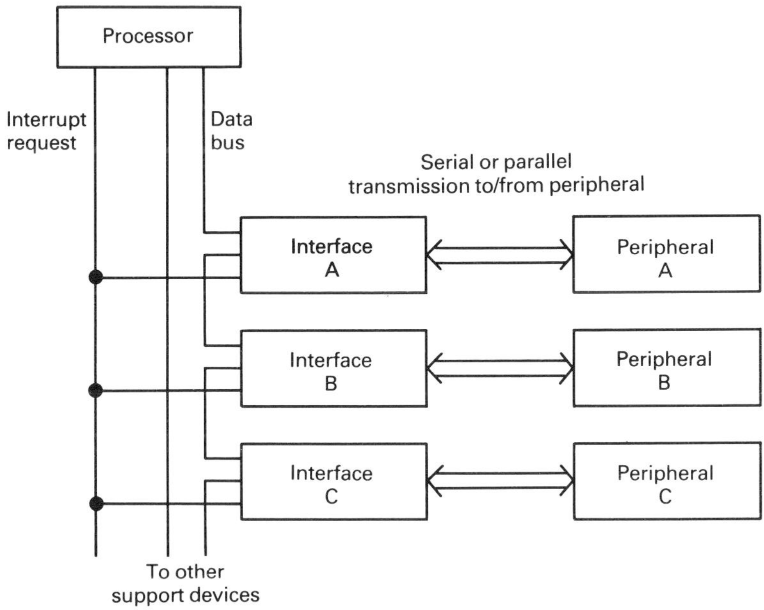

Fig. 1.19. A simple interrupt system.

In a simple interrupt system, once the processor has received an interrupt request it jumps to a program known as the Interrupt Service Routine (Fig. 1.20), automatically pushing the contents of the processor registers onto the system stack. The registers are then available for use in the interrupt service routine. At the end of this routine, the registers are automatically restored to their original values (the values that existed prior to the interrupt) by pulling their contents from the system stack. The interrupted program is then resumed from the point at which it was interrupted. The start address of the interrupt service routine is automatically loaded into the program counter from reserved memory addresses known as the interrupt vector.

The first function of the interrupt service routine is to identify the device that caused the interrupt and to branch to the interrupt routine

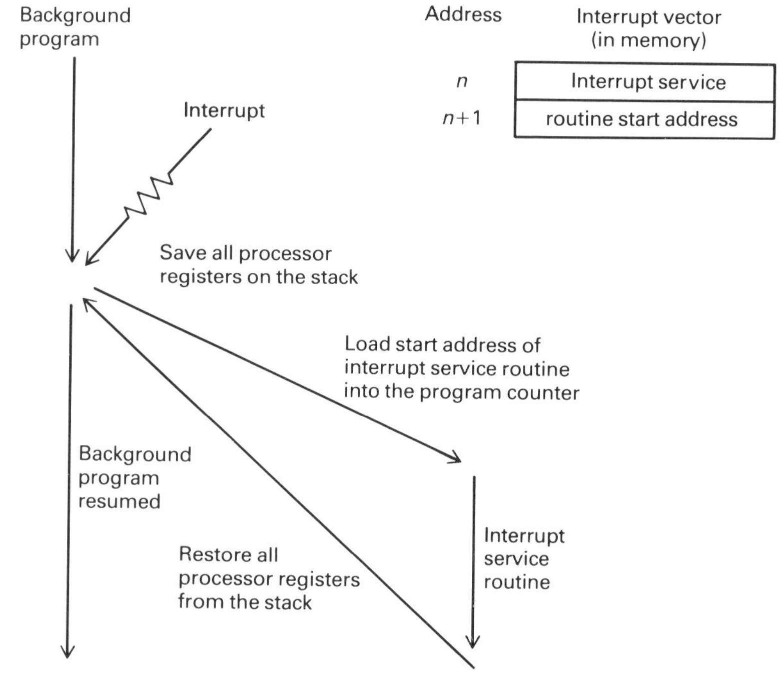

Fig. 1.20. Saving and restoring registers.

(device handler) for that peripheral. Whilst identifying the interrupting device, the interrupt service routine must not itself be interrupted as this would cause it to be restarted and the first interrupt to be lost. To prevent this happening, a mask is set to inhibit (disable) interrupts whilst the interrupting device is identified and the appropriate interrupt routine entered. The mask is cleared by the programmer immediately after entry to the device handler to make further interrupts possible.

There are several ways of identifying the interrupting device, the three most common being the use of polling, daisy chains or interrupt vectors supplied by an interrupt controller.

Once the processor has received an interrupt, it can, by software, poll the status flags of each interface to determine which caused the interrupt and then transfer control to the appropriate interrupt routine. The order of polling determines the priority, i.e. priority is determined by software.

Daisy chains provide an alternative method of identifying the interrupting device. After preserving registers, the processor generates an interrupt acknowledge signal on a control line which is gated to each interface in turn (Fig. 1.21).

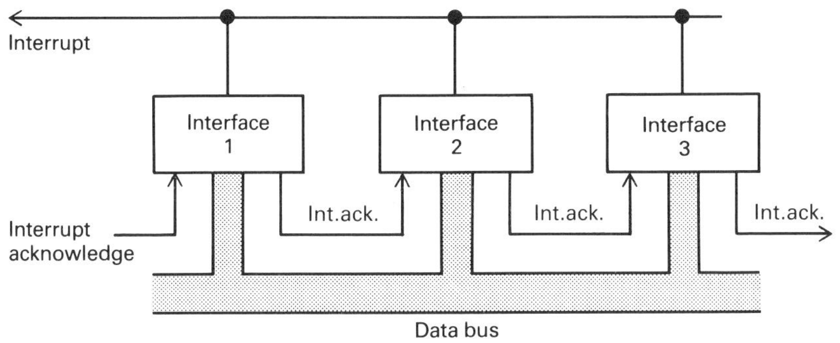

Fig. 1.21. Daisy chains.

If interface 1 generated the interrupt, it places its identification number on the data bus, and if not, passes the interrupt acknowledge signal to the next interface on the chain which responds in the same way. The processor then reads the data bus to identify the interrupting device and calls the correct interrupt routine.

The fastest method of responding to interrupts involves the interface or device controller supplying the identity of the interrupting device, or better still the start address of the interrupt routine for that device. The hardware must be capable of handling multiple interrupts and therefore of determining priority. Figure 1.22 shows the concept of a priority interrupt controller (PIC).

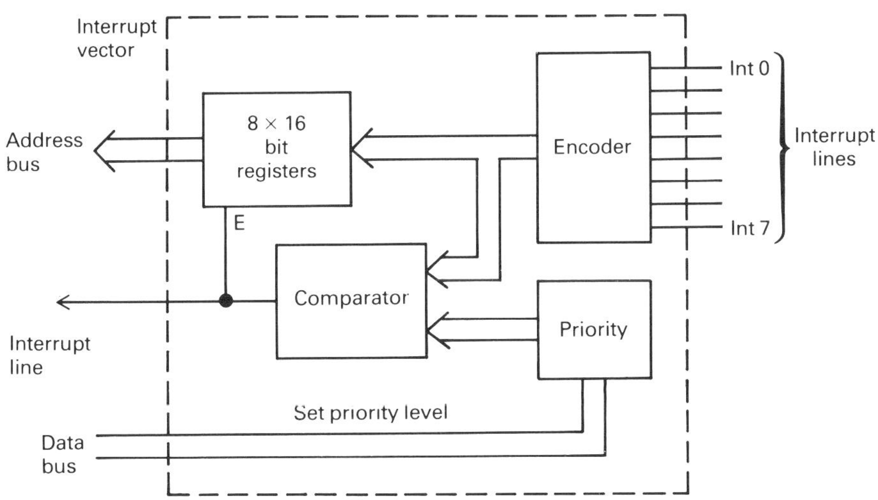

Fig. 1.22. Priority interrupt controller.

The user sets the priority level in the PIC after which only higher priority interrupts will affect the processor. When one of these occurs, the contents of the appropriate 16-bit register are gated onto the address bus, providing the processor with the start address of the device interrupt routine. By saving registers on the stack and moving the contents of the address bus to the program counter, the processor transfers control to the start of the device's interrupt routine. The registers in the PIC are loaded by the user when initializing the system and take the place of the interrupt vector held in reserved memory. This system provides a totally hardware method for handling interrupts and is extremely fast.

The type of interrupt described above is known as a maskable interrupt. On many systems, however, it is necessary to have an interrupt that can take precedence over all others. This is known as a non-maskable interrupt and is generated on a separate input line to the processor. The service routine for non-maskable interrupts is entered in a similar way to that for maskable interrupts, the start address being loaded into the program counter from reserved memory locations known as the non-maskable interrupt vector.

Figure 1.23 shows the pin connections for the 8-bit microprocessor including maskable (INT) and non-maskable (NMI) interrupts and an interrupt acknowledge signal (ACK).

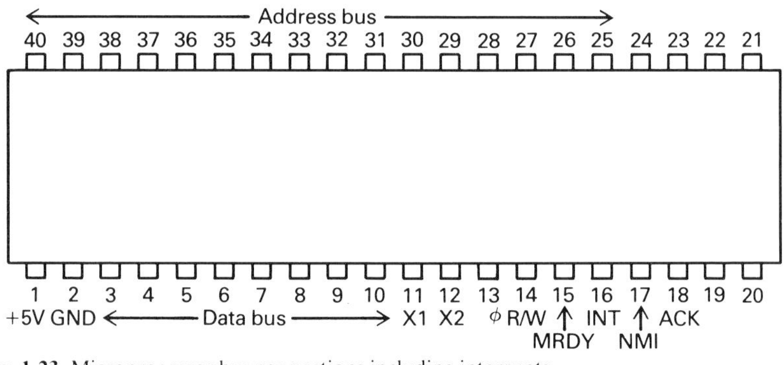

Fig. 1.23. Microprocessor bus connections including interrupts.

Direct memory access

Interrupts guarantee the fastest possible response to an input/output device. The service to the device is, however, performed by software that may not be fast enough for processes involving a large number of fast memory transfers (e.g. transfers to or from disk). To speed up the process, the software controller is replaced by a hardware Direct Memory Access Controller (DMAC), which takes control of the data, address and control buses while performing memory transfers. The DMAC must use the buses whilst they are not being used by the processor, and there are several different methods employed in direct memory access systems. The simplest is to suspend the processor for the period during which the DMAC has control of the buses. A device requesting a transfer sends an interrupt to the DMAC which generates a signal on the processor's DMA control line. On completion of the current instruction, the processor is put in dormant state (suspended) for a predefined time and the data and address buses floated. A DMA acknowledge signal is sent, via the control bus, to the DMAC which then uses the buses to send addresses and data to the memory.

DMACs contain registers that have their contents set by software from the processor and that define the addresses for the transfers. They also contain sequencing mechanisms for block transfers. For example, an 8-bit counter could be used to transfer 256-byte blocks. The counter, initially at zero, is decremented after each transfer and the transfer is complete only when it has returned to zero.

Many processors are capable of performing all three types of input/output and are provided with the necessary control pins as shown in Fig. 1.24.

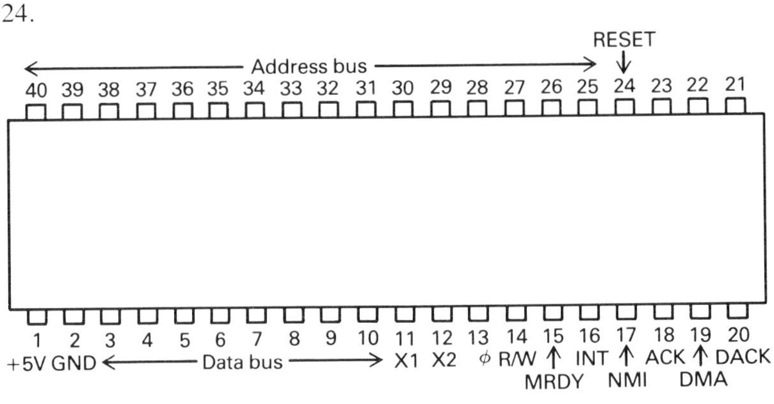

Fig. 1.24. Microprocessor bus connections including DMA and RESET.

1.9 SYSTEM RESET

Once a microprocessor has been connected to its power supply and clock, it will start executing instructions from whatever address is pointed to by its program counter. Most microcomputers on power up (and indeed at other times when no other course of action is possible), execute a program known as the system's monitor. This program, which resides in read only memory, is part of the architecture of the microcomputer and is used to initialize the system by setting up stack pointers and initializing interfaces. It then allows the user to enter simple commands. The roles and structure of systems' monitors vary from computer to computer and are discussed fully in Chapter 7.

The basic microcomputer hardware must, however, include a facility known as the system's reset which loads the start address of the system's monitor (or of some equivalent start-up routine) into the program counter. A reset pin provides this facility, loading the contents of a vector (the reset vector) into the program counter. The vector contains the start address of the monitor or start-up routine, which is then automatically entered if the reset pin goes high. This occurs either when the machine is powered up or when the reset button is pushed.

The remaining three pins cannot be generally categorized as their functions vary from processor to processor.

1.10 MOTOROLA M6809 PIN ASSIGNMENTS

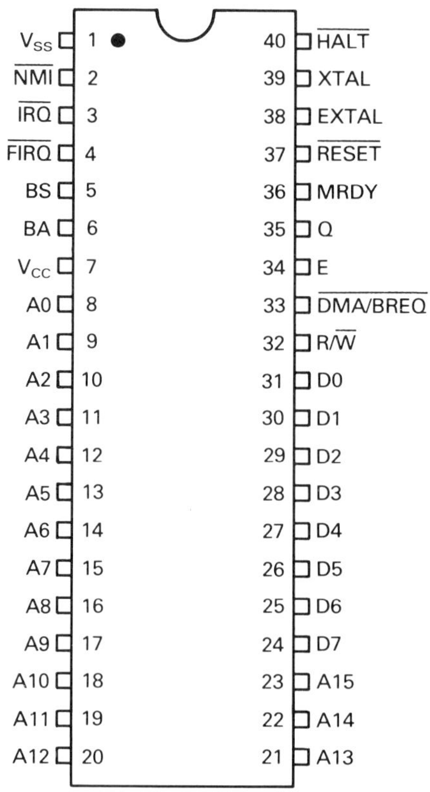

Fig. 1.25. The M6809 pin assignments.

Figure 1.25 shows the pin assignments for the M6809 microprocessor, the functions of which can be categorized into the following areas.

Power supply

Pin 1, V_{SS}, is 0 volts or ground; pin 7, V_{CC}, is the +5 volts supply.

Clock

The M6809 processor contains an internal clock (Fig. 1.26) which is triggered by connecting an external crystal between the XTAL (39) and EXTAL (38) pins.

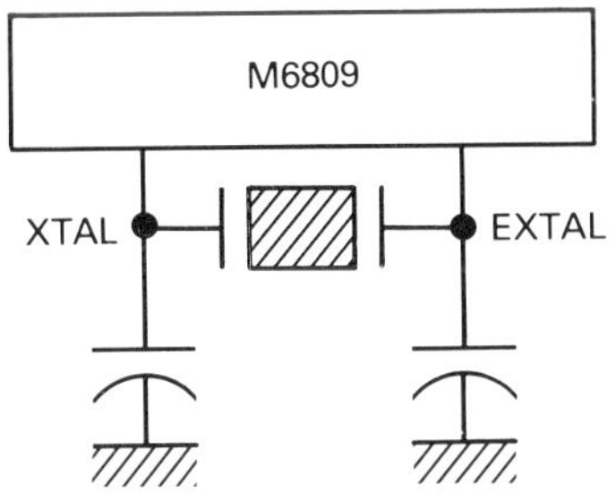

Fig. 1.26. M6809 clock.

In this mode the output pin E (34) gives a synchronizing signal which is used as the system's clock for support chips in the system. A further signal, the Quadrature output Q (35), is available to signal that the address and data are stable. Both E and Q are at a quarter of the crystal frequency.

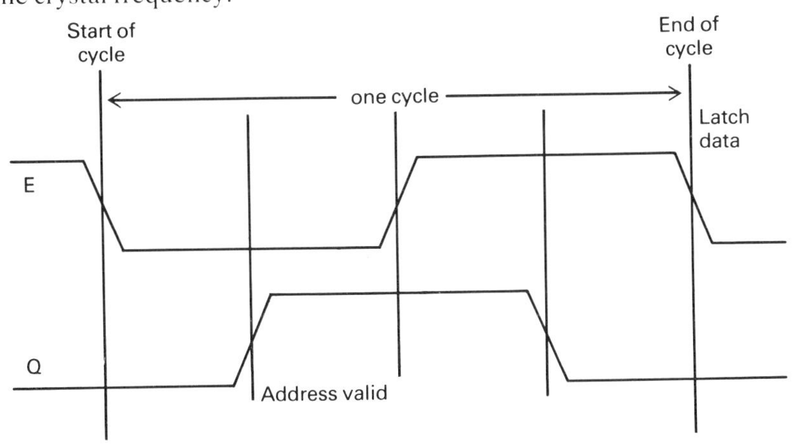

Fig. 1.27. M6809 clock cycle.

Addresses from the processor are valid on the leading edge of Q and data is latched on the falling edge of E (Fig. 1.27).

Address bus

Pins 8 – 23 are the 16 address bus lines A0 – A15 respectively.

Data bus

Pins 31 – 24 are the 8-bit data bus lines D0 – D7 respectively.

Data transfer and timing

$R/\overline{W}$	This output (pin 32) indicates the direction of transfer on the data bus. A low (0) indicates that the processor is writing data to the bus, and a high (1) that it is reading from it. The $R/\overline{W}$ signal is valid on the rising edge of Q.
MRDY	A low on this input (pin 36) stretches the E and Q clock signals to enable the processor to interface with slow memory chips.

Interrupts

There are three interrupt pins on the M6809 processor.

$\overline{\text{NMI}}$	A negative transition on this input pin (2) initiates an interrupt sequence in which the entire state of the machine is saved. The NMI vector addresses are FFFC and FFFD. After reset, an NMI will not be recognized until after the hardware stack pointer has been loaded.
$\overline{\text{IRQ}}$	The occurence of a low (0) on this pin (3) initiates an interrupt request provided that the interrupt mask bit in the condition code register is clear. All registers are pushed onto the hardware stack and the routine pointed to by the IRQ vector entered. The vector addresses are FFF8 and FFF9.
$\overline{\text{FIRQ}}$	The M6809 has a third interrupt line, the Fast Interrupt Request (pin 4). If the FIRQ mask bit (F) in the condition code register is clear, a low-level input on this pin will initiate an interrupt sequence in which only the condition code register and the program counter are stored on the hardware stack. The FIRQ interrupt

takes priority over the standard interrupt request. The FIRQ interrupt vector addresses are FFF6 and FFF7.

Suspension of processor and aquisition of MPU buses

$\overline{\text{HALT}}$ A low-level input (0) on this pin stops the processor after completion of the current instruction and places the buses in high impedance state. The processor stays in this state without losing data until the pin again goes high.

$\overline{\text{DMA/BREQ}}$ A low-level input on this pin causes the processor to be suspended at the end of the current instruction for up to 15 bus cycles or until the pin again goes high. The processor acknowledges this request by setting BA and BS high.

System reset

$\overline{\text{RESET}}$ A low-level input for greater than one bus cycle resets the CPU. The RESET vector addresses are FFFE and FFFF.

Microprocessor state definition

Two output pins, Bus Available (BA) and Bus Status (BS), are used to define the current state of the microprocessor (Fig. 1.28).

BA	BS	MPU state definition
0	0	Processor running normally
0	1	Interrupt or reset acknowledge. This state exists during the two memory read cycles taken to fetch the interrupt vector.
1	0	SYNC acknowledge is output whilst the processor is waiting for external synchronization on an interrupt line. (The SYNC instruction halts the processor until an interrupt is received. Any interrupt will restart the processor.)
1	1	Processor halted and/or buses available

Fig. 1.28. MPU state definition.

BA A high-level output on this line signals that the buses are available (bus outputs from the processor are in high impedance state) for the next cycle. After a high to low transition of this output there is a further dead cycle before the MPU reacquires the buses.

BS — This output when decoded in conjunction with the BA output specifies the MPU state (Fig. 1.28).

The M6809E microprocessor

A second version of this chip is the M6809E which has external clock inputs E and Q. Figure 1.29 shows the pin assignments for this processor.

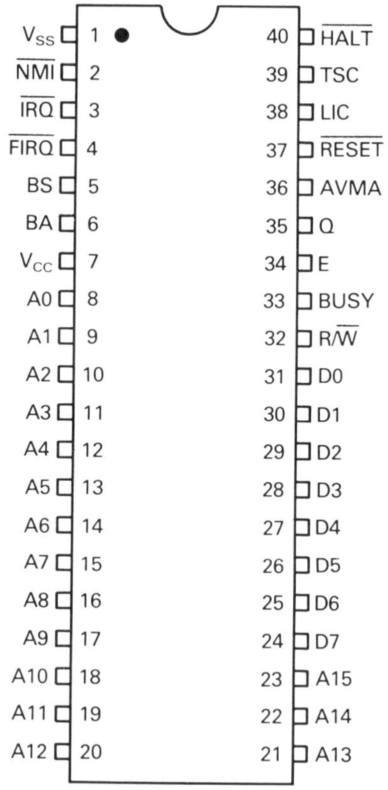

Fig. 1.29. Pin assignments for the M6809E.

Pin 39 is used as the TSC (Tri-State Control) input which forces the address, data and R/W buffers to go to high impedance state for DMA or memory refresh.

The LIC (Last Instruction Cycle) output is high during the last cycle of an instruction.

The BUSY signal indicates that the processor is performing functions that may change flags, and is used in multiprocessor applications to prevent flags that are being modified by one processor from being accessed by another at the same time.

The AVMA (Advanced Valid Memory Address) output is used to signify that the processor will use the buses in the following cycle and is used to allow efficient bus sharing in multiprocessor systems.

Chapter 2

Machine Code Instruction Sets

2.1 INTRODUCTION

This chapter describes basic instruction formats, addressing modes and the categories of instructions which go into making up a machine code instruction set. The M6809 is used to illustrate a typical instruction set. The assembly code and hexadecimal representation of machine code instructions are used to illustrate the categories of instructions and show how they are stored in memory.

2.2 INSTRUCTION FORMATS

Computers execute instructions which are stored in memory as a binary pattern. This pattern determines:

1 the operation to be performed,
2 the sources of data (called the operands), and
3 the destination of the result.

Some instructions, such as Add, Subtract or Multiply require two operands, whilst others like Increment or Rotate need only one (Fig. 2.1).

Operation code	Operand 1	Operand 2	Address of result
ADD	the contents of address 130	to the contents of address 153	& store the result at address 256
INCREMENT	the contents of address 130		& store the result at address 130

Fig. 2.1. General instruction format.

The binary pattern representing the instruction must therefore contain coded binary specifying:

1 the operation code,
2 the address of operand 1,
3 the address of operand 2, and
4 the address of the result.

A computer with a 16-bit address bus and 256 different instructions using separate fields for each of these elements would require 56 bits to store each instruction. Hence ways of reducing instruction lengths have to be found.

There are three basic methods for reducing instruction lengths:

1 making the address of one of the operands and the result implicit rather than explicit (implicit addresses may be registers or memory locations addressed through registers);

2 making the address of the result the same as that of one of the operands;

3 limiting addresses to be registers or the contents of registers.

Instructions in computers with short word lengths, like the Motorola 6809, generally use a register as one operand and as the address of the result. This gives rise to an instruction format containing an operation and only one operand or address.

Operation code	Operand or address
ADD to register A	the contents of address 165

Fig. 2.2. A one-address instruction.

The operation (op.) code itself may specify the register to be used, as shown in Fig. 2.2 or a separate field may be included for this purpose. Whilst on machines with long word lengths each instruction may be stored in a single word and fetched from memory with a single read, on 8-bit microprocessors a number of bytes may be used to store an instruction. The most common forms of instruction formats are described below.

Single-byte instructions

A single-byte instruction is one in which no operand field is required.

Op. code (8 bits)	Byte 1

Examples

Processor	Assembly code	Operation	Hexadecimal
Intel 8080	MOV A,B	B → A	78
M 6800	CLRA	0 → A	4F
M 6809	INCA	A + 1 → A	4C

Fig. 2.3. Single-byte instructions.

Two-byte instructions

A 2-byte instruction is one in which the byte following the operation contains either data or an address.

Op. code (8 bits)	Byte 1
Data or address (8 bits)	Byte 2

Examples:

Processor	Assembly code	Operation	Hexadecimal
Intel 8080	MVI D,data	data → D	16 data
M6800	ADDA address	A+(address) → A	9B address
M6809	ADDA data	A + data → A	8B data

Fig. 2.4. Two-byte instructions.

Three-byte instructions

In a 3-byte instruction, the two bytes following the operation code contain either a 16-bit data item or a 16-bit address.

Operation code	Byte 1
Data or address (8 bits)	Byte 2
Data or address (8 bits)	Byte 3

Processor	Assembly code	Operation	Hexadecimal
Intel 8080	LDA address	A ←(byte 3, byte 2)	3A low order address high order address
M6800	STAA address	A →(byte 2, byte 3)	B7 high order address
M6809	STA address	A →(byte 2, byte 3)	low order address

Fig. 2.5. Three-byte instructions.

Post-byte

Some operation codes on some microprocessors have to be followed by a byte that defines the register or set of registers to be used by the instruction. This is called the post-byte, and in addition to specifying the register(s) it may also define an operation to be performed on it (them). A post-byte may be used with any of the above formats giving 2-, 3- and 4-byte formats respectively.

Operation code
Post-byte

Operation code
Post-byte
Data or address

Operation code
Post-byte
Data or address
Data or address

Examples of Motorola 6809 instructions including a post-byte:

	TFR X,Y	LDA $23,X	LDA $1234,X
	Transfer X to Y	Load A with the contents of the address given by X+23	Load A with the contents of the address given by X+1234
	X→Y	(X + 23)→A	(X + 1234)→A
Op. code	1F	A6	A6
Post-byte	12	88	89
Operand		23	12 24
	The post-byte specifies the source and destination	The post-byte specifies the X register and an 8-bit offset	The post-byte specifies the X register and a 16-bit offset

Fig. 2.6. Post-byte.

2.3 ADDRESSING MODES

The operand field contains either data or an address and there are many ways in which this field can be interpreted during the execution of an instruction. These various methods are known as the addressing modes of the machine.

The requirements to be met in the design of instruction formats are:

1 the address field be as short as possible,

2 access be given to as large an amount of memory as possible,

3 the address should be able to be changed without changing the instruction, thus making program loops possible,
4 the addressing methods be as fast as possible, i.e. contain as few arithmetic operations as possible,
5 the methods adopted be reasonably simple and easy to use.

The most widely used addressing techniques are described below followed by a description of those available on the M6809.

Inherent or implied addressing

In inherent or implied addressing, the single-byte operation code specifies all the information needed for the instruction. Figure 2.7 shows how the M6809 instruction Clear Accumulator B is stored in one memory byte. The binary pattern for this instruction is 01011111 or in hexadecimal 5F.

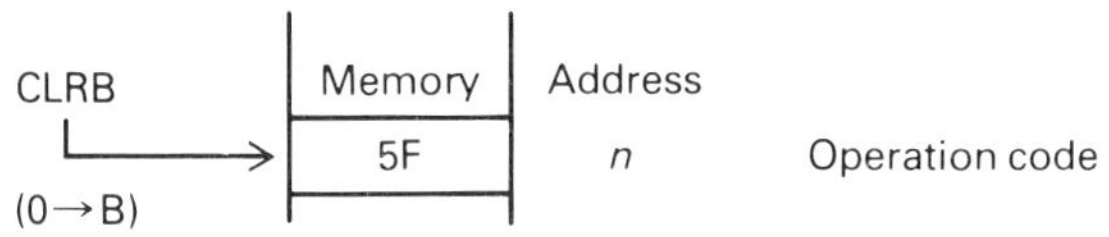

Fig. 2.7. An M6809 instruction using inherent addressing.

Immediate addressing

In immediate addressing, the effective address of the data is the location immediately following the operation code. Most processors with both 8- and 16-bit registers will accept either 8- or 16-bit arguments depending on the length of the register specified in the operation code. In assembly code programming, a # is usually used to indicate that the byte or bytes following the operation code contain the data. Figure 2.8 shows examples of instructions with 8- and 16-bit arguments on the M6809.

Direct addressing

In direct addressing, the address field is part of the instruction format. An instruction such as the M6800 instruction ADDA $43 will result in the contents of address $43 being added to the A register (a $ indicates hexadecimal).

A single-byte operand, however, allows only 256 memory locations to be addressed directly, and to enable large amounts of memory to be accessed in this way, a technique known as *paging* has to be used. With

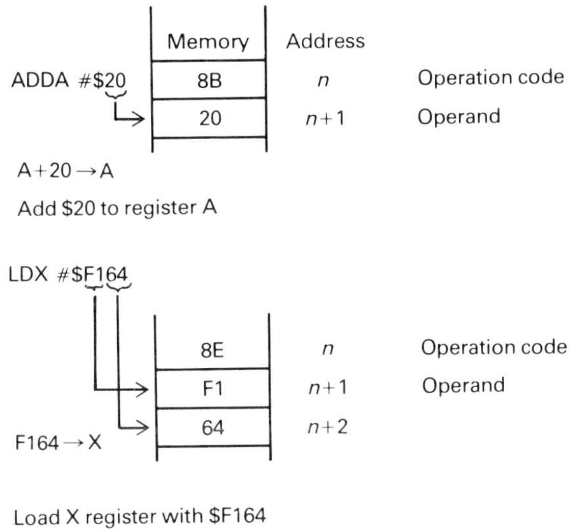

Fig. 2.8. M6809 instructions using immediate addressing.

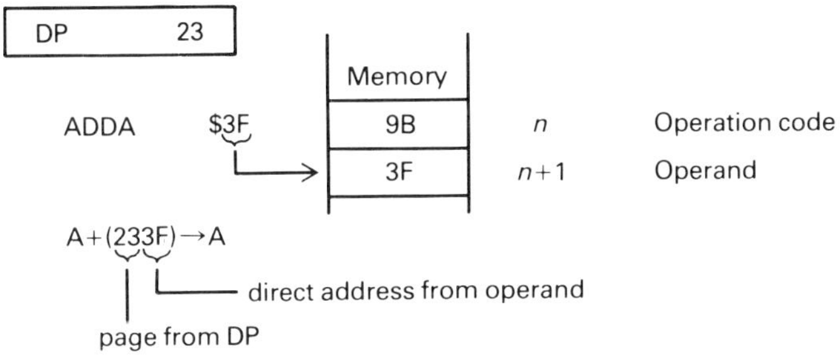

Fig. 2.9. An M6809 instruction using direct addressing.

this method the memory is divided into pages, the contents of each of which can be addressed directly. A register known as a direct page register is used to point to the current page and the address in the operand field supplies the position on the page.

Figure 2.9 above shows how the contents of address $233F might be added to accumulator A using a direct page register.

On the M6809, the direct page register is set to zero on reset and can only be loaded from another register using a Transfer (TFR) or Exchange (EXG) instruction. If this has not been done then direct addressing is from page 0.

Direct extended addressing

If 64K addresses are to be accessed directly, a 16-bit address field has to be used and the microprocessor has to fetch this in 2 bytes. On both the M6800 and the M6809 this process is known as *direct extended addressing* or often as just extended addressing (Fig. 2.10).

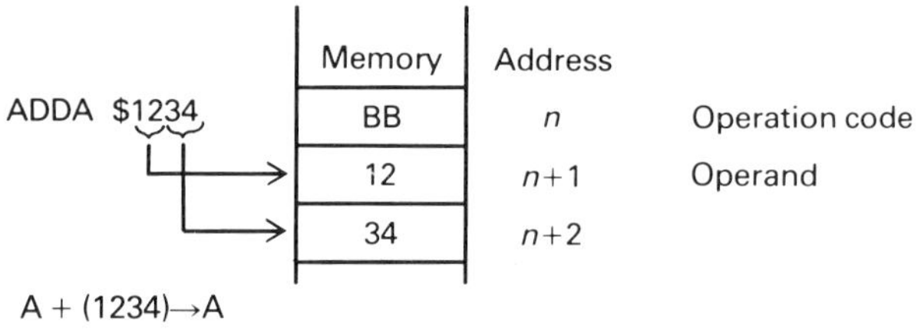

Fig. 2.10. An M6809 instruction using extended addressing.

Indexed addressing

In this mode the contents of the specified base register are added to the address in the operand field to give the effective address.

On the M6809, the base register may be either of the two index registers or the two stack pointers. The instruction ADDA $60, X where the X register contains $1235 will add the contents of address $1295 to accumulator A, i.e.

$$A+(60+X)\rightarrow A$$

Type	Form	Assembler form	Post-byte op. code
Constant two's complement offset from R	No offset	,R	1RR00100
	5-bit offset	n,R	0RR*nnnnn*
	8-bit offset	n,R	1RR01000
	16-bit offset	n,R	1RR01001
Accumulator Offset from R	A register	A,R	1RR00110
	B register	B,R	1RR00101
	D register	D,R	1RR01011
Auto-increment /decrement R (N.B. no offset)	Increment by 1	,R+	1RR00000
	Increment by 2	,R++	1RR00001
	Decrement by 1	,−R	1RR00010
	Decrement by 2	,−−R	1RR00011

RR: 00=X, 01=Y, 10=U, 11=S

Fig. 2.11. M6809 indexed addressing post-bytes.

The M6809 has various indexed addressing modes and requires that the operation code be followed by a post-byte to differentiate between the various modes (Fig. 2.11). Two examples of instructions using indexed addressing are given in Fig. 2.6.

A special form of indexed addressing available on the M6809 is used in the 'Load Effective Address' instructions in which the effective address rather than the data at that address is loaded into the pointer register. These instructions can have 5-, 8- or 16-bit offsets.

Relative addressing

A specialized form of indexed addressing involves using the program counter as an index register. The effective address is then the sum of the address of the next instruction given by the program counter and the offset specified in the operand field of the instruction. The effective address will therefore maintain its position in memory relative to the instruction using it even if the routine containing the instruction is moved. Programs written using this technique are said to be *relocatable*, since provided the program and data are moved together, they can be positioned almost anywhere in memory.

An example of an M6809 instruction is the 3-byte instruction

ADDA $15,PC

where PC signifies to the assembler that the numeric address ($15) is a two's complement number to be added to the contents of the program counter to form the effective address.

There are two possible post-byte operation codes for use with relative addressing. These specify either an 8-bit or 16-bit offset (Fig. 2.12).

Type	Form	Assembler form	Post-byte op-code
Constant two's Complement Offset from PC	8-bit offset 16-bit offset	*n*,PC *n*,PC	1XX01100 1XX01101

X = don't care

Fig. 2.12. M6809 relative addressing post-byte operation code.

The instruction ADDA $15,PC will therefore add the contents of the address of the next instruction + 15, to the A register (Fig. 2.13).

(NB This is the address of the current op. code + 18 since the instruction itself occupies 3 bytes.)

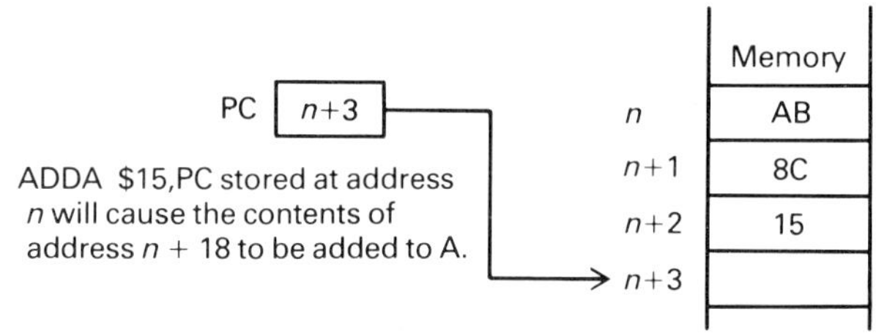

Fig. 2.13. M6809 relative addressing.

Relative addressing is also used with branch instructions, the byte(s) following the operation code being the two's complement offset which may be added to the program counter if the branch condition is true.

The M6809 can have either 8- or 16-bit offsets, giving what are known as short or long branches (Fig. 2.14).

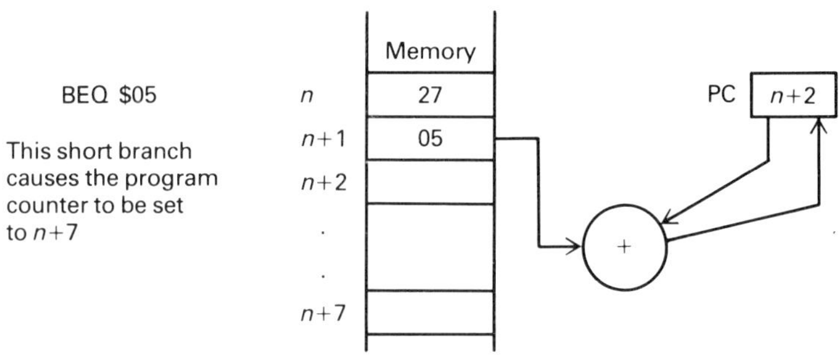

Fig. 2.14. M6809 branch if equal to zero (Z flag = 1).

Indirect addressing

In indirect addressing, the operand of the instruction specifies the memory location containing the effective address. On a byte-based system, the operand points at the first of two bytes containing the effective address.

For example ADDA [$1000] will cause the CPU to add the contents of the address given in locations $1000 and $1001 to the A register, i.e. A+(($1000,$1001))→A. (See Fig. 2.15.)

On the M6809 indirect addressing is restricted to indexed, relative and extended addressing modes. The instruction ADDA [$1000] above is an example of extended indirect addressing. Figure 2.16 shows the post-byte operation codes for indexed indirect addressing.

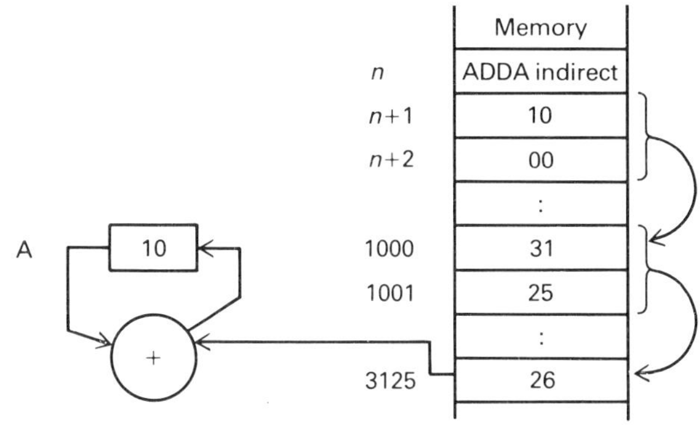

After completion of the instruction the A register will contain $(36)_{16}$ i.e. $10_{16} + 26_{16}$

Fig. 2.15. Indirect addressing.

Type	Form	Assembler Form	Post-byte op. code
Constant two's complement offset from R	No offset 8-bit offset 16-bit offset	[,R] [*n*,R] [*n*,R]	1RR10100 1RR11000 1RR11001
Accumulator offset from R	A register B register D register	[A,R] [B,R] [D,R]	1RR10110 1RR10101 1RR11011
Auto-Increment & -Decrement R	Increment by 2 Decrement by 2	[,R++] [,−−R]	1RR10001 1RR10011

RR: 00=X, 01=Y, 10=U, 11=S

Fig. 2.16. M6809 indexed indirect addressing post-bytes.

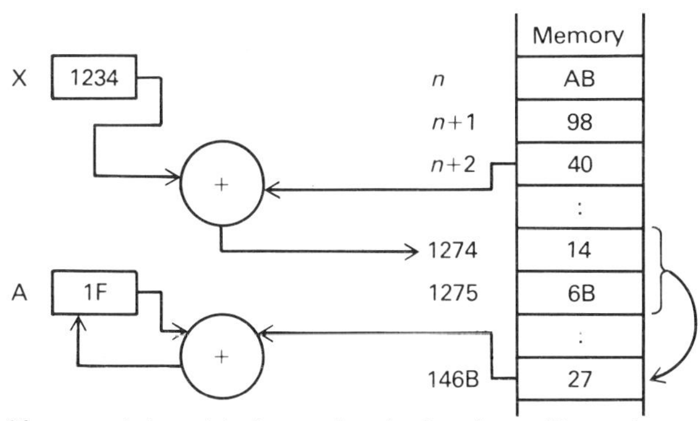

After completion of the instruction the A register will contain $(46)_{16}$ i.e. $1F_{16} + 27_{16}$

Fig. 2.17. ADDA with indexed indirect addressing.

The instruction ADDA [$40,X] where X register contains $1234 will therefore add the contents of the address pointed to by the bytes 1274 and 1275 to the A register (Fig. 2.17).

Figure 2.18 shows the post-bytes for 8-bit and 16-bit offsets used with relative indirect addressing.

Type	Form	Assembly Code	Post-byte op. code
Constant two's complement offset from PC	8-bit offset 16-bit offset	[*n*,PC] [*n*,PC]	1XX11100 1XX11101

XX = don't care

Fig. 2.18. M6809 relative indirect addressing post-bytes.

Register addressing

Many microprocessors use register addressing which may be either direct or indirect. Register direct addressing is identical to direct or extended addressing except that the effective address is that of a register, for example the instruction ADDA B would add the contents of the B register to those of the A register leaving the result in the A register.

With register indirect addressing the effective address is held in a register rather than in a memory location, so that an instruction such as ADDA (H) will add the contents of the address specified in the H register (usually 16 bits) to the register A.

These addressing modes have the advantage that the instructions are both shorter and faster in execution than with direct or indexed addressing, but the disadvantage that programs are frequently longer.

Neither register direct nor register indirect addressing are available on the M6809 but both can be illustrated using Intel 8080 instructions. The instruction MOV B,D uses register direct addressing to transfer the contents of the D register to the B register, MOV M,B uses the register indirect mode to transfer the contents of the B register to the memory location whose 16-bit address is held in the two 8-bit registers H and L (referred to as one 16-bit register M).

Bit addressing

Many microprocessors, including the Zilog Z80, have a number of instructions that allow individual bits to be tested, set or reset. For example the instruction SET 1,A will set bit 1 of the A register to 1. Individual bit addressing is not available on the M6809.

Figure 2.19 compares the addressing modes available on the M6800, M6809, Intel 8080 and Zilog Z80 microprocessors.

Addressing mode	M6800	M6809	Intel 8080	Z80
Inherent (Implied)	Yes	Yes	Yes	Yes
Immediate	Yes	Yes	Yes	Yes
Immediate extended	Yes	Yes	Yes	Yes
Direct	Yes	Yes	Yes	Yes
Direct extended	Yes	Yes	No	Yes
Indexed	Yes	Yes	No	Yes
Relative	(1)	Yes	No	(1)
Indirect	No	Yes	No	No
Register direct	No	No	Yes	Yes
Register indirect	(2)	(2)	Yes	Yes
Bit	No	No	No	Yes

(1) only on branch instructions
(2) partially achieved by indexed addressing with zero offset

Fig. 2.19. A comparison of addressing modes.

2.4 MACHINE CODE INSTRUCTION SETS

Machine code instruction sets are made up of four categories of instructions:

1 data manipulation
2 data transfer
3 program manipulation
4 status management

The following sections describe each of these categories in turn and illustrate each with M6809 instructions.

Data manipulation

There are five types of data manipulation instructions: arithmetic, logical, comparison, shift and special purpose.

Arithmetic

Arithmetic instructions manipulate data stored in registers and/or memory. Typical instructions included in this group are shown in Fig. 2.20.

Operation	M6809 instruction	Description
Add	ADDB	B+M→B
Add with carry	ADCB	B+M+C→B
Subtract	SUBA	A−M→A
Subtract with carry	SBCA	A−M−C→A
Negate	NEGB	−B→B
Increment memory/register	INC	M+1→M
Decrement memory/register	DECA	A−1→A
Multiply	MUL	A*B→D (unsigned)

Fig. 2.20. M6809 arithmetic instructions.

Logical

In addition to arithmetic functions, logical operations can be performed on data held in registers or memory. Examples of logical operations are given in Fig. 2.21.

Operation	M6809 instruction	Description
And	ANDA	A.M→A
Or	ORB	B+M→M
Exclusive Or	EORA	A⊕M→A
Complement	COM	$\overline{M}$→M

Or and Exclusive Or operate on A, B and the condition code register. When operating on the condition code register only immediate addressing can be used.

Complement operates on either the selected register or memory.

Fig. 2.21. M6809 logical operations.

Comparison

This group of instructions allows data to be tested without changing it. Such instructions set or clear the flags in the condition code register for later use (often conditional jumps). Figure 2.22 gives typical examples of this group of instructions.

Operation	M6809 instruction	Description
Compare	CMPA	Compute A–M
Bit test	BITA	Compute A.M
Test	TSTA	Compute A–0

M = the contents of a memory location

Fig. 2.22. M6809 comparison instructions.

Shift

There are three basic types of shift operations, Arithmetic Shifts, Logical Shifts and Rotates or Cyclic Shifts. All can be either to the left or to the right and are performed on the contents of a register or a memory location. On many systems, including the M6809, the contents of the carry flag are affected by shift operations as shown in Fig. 2.23.

Operation	M6809 instruction	Description
Logical left shift	LSLA	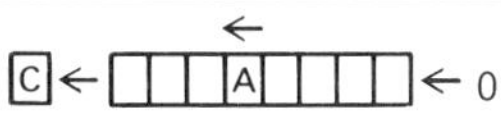
Logical right shift	LSRA	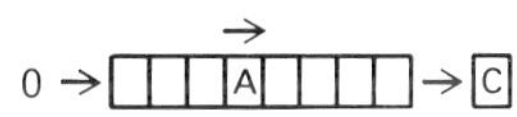
Arithmetic left shift	ASL	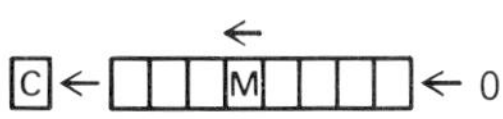
Arithmetic right shift	ASRB	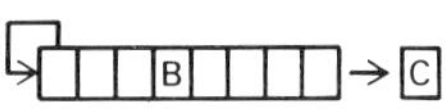
Rotate register or memory left	ROLA	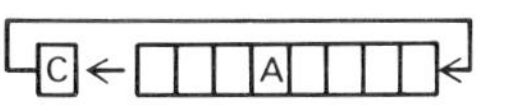
Rotate register or memory right	ROR	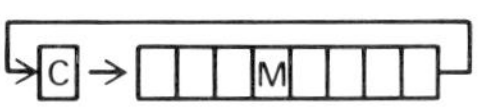

All instructions operate on the A or B registers or memory.

Fig. 2.23. M6809 shift operations.

Special purpose

Special purpose instructions are usually used in chips designed for specific applications. For example, instructions to perform decimal arithmetic, keyboard scans and floating point conversions are used in calculator applications (see Fig. 2.24).

Operation	M6809 instruction	Description
Decimal adjust	DAA	Used after addition to convert the A register contents to BCD format

Fig. 2.24. M6809 decimal adjust.

Data transfer

There are four types of instructions within this group: memory transfer, internal transfer, input/output and stack instructions.

Memory transfer

Memory transfer instructions are used to load and store registers and to clear memory locations or registers. Figure 2.25 gives examples of M6809 memory transfer instructions.

Operation	M6809 instruction	Description
Load register	LDA	M→A
Store register	STA	A→M
Clear register or memory	CLR	0→M

Fig. 2.25. M6809 memory transfer instructions.

Internal transfer

Internal transfer instructions are used to transfer data from one register to another or to exchange the contents of two registers. Either these instructions contain a binary pattern specifying the source and destination registers or a post-byte is used for this purpose. Figure 2.26 shows the M6809 internal transfer instructions which will move data between any pair of 8-bit registers or between any pair of 16-bit registers.

Operation	M6809 instruction	Description
Transfer	TFR R1,R2	R1→R2
Exchange	EXG R1,R2	R1←→R2

R1 and R2 may be any of the 8-bit registers A, B, CC, DP or any of the 16-bit registers X, Y, U, S, D or PC. Bits 4 to 7 of the post-byte represent the source register and bits 0 to 3 the destination;

0000=D, 0001=X, 0010=Y, 0011=U, 0100=S
0101=PC, 1000=A, 1001=B, 1010=CC, 1011=DP

All other combinations are undefined and invalid.

Fig. 2.26. M6809 internal transfer instructions.

Input/output

There are two basic forms of input/output systems, memory-mapped and isolated input/output.

In memory-mapped input/output, the I/O port is treated in exactly the same way as a memory location and any instruction that operates on memory will affect a selected port. Thus a store instruction is used for output and a load for input. The Motorola 6809 has memory-mapped input/output and therefore no special I/O instructions.

In isolated input/output, the ports are treated separately from memory and additional hardware control signals are needed. Special input/output instructions have therefore to be included in the instruction set. Typical instructions are Read, Input or In to transfer data from a port to a selected register and Write, Output or Out to transfer from the selected register to a port.

Stack instructions

There are basically two stack instructions:

Push, which places the contents of the specified register(s) onto the stack and decrements the stack pointer, and

Pull, which places the contents of the top of the stack into the specified register(s) and increments the stack pointer.

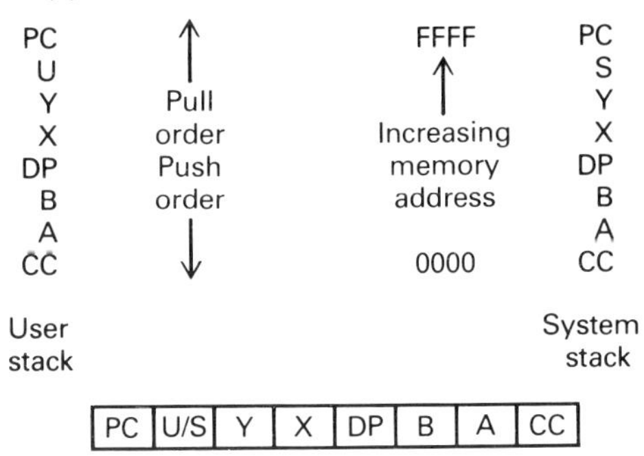

Post-byte: the bits set to 1 specify the register(s) to Push or Pull

Examples

Operation	M6809 instruction	Description	Hexadecimal
Push	PSHS X,Y,A	Push registers onto S stack	34 32
Pull	PULU X,A	Pull registers from U stack	37 12

Fig. 2.27. M6809 stack instructions.

The Push and Pull instructions on the M6809 transfer the contents of any single register or set of registers to or from either the system stack (S) or the user stack (U). The post-byte specifies which registers are to be pushed or pulled.

The system stack is also affected by interrupts, subroutine calls and return instructions.

Program manipulation

There are four categories of program manipulation instructions: unconditional jumps, conditional jumps, subroutine calls, halts and no operations.

Unconditional jumps

Unconditional jumps or branches, load the program counter with the effective address, thus executing the instruction stored at that address during the next instruction cycle. In addition to a straightforward jump instruction, the M6809 has two types of branch instructions, those with an 8-bit relative offset and the second type with a 16-bit offset known as long branches (Fig. 2.28).

Operation	M6809 instruction	Description
Jump Always	JMP	EA→PC
Branch Always	BRA *nn*	PC+*nn*→PC
Long Branch Always	LBRA *nnnn*	PC+*nnnn*→PC

EA = effective address

Fig. 2.28. M6809 branch instructions.

Conditional jumps

Conditional jumps or branches load the program counter with the effective address, providing that the specified condition of the status flags exists, e.g. branch to the effective address if a particular flag or group of flags are in specified clear or set conditions. Figure 2.29 lists the M6809 conditional branch instructions.

Subroutine

There are basically only two types of instructions used with subroutines:

Call or Branch to Subroutine, which acts like an unconditional branch but which also saves the contents of the program counter

Operation	M6809	Operation	M6809
Simple conditional branches			
Branch if Carry Clear	BCC	Branch if Carry Set	BCS
Branch if Overflow Clear	BVC	Branch if Overflow Set	BVS
Branch if Equal (Z=1)	BEQ	Branch if Not Equal (Z= 0)	BNE
Branch if Minus (N=1)	BMI	Branch if Plus (N=0)	BPL
Signed conditional branches			
Branch if Greater Than	BGT	Branch if Less than or Equal to	BLE
Branch if Greater than or Equal to	BGE	Branch if Less Than	BLT
Branch if Equal	BEQ	Branch if Not Equal	BNE
Unsigned conditional branches			
Branch if Higher	BHI	Branch if Lower of Same	BLS
Branch if Higher or Same	BHS	Branch if Lower	BLO
Branch if Equal	BEQ	Branch if Not Equal	BNE

All conditional long branches have the short branch operation code prefixed by $10 and use a 16-bit offset.

Fig. 2.29. M6809 conditional branch instructions.

so that the calling program can be resumed correctly on completion of the subroutine, and Return which restores the value of the program counter stored during the subroutine call and hence causes a return to the main program. There are three main types of subroutine calls:

1 Jump & Mark Place or Jump & Save, in which the return address (the contents of the program counter) are stored at the address specified in the call and the execution continues at that address + 1. This method has the disadvantage that the subroutine cannot be recursive (cannot call itself) and that it cannot be re-entrant (it cannot be shared between two simultaneous programs or background and foreground programs).

2 Jump & Link, in which the call places the return address in a special purpose link register and transfers control to the specified address. This method again does not allow subroutines to be re-entrant nor immediately recursive.

3 Call instructions push the contents of the program counter onto the stack thus allowing the subroutines to be both re-entrant and recursive. The M6809 uses this method for calling subroutines.

Operation	M6809 instruction	Description
Branch to Subroutine	BSR	PC→System stack PC+nn→PC
Jump to Subroutine	JSR	PC→System Stack M→PC
Return from Subroutine	RTS	System stack→PC

The Branch to Subroutine uses either 8-bit or 16-bit offsets. The Jump to Subroutine uses direct, direct extended or indexed addressing modes.

Fig. 2.30. M6809 subroutine instructions.

Halt and No Operation

A Halt instruction is used to suspend the processor until some external signal is received to restart it. A No Operation performs no function but takes a precise time (e.g. two clock cycles) to increment the program counter. (See Fig. 2.31.)

Operation	M6809 instruction	Description
Logically AND next byte with condition code register and wait for interrupt.	CWAI	AND condition code register & next byte. Save all registers on hardware stack & wait for interrupt.
Synchronize	SYNC	Halt processor until an interrupt is received
No operation	NOP	No operation

Fig. 2.31. M6809 halt and no operation instructions.

Status management

The fourth and last group of instructions are used to set or clear flags, designate register functions and handle interrupts, and are known as status management instructions.

Flag management

Typical flag management instructions are Clear Carry Flag and Set Carry Flag, each instruction specifying the flag to be either cleared or set.

The M6809 has no special instructions to clear or set individual condition code flags. This function is achieved by performing logical operations on the condition code register, e.g. the carry flag is cleared by using the instruction ANDCC #%11111110.

Designate register functions

On some computers it is possible to specify the function of a register by software, for example to specify that register F be used as the program counter. This facility is more usually found on mainframe computers than on microprocessors and is not present on the M6809.

Interrupt handling

There are two distinct categories of interrupts, hardware interrupts which are generated by an event external to the processor, and software interrupts caused by the execution of a software interrupt instruction in a program.

There are two types of hardware interrupt, maskable and non-maskable, and most processors have special purpose instructions to enable and disable maskable interrupts.

The M6809 processor chip has two maskable interrupt pins, $\overline{\text{IRQ}}$ and $\overline{\text{FIRQ}}$, and a non-maskable interupt pin, $\overline{\text{NMI}}$. The IRQ and NMI interrupts store all the registers on the system stack, whilst an FIRQ interrupt stores only the condition code register and program counter. IRQ and FIRQ interrupts can be enabled or disabled by clearing (0) or setting (1) the appropriate flags in the condition code register. Non-maskable interrupts cannot be masked and are therefore of higher priority than both IRQ and FIRQ interrupts.

The IRQ interrupt flag (I) is set to 1 by any interrupt or by a system reset. The FIRQ interrupt flag (F), however, is only set by an NMI, FIRQ, high priority software interrupt or system reset thus making it of higher priority than an IRQ interrupt. The M6809 does not have special instructions to enable/disable interrupts, but uses logical operations on the condition code register to clear and to set the appropriate flags. Following an interrupt, further interrupts are inhibited until the associated flag is cleared by software. The interrupted program is resumed at the end of the interrupt service routine by execution of a Return From Interrupt instruction (RTI) which restores all the registers with the values pushed onto the stack at the time when the interrupt was received. Figure 2.32 shows the sequence of operations that occur in handling IRQ interrupts.

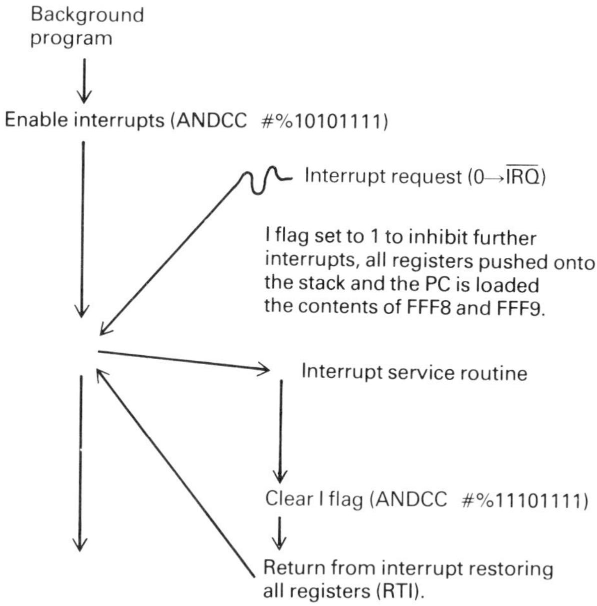

Fig. 2.32. M6809 IRQ interrupt handling.

Software interrupt instructions increment the program counter, store all the registers on the system stack and pass control to the interrupt service routine by means of a vector table. The M6809 has three software interrupt instructions, SWI, SWI2 and SWI3. The SWI instruction inhibits both regular and fast interrupts by setting both the I and F flags, whilst SWI2 and SWI3 instructions do not. Figure 2.33 gives the vector addresses for the various M6809 interrupts.

Most significant byte		Least significant byte	Interrupt type
FFFC	and	FFFD	for NMI
FFFA	and	FFFB	for SWI
FFF8	and	FFF9	for IRQ
FFF6	and	FFF7	for FIRQ
FFF4	and	FFF5	for SWI2
FFF2	and	FFF3	for SWI3

Fig. 2.33. M6809 interrupt vector addresses.

2.5 EXAMPLE MACHINE CODE PROGRAM

The hand-coded program in Fig. 2.34, which uses indexed addressing to summate a table of \$10 numbers, illustrates the way in which programs are both translated and stored.

Assembly Language	Comment	Address	Hexidecimal machine code
LDB #$10	Load B (Counter) with the length of the table	0800 0801	C6 10
LDX #$900	Load X with the start address of the table	0802 0803 0804	8E 09 00
CLRA	Total=0	0805	4F
LAB ADDA ,X+	Add number from table and increment address	0806 0807	AB 80
DECB	Counter=Counter−1	0808	5A
BNE LAB	If Counter>0 then goto LAB	0809 080A	26 FB
SWI	End of program. Return to System monitor	080B	3F

The first column shows the assembly language instructions and the last two columns give the machine code instructions and their corresponding addresses.

Fig. 2.34. Example machine code program.

Chapter 3

Assembly Language Programming

3.1 INTRODUCTION

In the preceding chapter, a typical assembly code instruction set and range of addressing modes were described. The following definition of labels, assembler directives, data types and comments completes the description of the format of assembly language instructions.

The chapter then outlines the stages in software development and the tools and techniques available to the low-level language programmer. Both pseudo-code and simple M6809 example programs are included in this chapter to illustrate possible program structures. Example programs given in Chapters 5 – 7 further illustrate programming techniques and show typical application areas for assembly language programming.

3.2 ASSEMBLERS

The primary function of an assembler is to translate source code instructions written in mnemonic form, with mnemonically named operands, into binary object code. Most assemblers take two passes (read the source code twice), the first assigning numeric addresses to mnemonic names and the second producing the object code.

An assembly code instruction has up to five fields as shown in Fig. 3.1. Each field is separated from the next by a delimiter character (e.g. a space as for the M6809).

The sequence number is an optional field sometimes provided to enable the programmer to number the lines of code. On the Motorola

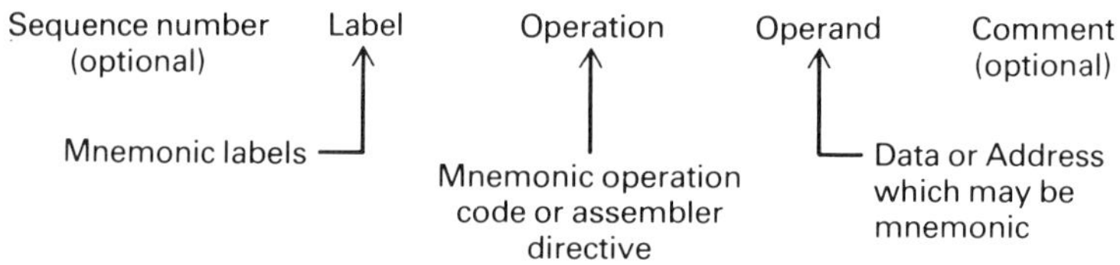

Fig. 3.1. Assembly language instruction fields.

M6809 assembler it is a number, of up to five digits but less than 65536, followed by a space.

The label field is used to mark a line in conjunction with a Jump, Branch or Call instruction. Labels are usually up to five or six characters long, consist of alphabetical or numeric characters and start with an alphabetical character. On the M6809 assembler a '.' (period) or a '$' (dollar sign) may also be included and a label may start with a period. Certain reserved symbols are not allowed in the label field. Typically these are the register and reserved assembler mnemonics. On the M6809 the reserved mnemonic PCR and the register mnemonics S, U, X, Y, PC, A, B, D, DP and CC are not permitted.

The operation field of an assembly code instruction contains either a mnemonic operation code or an assembler directive. Mnemonic operation codes were described in Chapter 2 and shown to specify both the instruction to be executed and the number, and length, of operands following it. Assembler directives are used to control the assembly process rather than being translated directly into machine code instructions.

Typical assembler directives are as follows.

1 The DATA directive allows fixed data to be assigned and named. There are many different variations of data directive to allow for different forms of numeric data and character strings. The M6809 data directives are:
Form Constant Byte (FCB) for 8-bit numbers;
Form Double Byte (FDB) for 16-bit numbers and addresses;
Form Constant Character string (FCC) for 7-bit ASCII characters.

M6809 examples:

```
TABLE FDB $1234
```

stores $12 and $34 in the next 2 bytes and labels the first TABLE.

```
CONST FCB $3A
```

stores $3A in the next byte called CONST.

```
EXIT FCC /EXIT/
```

stores the letters E, X, I and T in ASCII format, in the next 4 bytes, and labels the first one EXIT.

2 The EQUATE directive assigns mnemonic names to addresses or data. Unlike the DATA directive the EQUATE does not reserve memory, it simply enters a name into the Symbol Table (a table of symbolic names and their corresponding addresses created when the source code is assembled).

M6809 example:

```
ERROR EQU $5A00
```

3 The END directive indicates the end of the assembly language program to the assembler.
4 The optional program NAME directive is usually the first statement of an assembly language program.

M6809 example:

NAM EXAMPLE FIND STRING

Program name (EXAMPLE) — Comment (FIND STRING)

5 The ORIGIN directive allows the programmer to specify an address from which the assembler will start to store the object code. Origin directives can be used to store different segments of program or data in different areas of memory.

M6809 examples:

```
        ORG $800
```

specifies that the code that follows, when assembled, should be loaded in memory starting at address $800.

```
        ERROR EQU $5A00
              ORG ERROR
```

specifies that the routine following the ORG directive will start at address $5A00.

6 The RESERVE directive is used to allocate memory to variables, giving a specified name to the first location in each reserved area. No data is placed in the reserved locations.

On the M6809, the Reserve Memory Byte directive allocates the specified label to the first of the reserved locations:

```
        TABLE RMB 20.
```

will reserve 20 bytes, labelling the first one of them TABLE.

Most processors also have machine-specific directives. the M6809 has several, for example SETDP, which specifies which page in memory is to be treated as the direct addressing page. Whenever an address on this page is encountered during subsequent assembly, it is converted into a direct address. The program must, however, still contain code to set the DP register.

The operand field can contain either data or addresses, which can be in numeric, character or symbolic forms.

Numeric data or addresses can be in the following forms.

1 Decimal. Nearly all assemblers assume that numeric data is in decimal unless instructed otherwise, e.g.

ADDA #14 $A+14_{10} \rightarrow A$

2 Hexadecimal. Data in this form is indicated by preceding the number with '$' or following it by an 'H', e.g.

ADDA #$14 $A+14_{16} \rightarrow A$

When using the 'H' notation, data starting with a letter (A to F) must be preceded by a zero to distinguish it from a symbolic name, e.g.

ADDA #0A3H $A+A3_{16} \rightarrow A$

3 Binary numbers are usually preceded by '%' or followed by 'B', e.g.

ADDA #%00001110 $A+14_{10} \rightarrow A$

4 Octal numbers are usually preceded by '@' or followed by either 'O' or 'Q' e.g.

ADDA #@14 $A + 14_8 \rightarrow A$

Note that using the O suffix is dangerous as it can easily be entered as zero.

Data may also be specified as being in ASCII form, the single character being surrounded by either quotation marks or as in the M6809 preceded by an apostrophe, e.g.

LDA 'A $41_{16} \rightarrow A$

The data and address forms specified above may be used together with arithmetic and logical operators to produce an expression. Addition and subtraction are permitted on most assemblers, giving rise to instructions of the form:

ADDA TABLE+2

which, if TABLE is a label at address $200, will add the contents of address $202 to the A register.

Whilst simple expressions of this form are relatively clear, as the range of operators increases so does the complexity of the operand field. On the M6809 as well as + (addition), − (subtraction), * (multiplication) and / (integer division) operators, brackets can be used and there are eight special two-character operators given below:

!∧ exponentiation	!. logical and
!< shift left	!+ logical or
!> shift right	!X logical exclusive or
!L rotate left	!R rotate right

The PCR directive in the operand field of an M6809 assembly language instruction causes the assembler to convert the preceding mnemonic into a relative address. Thus an instruction such as

ADDA TABLE,PCR

will be assembled into machine code using relative addressing with the offset from the current value of the program counter being calculated automatically.

The last field in the assembly code instruction is the optional comment field which is only printed on the assembly language source code listing for documentation purposes. This field can contain any printable ASCII character.

3.3 STAGES IN SOFTWARE DEVELOPMENT

The software development process can be subdivided into seven different but overlapping stages:

1 problem definition;
2 program design;
3 coding;
4 program verification;
5 testing;
6 documentation;
7 program maintenance and modification.

None of these stages can be isolated from either preceding or following stages, the whole process being an iterative one, with the final objective of an error-free solution to the existing problem.

Problem definition is the expression of the requirements that need to be achieved. These may be in terms of what functions the computer program is expected to fulfil, what time response constraints have to be met and what hardware limitations are dictated by the total product specification. For example, if a microprocessor-based controller is being designed for a washing machine, then the program length may be critical as this will determine the overall memory requirements. These in turn dictate the number, or size, of memory chips and hence affect the overall cost of the washing machine, perhaps even being a critical factor in its viability against rival products.

Program design is the preparation of an outline specification for the method to be adopted in the computer program. This stage is often greatly aided by the use of pseudo-code or structured English and will be (more or less) independent of the programming language to be used. This stage is often the longest of the processes in software development and is the source of information for both coding and documentation. The choice of programming language is an intrinsic but final stage in program design and will usually be dictated by the problem definition. If the problem does not involve real-time responses, or extensive bit handling, or a critical memory size, or specific device handling routines not normally found within a high-level language or operating system, then it will probably be most economically solved by the use of an appropriate high-level language. If, however, one or more of these features is required, then assembly language programming will be employed for either the complete program or segments that cannot be written in the high-level language.

Coding is the process of converting the program design into the decided form for input to the computer. Often because of constraints imposed by the product specification, programs that have to be written in assembly code are developed on systems other than the one on which they are to be run. It is then only the object code, or binary, that is transfered to the target system. The system on which the programs are written is known as the development system (or host) and will incorporate both hardware and software features to aid with coding and program verification.

There are two types of development systems, those with the same processor as the target system and those with a different one. A development system using the same microprocessor as the target can have a visual display unit, disk backing store and PROM programmer, enabling it to run an assembler and screen editor, and letting the programmer save both source and object code programs on backing store for later use or modification. Programs can be assembled, run and tested on this system, enabling simple program verification (or debugging) to be performed. Errors found at this stage can be easily corrected using the editor and the program re-assembled and re run.

A development system using a different processor to that of the target system will have the same hardware configuration, but will use an editor, cross-assembler and simulator for program development. A cross-assembler is a program that runs on one processor but accepts assembly code and produces object code for another. With this type of development system the object code has to be loaded into the target system or the target system's processor has to be simulated on the development system. A simulator is the program that converts the target system's machine code or assembly language into that of the host and monitors target system registers during execution in the host.

There are two stages in program verification, that of achieving a program which will assemble without errors and then that of making the program perform according to its design specifications. Both types of development systems described above aid in producing programs that assemble without errors, and both can incorporate hardware and software facilities to monitor the execution of the program. A Debugger is the name for a utility program that provides the programmer with tools to help him verify his program at run time.

The simplest of these tools is the *trace* facility, which allows the values of all registers and other selected variables to be displayed during program execution. The contents of the registers and variables may be displayed either after each instruction has been executed or at a frequency defined by the programmer.

The *single step* facility allows the programmer to execute the program one instruction at a time, or one memory read/write cycle at a time, and to examine the state of the machine at each step.

The *breakpoint* facility lets the programmer halt the program automatically at specified points during its execution, and examine or change the contents of registers whilst the program is halted. The program execution can then be resumed either in the normal way or in single step mode.

Memory, register and stack *dumps* are provided by utility programs which list the contents of a memory block, the processor registers or the system stack, respectively, on an output device such as a printer.

The responses of target systems with real-time operations, perhaps including specialized hardware and using interrupts, cannot be reproduced by software tools on development systems which are of a different configuration to that of the target system. All the software aids described above either slow down or halt the program execution. For these real-time applications areas, hardware debugging tools which monitor the performance of the actual target system are available.

One such tool is a logic analyser, a digital device which runs in parallel with the target system. It is attached to the processor's data, address and control buses and is used to display their contents on a VDU screen in binary, hexadecimal or mnemonic form. The logic analyser is usually set to display the bus states after being triggered by a specified event, such as the occurrence of a given address on the address bus or of a particular operation code on the data bus. The analyser then displays the bus states leading up to that event for a predefined number of cycles of the target system.

An in–circuit emulator is hardware which is either free-standing or which when fitted to a development system allows a target system with the same processor to be attached. The target system's processor chip is removed and a multiway umbilical cable used to connect its processor buses to the development system. A bit map within the in-circuit emulator hardware is then used to switch out existing development system hardware and replace it by the target system (the addresses used are those of the target system). Debugging and testing facilities available on the development system can then be used on programs actually running in the target system.

Software development must produce more than just a working program. It must provide documentation that allows the program to be used and to be maintained, modified and extended. Assembly language programs should be as self-documenting as possible and should include:

1 the program name;
2 the programmer's name;
3 the date of the last amendment to the program;
4 a brief description of the program;
5 the high-level pseudo-code produced during program design;
6 the assembly code, using meaningful labels and variable names and commented in such a way as to relate it to the high-level pseudo-code.

Program maintenance and modification may be necessary either because of a fault in the program which was not detected in the debugging or testing stages, or because the problem definition was incomplete or has been changed. Program maintenance therefore involves redesign, recoding, verification, testing and updating of documentation.

It is at this stage of software development that good documentation pays and time spent in documenting the program initially is rewarded. The advantage of self-documentation is also evident in this phase; for however many years may have elapsed between the program being written and a modification being required, if the program exists the documentation cannot have been lost or destroyed.

3.4 TOP–DOWN DESIGN AND MODULAR PROGRAMMING

In top–down design the programmer first designs the overall solution to the problem and does not worry about details until after the overall design has been completed. This leads naturally to a modular program design in which a main program segment calls other lower level segments, or subroutines, which perform the more detailed tasks. Whilst the main program segment is being written, the individual subroutines may be left as single return instructions so that the logic of the main segment can be checked. After this stage has been completed, the subroutines in the first level down can each be written separately.

These may include calls to even lower level subroutines which may be left as stubs (single return instructions) and written at a later time.

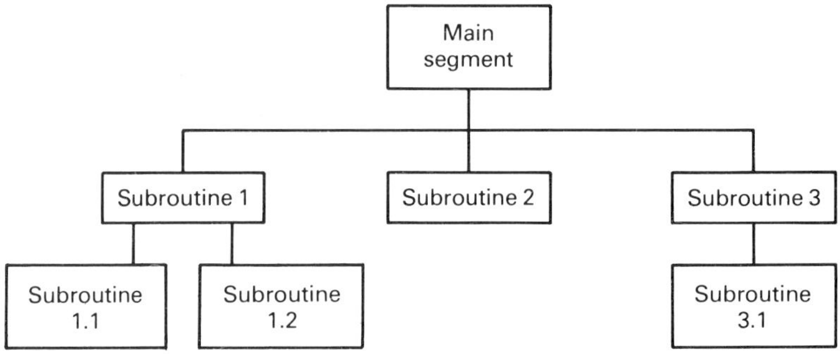

Fig. 3.2. A modular program structure

The main advantage of this top–down method is that programs are easier to test, because only small segments are tested at one time and testing is spread over the entire design period. The disadvantages are that it may not result in generally useful subroutines, and may not take the best advantage of existing software.

Before adopting a top–down approach to program design, a detailed study should be made of any systems software that may be resident on the target system. The programmer will then be aware of any subroutines in the system's software that can be called by the applications program. Similarly the programmer should be familiar with relevant subroutines available in any accessible software library. Thus, whilst top-down design is generally a good practice to adopt, particularly for large programs, it should not be followed to the exclusion of all other considerations.

3.5 STRUCTURED PROGRAMMING

To enable program modules to be easily understood and modified, they should be organized and logical and have a clear sequence of operations without any hidden effects. They should be written using easily recognizable blocks or structures which should have only a single entry and exit point.

There are usually only four basic structures used in assembly language programming:

1 sequential
2 conditional

3 loop
4 case

A sequential structure

This is a linear structure and consists of instructions, or groups of instructions, which are executed consecutively. A very simple example of this structure is a program to summate three numbers, the pseudocode for which is

```
begin
        total = number 1
        total = total + number 2
        total = total + number 3
end
```

The block, in this case the entire program, is bounded by begin and end, and statements within the block are indented.

A conditional structure

A conditional structure is used when the sequence of instructions to be executed depends on the result of a test. The condition tested for can be either true or false and may be made up of several criteria joined in a Boolean expression. The format for this structure is:

```
if (condition is true)
     then begin
                execute block of instructions A
          end
     else begin
                execute block of instructions B
          endif
```

The begins and ends may be omitted as the structure will be clear through identations. This structure has only a single entry point (at the 'if' condition) and a single exit point. The instruction immediately following the structure is the next to be executed irrespective of the route taken through it, and exit from either block of instructions, other than through the structure, is not permitted.

In situations where an action is to be taken if a condition exists and no alternative is required, the structure is reduced to:

```
if (condition is true) then execute block of instructions
```

The condition tested for can be inverted modifying the structure to:

if (condition is false) then continue
  else execute block of instructions

The following example program illustrates the use of the 'if then else' structure. It checks the contents of a memory location (ASCII). If the contents are found to be valid ASCII code for a hexadecimal character, they are converted into the equivalent binary number. The B register is used as a flag, being set to $FF if the contents were hexadecimal and to $00 if they were not. (See Program 3.1.)

```
00010        NAM    ASCII TO BINARY
00020 *PROGRAMMER P.J.THEWLIS
00030 *22 FEBRUARY 1984
00040 *PROGRAM CONVERTS CONTENTS OF LOCATION ASCII TO BINARY IF IT IS
00050 *A VALID HEXADECIMAL CHARACTER AND SETS THE B REGISTER TO ZERO.
00060 *IF IT IS NOT A VALID HEXADECIMAL CHARACTER THE B REGISTER IS
00070 *SET TO FF.
00080 *
00090 *BEGIN FLAG=NOT HEXADECIMAL
00100 *      IF ASCII>"F" OR <"0" THEN END
00110 *         ELSE IF ASCII>="A" THEN ASCII=ASCII-$37
00120 *                                 FLAG =HEXADECIMAL
00130 *                            ELSE IF ASCII<="9" THEN ASCII=ASCII-$30
00140 *                                                    FLAG =HEXADECIMAL
00150 *END
00160 *
00170 *DATA     ASCII 0 TO 9 = HEXADECIMAL 30 TO 39
00180 *         ASCII A TO F = HEXADECIMAL 41 TO 46
00190 *
00200       ORG    $800
00210 ASCII EQU    $0900
00220 BEGIN LDB    #$FF
00230       LDA    ASCII
00240 IF1   CMPA   #$46     TEST > "F"
00250       BGT    EXIT     NOT HEXADECIMAL CHARACTER
00260       CMPA   #$30     TEST < "0"
00270       BLT    EXIT     NOT HEXADECIMAL CHARACTER
00280 ELSE1 CMPA   #$40     HEXADECIMAL A TO F
00290 IF2   BLE    ELSE2    NOT ALPHA
00300       SUBA   #$37     CONVERT TO BINARY
00310       CLRB            FLAG=HEXADECIMAL
00320       JMP    EXIT
00330 ELSE2 CMPA   #$3A     HEXADECIMAL 0 TO 9
00340 IF3   BGE    EXIT
00350       SUBA   #$30     CONVERT TO BINARY
00360       CLRB            FLAG TO HEXADECIMAL
00370 EXIT  STA    ASCII
00380       END
00390
```

Program 3.1. Lines 10–30: program name, programmer, last update. Lines 40–70: program description. Lines 90–150: pseudo-code. Lines 170 & 180: data. Lines 200–380: assembly language program.

A loop structure

There are several possible loop structures. The 'while do' structure is one of the most common having the form:

while (condition is true) do
    execute block of instructions

An alternative structure is that of the 'until do' which has the form:

until (condition is true) do
    execute block of instructions

In both of the above structures the condition is tested before the block of instructions is executed, whilst in the 'repeat until' or 'do while' structures the condition is checked at the end of the loop.

repeat execute block of instructions
until (condition is true)

do execute block of instructions
while (condition is true)

These two structures are the more straightforward and efficient to implement in assembly language through the use of conditional branch

```
       NAM    BLOCKMOVE
*PROGRAMMER P.J.THEWLIS
*23 MARCH 1984
*PROGRAM TO MOVE A BLOCK OF LESS THAN 255 BYTES FROM ONE MEMORY
*AREA TO ANOTHER AT A HIGHER ADDRESS.
*
*BEGIN COUNTER=LENGTH OF BLOCK
*      INDEX1=START ADDRESS OF BLOCK PRIOR TO MOVE
*      INDEX2=DESTINATION ADDRESS FOR FIRST BYTE
*      DO  MOVE CONTENTS OF INDEX1+COUNTER TO INDEX2+COUNTER
*          DECREMENT COUNTER
*      WHILE COUNTER>=0
*END
*
*DATA BSTRT AND BSTRT+1 CONTAIN THE 16 BIT START ADDRESS OF
*     THE BLOCK PRIOR TO THE MOVE.
*     BDEST AND BDEST+1 CONTAIN THE 16 BIT DESTINATION ADDRESS
*     FOR THE FIRST BYTE IN THE BLOCK.
*     BLEN CONTAINS THE BLOCK LENGTH.
*
       ORG    $900
BSTRT  FDB    $0800
BDEST  FDB    $0A00
BLEN   EQU    $06
BEGIN  LDX    BSTRT    START ADDRESS OF BLOCK PRIOR TO MOVE
       LDY    BDEST    DESTINATION ADDRESS FOR FIRST BYTE
       LDA    #BLEN     BLOCK LENGTH
DO     LDB    A,X
       STB    A,Y       MOVE BYTE
       DECA             DECREMENT COUNTER
WHILE  BGE    DO
       END
```

Program 3.2.

instructions at the end of the block of instructions. As with the 'if' structure, the test in any of the loop structures can be inverted to test for false.

The block move program in Program 3.2 illustrates the 'do while' structure.

In some applications, such as monitors and terminal controllers, it is required to perform loops endlessly. This is accomplished using the 'do forever' structure:

do-forever execute block of instructions

A case structure

In high-level languages the case structure is commonly used:

case I of B0,B1,. . .B*n*

where I is an index and B0 to B*n* are blocks of instructions, procedures or subroutines. The block B0 is executed if I=0, block B1 if I=1 and so on. If I is greater than *n*, negative or on completion of one of the blocks, the next instruction is executed. In assembly language this structure may be implemented using a jump table, a table containing the start addresses for each block. The blocks are written as subroutines.

n start address of B0
n+2 start address of B1
n+4 start address of B2
.
.
.

An accumulator is loaded with the index for the case number and an index register with the base address of the jump table. Since each case number pointer in the jump table occupies two memory locations, the index has to be multiplied by 2 before the jump to subroutine is made:

```
        LDA   CASENUM
        LDX   #TABLE
        CMPA  #FIRST     check case number > smallest
        BLT   NEXT       if not goto next instruction after case
        CMPA  #LAST      check case number < largest
        BGT   NEXT       if not goto next instruction after case
        LSLA             multiply pointer by 2
        JSR   (A,X)      jump to appropriate subroutine
NEXT
```

Chapter 4

Memory Systems

4.1 INTRODUCTION

There are three main types of memory chips used in microcomputer systems.

Read only memory

Read Only Memory (ROM) chips are the simplest and cheapest form of memory. Their contents are fixed at manufacture to a specified pattern (called a mask) and cannot afterwards be changed. The contents of these chips are not affected when power is removed, and the chip is said to be non-volatile.

Programmable read only memory

Programmable Read Only Memory (PROM) chips, like ROMs cannot have their contents changed under normal operation. The user can, however, 'program' or 'blow' them by using special hardware called a PROM programmer. A program written on a development system is blown into PROM chips which are then inserted into the circuitry of the target system. These chips are non-volatile, but most can only be programmed once making them expensive to use for software development.

PROM chips that can have their contents erased and which can be reprogrammed are called EPROMs (Erasable Programmable Read Only Memory). These chips are programmed in a similar way to PROM chips, are non-volatile, and in normal operation cannot have their contents changed or erased. They have a 'window' above the integrated circuit and their entire contents can be erased by shining ultraviolet (UV) light through it and onto the integrated circuit for about 15 minutes.

Random access memory

Random Access Memory (RAM) chips can have data either written to, or read from, the specified address. Data is not lost during a memory read (a non-destructive read) although the chip's entire contents are lost when power is removed (the chip is volatile).

4.2 READ ONLY MEMORIES

Read only memories are manufactured in varying sizes, with typically up to 64K bits per chip. Common ROM chips are listed in Fig. 4.1.

Chip number	Size	Organization
MCM68308	8K bits	1K bytes
MCM68316	16K bits	2K bytes
MCM68332	32K bits	4K bytes
MCM68364	64K bits	8K bytes

Fig. 4.1. Typical ROM chips.

ROM chips are mask-programmable usually with TTL-compatible tri-state outputs. To read the contents of a memory location, the required address has to be sent to the chip via the address bus and the chip selected. The data will then be available on the chip's data pins after a short delay. These pins are connected to the data bus thus

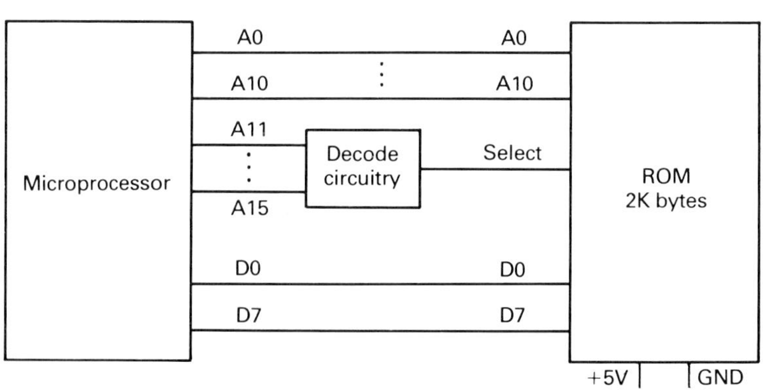

Fig. 4.2. ROM connections.

allowing the processor to gate the contents of the selected memory location to either its instruction or data registers. Figure 4.2 shows the address and data bus connections between a microprocessor and a 2K byte ROM chip.

The decode circuitry on the higher address lines in this configuration could allow up to 32×2K ROM chips to be incorporated into the system.

A ROM takes time to access a memory location, typically about 350 nanoseconds. This delay between the address being present and the data becoming available is known as the memory access time. The processor reads the data on the falling edge of the clock pulse which coincides with the end of the memory cycle. For the data to be read correctly, the ROM chip must place data on the bus some time before this (the data set up time) and must maintain it for the data hold time afterwards. Figure 4.3 shows the timing diagram for a ROM.

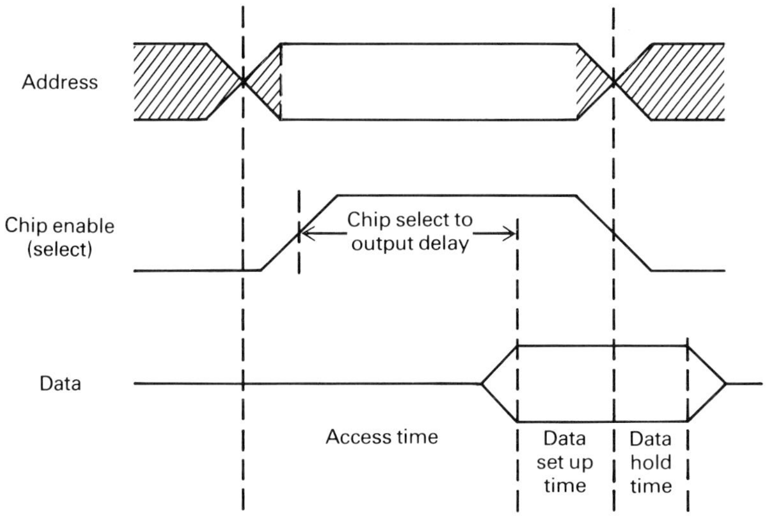

Fig. 4.3. ROM timing diagram.

4.3 THE MOTOROLA MCM68316 2K×8 bit ROM

The pin assignments for the MCM68316 2K byte ROM are given in Fig. 4.4 next page.

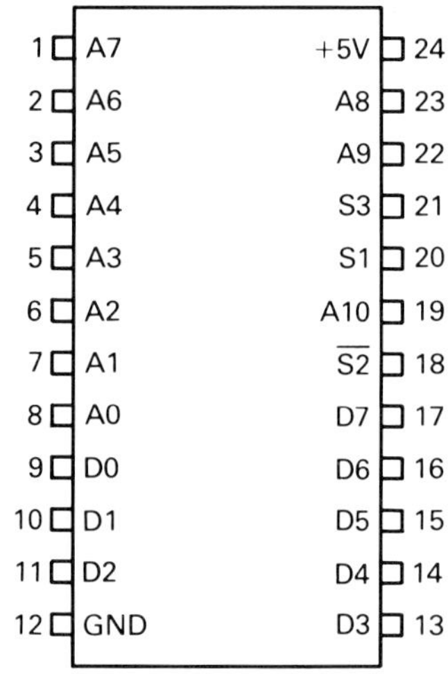

Fig. 4.4. MCM68316 pin assignments.

This 24-pin chip has a +5V power supply (+5V), ground (GND), 11 address pins (A0–A10), eight data pins (D0–7) and three chip select inputs (S1–S3) the active levels of which are specified by the user and incorporated in the chip at the time of manufacture. Figure 4.5 shows the internal organization of this typical ROM chip.

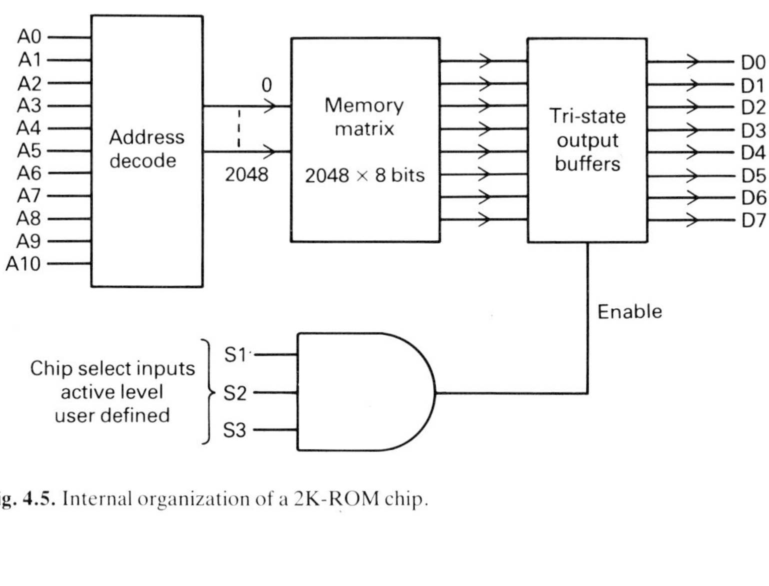

Fig. 4.5. Internal organization of a 2K-ROM chip.

4.4 CONNECTING MCM68316 ROMs to an M6809 PROCESSOR

Figure 4.6 below is the timing diagram for an M6809 memory read.

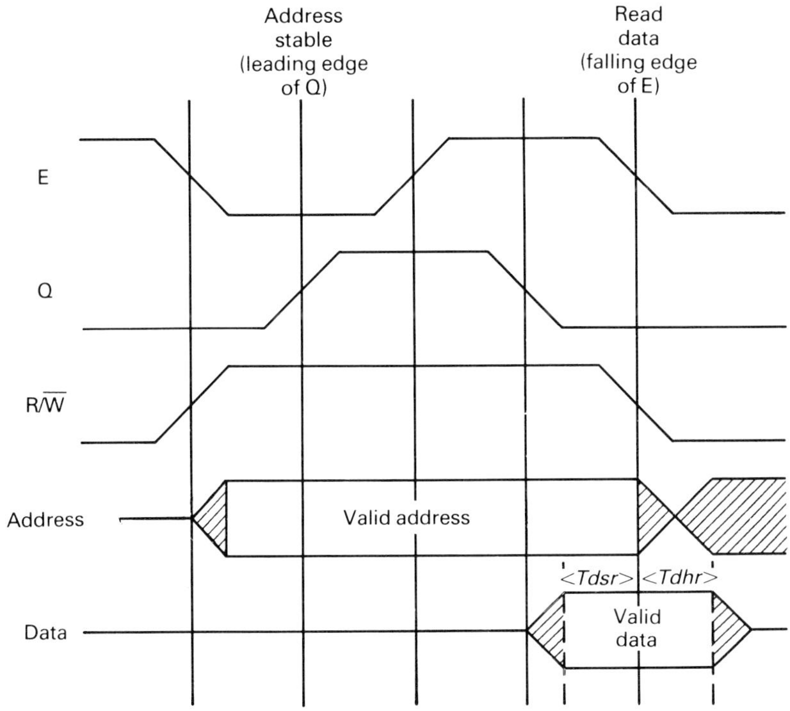

Fig. 4.6. Timing diagram for an M6809 memory read.

The address is valid when Q + E = 1 (see page 21). This logic signal, which is easily produced, can be used to ensure that any address decoding circuitry is enabled only when there is a valid address on the address bus. Data from the selected ROM is put on the bus and maintained both whilst the chip is selected and for the data hold period (*Tdhr*) after its select inputs are made inactive. Thus a second easily produced control signal $R/\overline{W}.E=1$ is used together with the output from the address decoding circuitry to enable the ROM output and to provide the two chip select signals needed to control its operation.

Figure 4.7 shows the memory circuitry for a microcomputer with an M6809 microprocessor and with three MCM68316 ROM chips giving 6K bytes of memory at the top of the address range.

	Address range	A15	A14	A13	A12	A11	A10–A0
ROM 1	F800–FFFF	1	1	1	1	1	X
ROM 2	F000–F7FF	1	1	1	1	0	X
ROM 3	E800–EFFF	1	1	1	0	1	X

X = don't care (internally decoded in ROM)

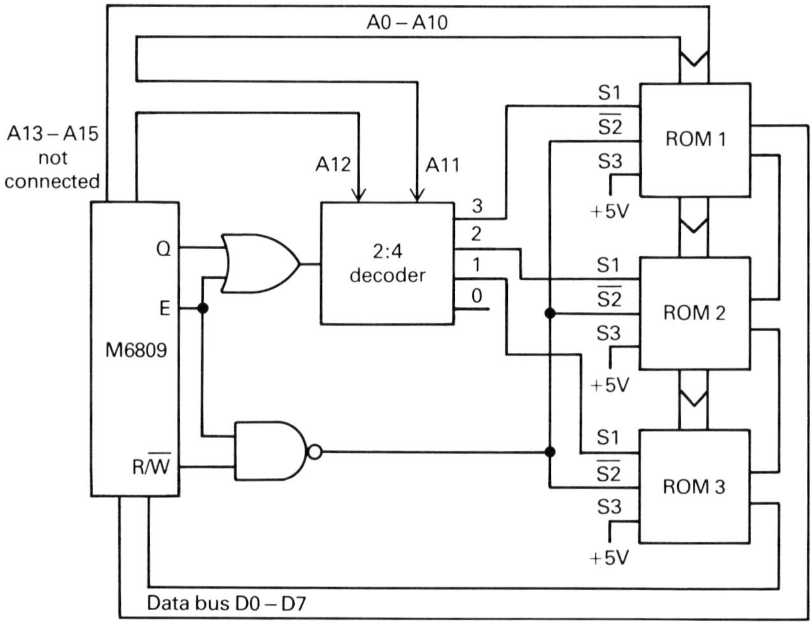

Fig. 4.7. Memory circuitry for a microcomputer with 6K of ROM.

4.5 COMPATIBLE ROM FAMILIES

A family of ROM chips, such as the Motorola ROMs listed in Fig. 4.1 are pin-compatible with each other and with other types of memory chips (Fig. 4.8).

4.6 UV-ERASABLE PROMS

UV-erasable PROMs which are usually NMOS chips are produced in various sizes (Fig. 4.9).

EPROM chips are programmable by the user using special hardware known as an EPROM programmer and then incorporated into the

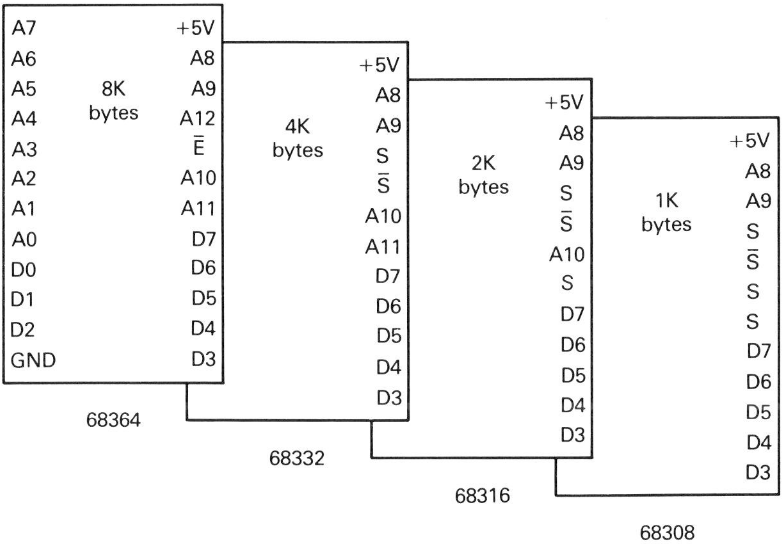

Fig. 4.8. Motorola ROM compatibility.

Chip number	Size	Organization
MCM2708	8K bits	1K bytes
MCM2716	16K bits	2K bytes
MCM2532	32K bits	4K bytes
MCM68764	64K bits	8K bytes

Fig. 4.9. Typical EPROM chips.

target system. They can be erased ready for programming by exposure to high-intensity ultraviolet light. After erasure every bit of each byte is in the logical 1 state and data can be entered by programming logical 0 into the required bits.

4.7 THE MOTOROLA MCM2716 EPROM

The pin assignments for the MCM2716 2K byte EPROM are given in Fig. 4.10 overleaf.

This chip has two modes of operation:

1 Read Mode when it is in position in the target computer system and being used in a similar way to ROM, and

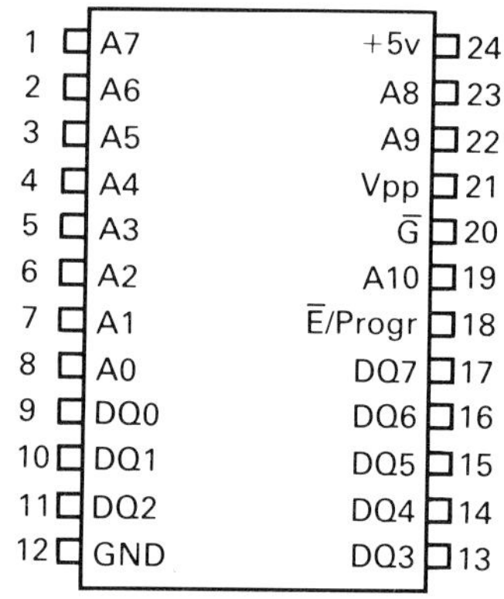

Fig. 4.10. MCM2716 pin assignments.

2 Program Mode when it is removed from the target system and is being programmed. Figure 4.11 shows the internal organization of this chip.

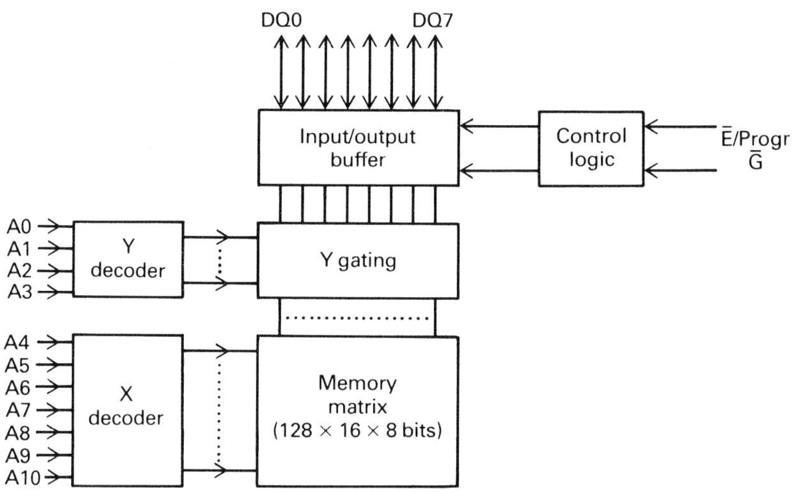

Fig. 4.11. The internal organization of a 2K EPROM.

In read mode (Figure 4.12) the chip requires a +5V power supply (pin 24), ground (pin 12) and a further +5V supply V_{pp} on pin 21. The +5V supply (called V_{CC} on pin 24) must be both applied before or at the same time as V_{pp} and switched off with or after V_{pp}. The 11 address pins (A0 – A10) and the data pins (DQ0 – DQ7) are identical in positions to those of the 2K byte ROM. Pin 20, $\overline{G}$, is an active low output enable, and pin 8, $\overline{E}$/Progr, is used to switch the chip into standby mode,

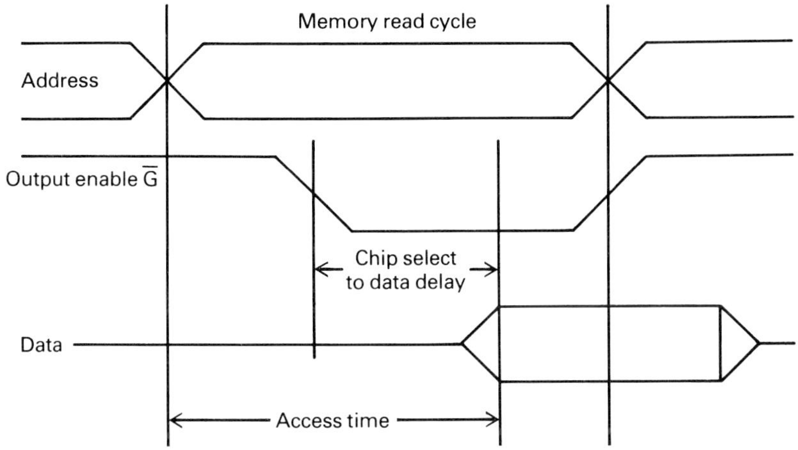

Fig. 4.12. EPROM read timing diagram.

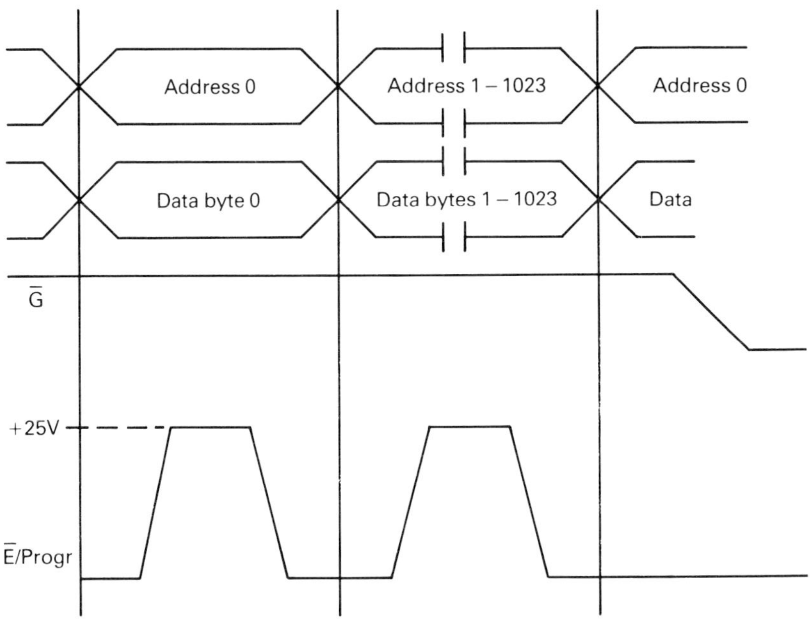

Fig. 4.13. Program mode timing diagram.

reducing its power consumption and putting the outputs into high impedance state irrespective of signal on $\overline{G}$. Thus $\overline{E}$/Progr can also be used as an output enable. When the outputs are not enabled ($\overline{G}=1$) they are in high impedance state.

This chip can be connected to an M6809 processor in much the same way as the MCM68316 ROM, although it should be noted that the enable on pin 20 has to be inverted.

In program mode (Figure 4.13) the $\overline{G}$ enable is set high. The chip is addressed in the same way as in the read mode and the data to be written to the chip is loaded though the DQ0 – DQ7 terminals. The data is written (burnt) into the chip by applying a +25V pulse of 50 milliseconds duration on the $\overline{E}$/Progr input.

4.8 COMPATIBLE EPROM FAMILIES

A family of EPROM chips are compatible with each other and with other types of memory chips. Figure 4.14 shows the industry standard pin assignments for 8K, 16K, 32K and 64K bit chips.

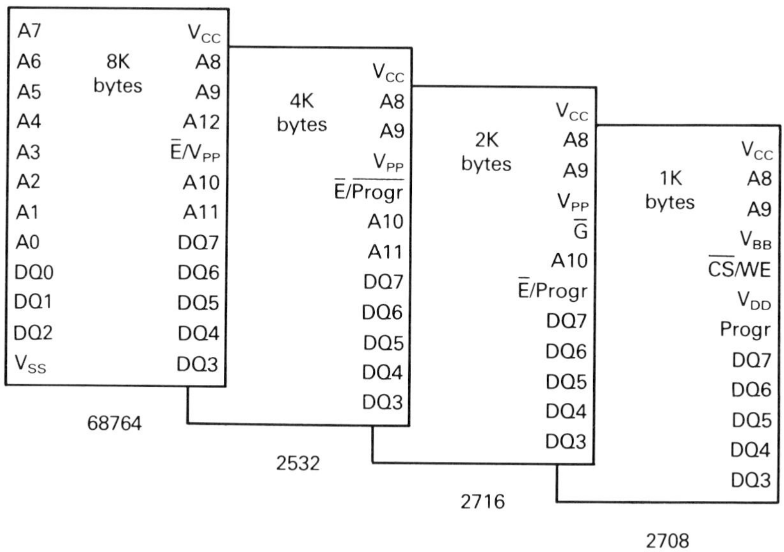

Pin names

A = Address

$\overline{E}$/Progr = Dual function Enable

V_{PP} = +25V program voltage

DQ = Data input/output

V_{CC} = +5V supply

V_{SS} = Ground

Fig. 4.14. Industry standard EPROM pin assignments.

Programming details vary slightly from chip to chip, the main variations being as follows.

The programming pulse width for the 2708 is defined by 0.1

milliseconds < *Tpw* < 1.0 milliseconds, and since each byte requires a programming time of at least 100 milliseconds, there must be between 100 and 1000 successive writes to each of the 1024 bytes that are to have data written to them. The $\overline{CS}$/WE pin is held at +12V throughout this operation. V_{DD} is a +12V supply and V_{BB} a −5V supply.

The $\overline{E}/\overline{Progr}$ terminal on the 2532 is first raised to +25V and it is a 50 milliseconds low pulse that causes data to be written into the chip.

On the 68764 the $\overline{E}/V_{PP}$ pin is raised to between 2 and 6 volts allowing the data to be set up on the DQ terminals. After the address and data have been set up a 25 volt programming pulse of 50 milliseconds duration is applied to the $\overline{E}/V_{PP}$ pin.

4.9 RANDOM ACCESS MEMORIES

There are two basic forms of random access memory, static and dynamic. Static RAM chips contain a large number of bistable elements each of which is used to store one data bit, whilst on Dynamic RAM the data is stored as an electrical charge on the gate capacitance of an MOS transistor. This charge has to be periodically 'refreshed' to prevent the signal decaying and the data being lost.

The circuitry in dynamic RAMs is simpler than that of static RAMs thus enabling more storage capacity on each chip (or for chips to be cheaper). A disadvantage with this type of memory is that the 'refresh' signal, which is often generated by the processor and may be as frequent as a hundred thousand times a second, causes the processor to execute instructions more slowly since each clock cycle has to include the refresh function.

4.10 STATIC RAM CHIPS

CMOS or NMOS Static RAM chips can be organized in much the same way as ROMs and PROMs, storing data in the form of an array of $n \times m$ bits. The organization of some static RAM chips are given in Fig. 4.15.

Chip number	Size	Organization
MK4801	8K bits	1 K bytes
HM6116	16K bits	2K bytes
HM6264	64K bits	8K bytes
MCM2114	4K bits	1K×4 bits
MCM2147	4K bits	4K×1 bit
HM6167	16K bits	16K×1 bit

Fig. 4.15. Static RAM chips.

Static RAM chips can be either byte-, nibble- or bit-organized as shown above. Each type is briefly described in the following sections.

4.11 BYTE-ORGANIZED STATIC RAM CHIPS

Byte-organized static RAM chips are designed to be fully interchangeable with other types of memory chips. Typical of this family of chips is

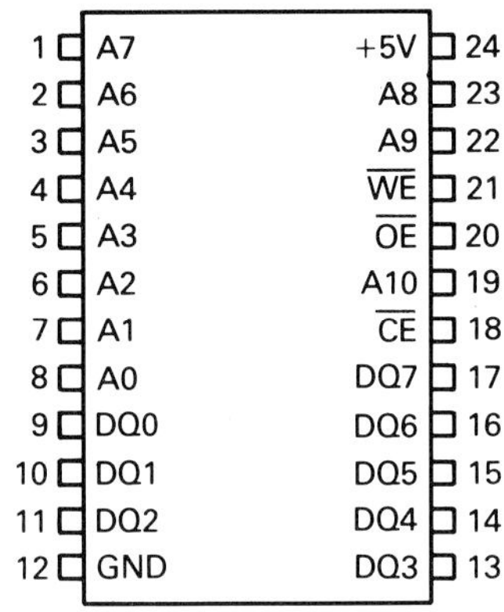

Fig. 4.16. HM6116 pin assignments.

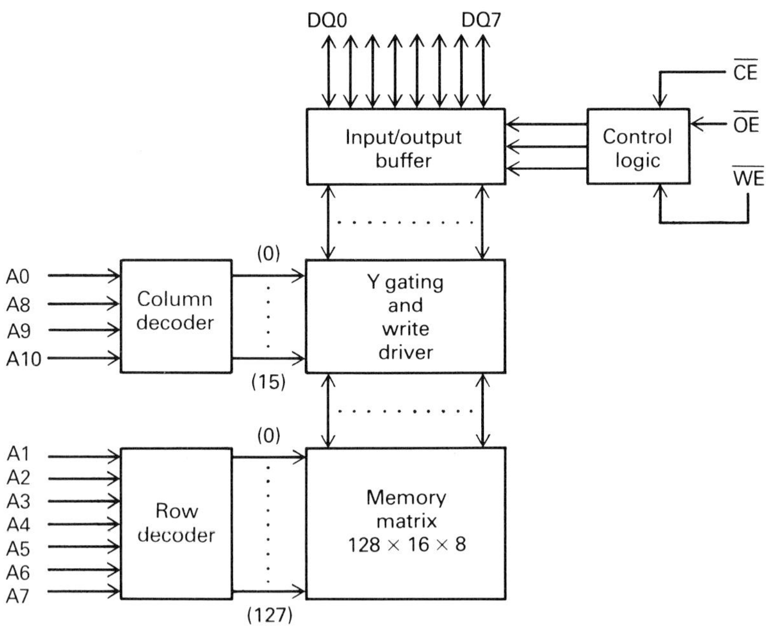

Fig. 4.17. Internal organization of a 2K-byte static RAM chip.

the Hitachi HM6116 2K×8-bit static RAM, the pin assignment for which is given in Fig. 4.16.

This chip is compatible with the 2K byte EPROM (2716) and the 2K byte ROM (68316). Again this 24-pin chip has a single +5V power supply, 11 address pins (A0–A10) and eight data pins (DQ0–DQ7). It also incorporates a single chip select input ($\overline{CE}$), an active low write enable ($\overline{WE}$), and an active low output enable ($\overline{OE}$). Figure 4.17 shows the typical internal organization of a 2K byte static RAM chip.

When data is being read from the chip, the chip select input ($\overline{CE}$) is low, the write enable ($\overline{WE}$) high, and the output enable ($\overline{OE}$) used as the timing signal to enable the outputs. When writing data $\overline{CE}$ is low, $\overline{OE}$ is high and $\overline{WE}$ is used to control the transfer.

4.12 CONNECTING THE HM6116 STATIC RAM TO AN M6809 PROCESSOR

The timing diagrams for a memory read from byte-organized static RAM and ROM are similar (cf Fig. 4.6). The address is valid whilst $Q + E = 1$ and this signal is used to generate the $\overline{CE}$ signal which must be low whilst the address is stable. The data output is controlled by the R/W.E signal which is inverted and supplied to the $\overline{OE}$ terminal.

A typical timing diagram for a write to a static RAM chip is shown in Fig. 4.18 overleaf.

Data is written to the chip on the rising edge of the write pulse which must be longer than the specified minimum (*Twp*). Data must be available at least *Tdw* (the data write set up time) before the end of the write pulse and be held for at least a period *Tdh* (the data hold time) after it.

Other timing constraints, such as the minimum period between a stable address and the start of the write pulse (*Tas*) and between the end of the write pulse and the end of the write cycle (*Twr*), have to be met and the reader should consult the memory chip and processor data sheets for further detailed timing criteria.

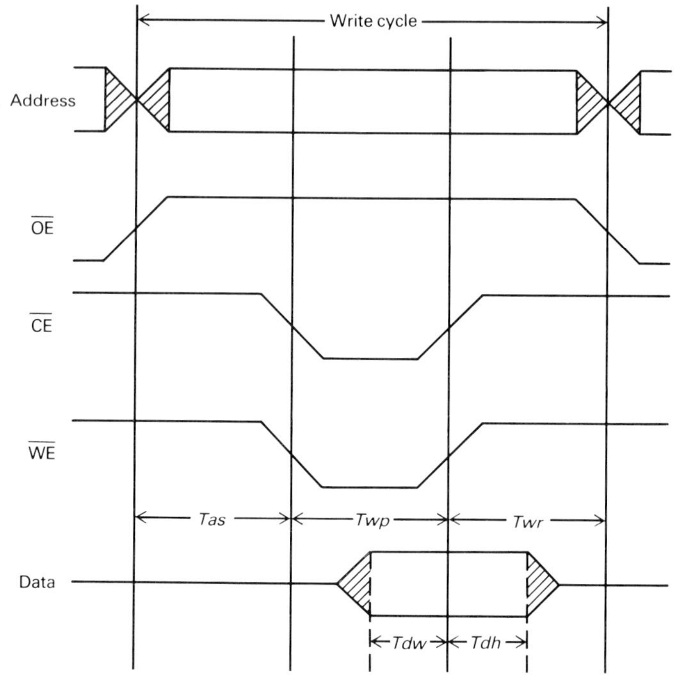

Fig. 4.18. Timing diagram for a static RAM write cycle.

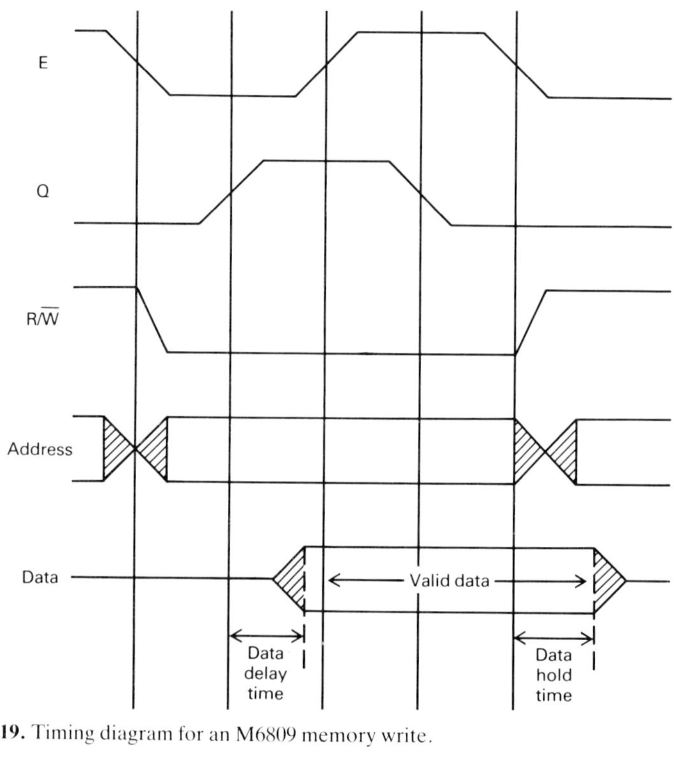

Fig. 4.19. Timing diagram for an M6809 memory write.

Figure 4.19 opposite shows the timing diagram for an M6809 memory write.

The address is again stable when Q+E=1. This signal is used as the enable for the address decoding circuitry which in turn provides the RAM chip enable signal during both read and write operations.

	Chip	Address range	A15	A14	A13	A12	A11	A10–A0
ROM 1	68316	F800–FFFF	1	1	1	1	1	X
ROM 2	68316	F000–F7FF	1	1	1	1	0	X
ROM 3	68316	E800–EFFF	1	1	1	0	1	X
RAM 1	6116	E000–E7FF	1	1	1	0	0	X
RAM 2	6116	D800–DFFF	1	1	0	1	1	X

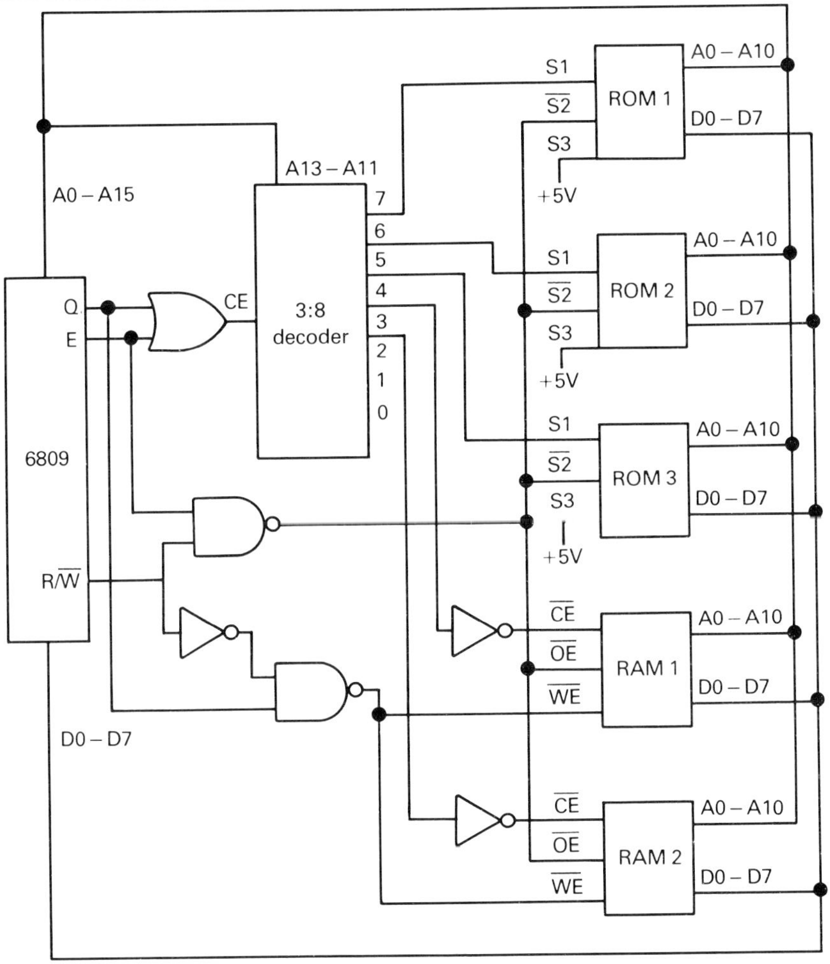

Fig. 4.20. Microcomputer with 6K of ROM and 4K of RAM.

The output enable signal derived for the memory read ($\overline{R/\overline{W}.E}$) is high throughout the write operation, as required, leaving only the write enable ($\overline{WE}$) input to be obtained. The derived $\overline{Q.R/\overline{W}}$ signal is used for this purpose as it meets the timing requirements for the write enable of the HM6116 memory chip.

The microcomputer system shown in Fig. 4.7. can be extended to include 4K of RAM in two 2K byte HM6116 static RAM chips at the addresses given on the previous page in Fig. 4.20.

Note that the decoding has been extended by using a 3:8 decoder to allow for the increased occupation of the available address space. Additional logic has been used to derive the $\overline{Q.R/\overline{W}}$ write signal.

4.13 NIBBLE-ORGANIZED STATIC RAM CHIPS

Static RAMs are also organized as $n \times 4$ bit chips, two of which are used in parallel to produce n bytes of read/write memory. Two commonly used chips are the 2112, a 16-pin 256×4-bit chip, and the 2114 an 18-pin 1K×4-bit chip, the pin assignment of which is given in Fig. 4.21.

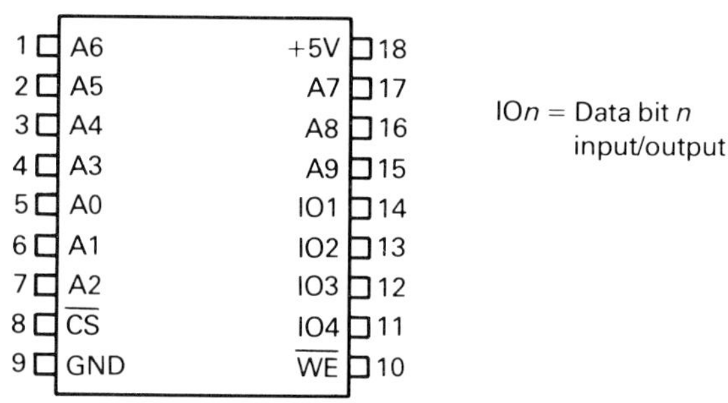

Fig. 4.21. Pin assignments for 2114 series 1K × 4-bit static RAM.

4.14 BIT-ORGANIZED STATIC RAM CHIPS

The third type of static RAM is the bit-organized chip. Figure 4.22 shows the pin connections for the MCM2147 which is a typical 4K×1 bit static RAM chip.

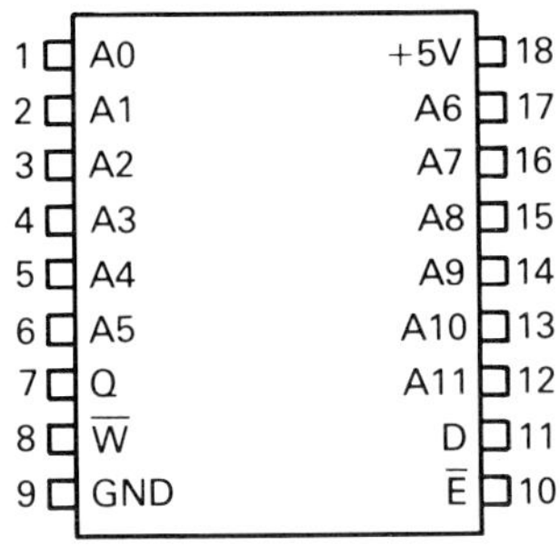

Fig. 4.22. MCM2147 pin assignments.

This 18-pin chip stores 4096 data bits, has 12 address lines (A0–A11), a single +5V power supply (V_{CC}) and ground (GND). The chip is selected with the $\overline{E}$ terminal, which when high places the chip into low-power standby mode saving power by up to 85%. The write enable pin ($\overline{W}$) controls the direction of transfer on the data input (D) and data output (Q) terminals. Figure 4.23 shows the internal organization of this chip.

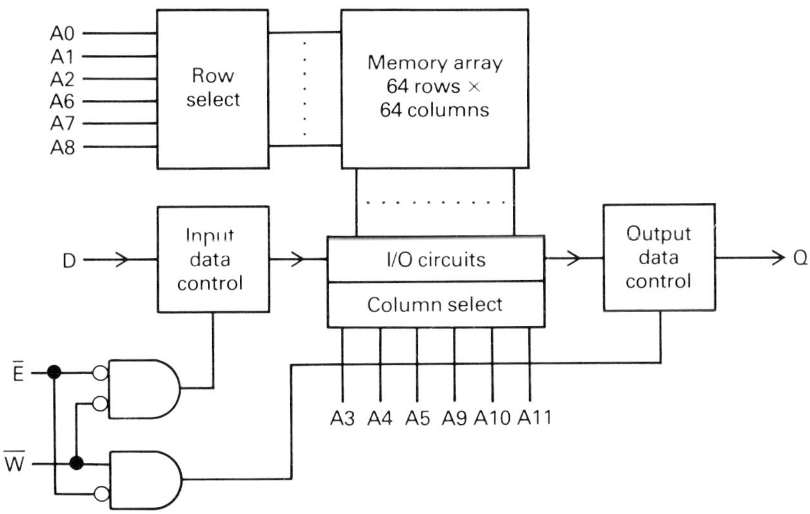

Fig. 4.23. Internal organization of a 4K bit-organized static RAM.

On an 8-bit microcomputer system, eight of these chips are used in parallel to give 4K bytes of random access memory, each chip providing 1 bit of the selected byte as shown in Fig. 4.24.

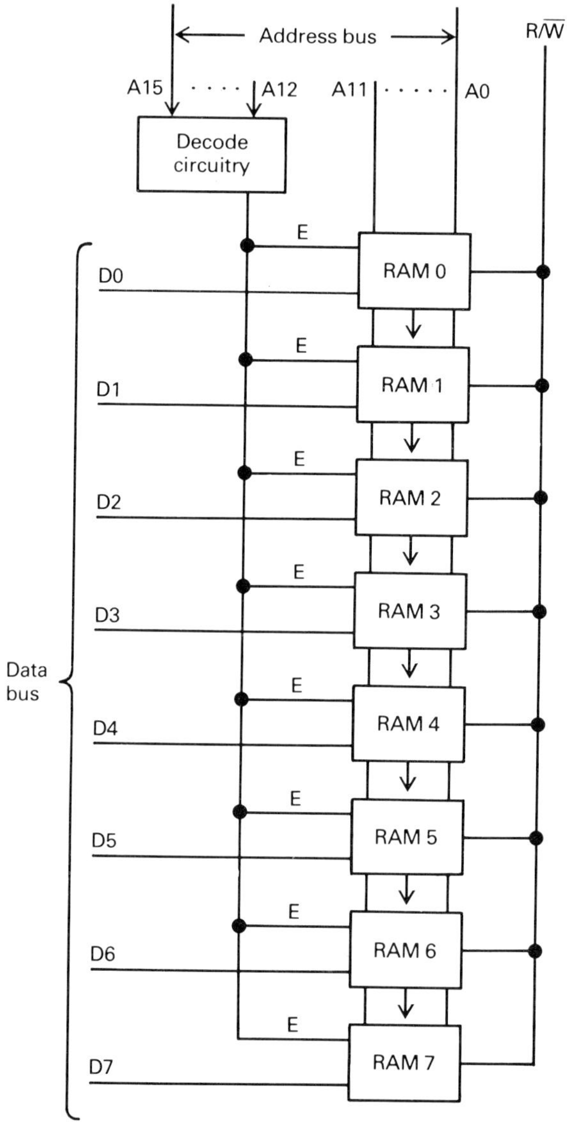

Fig. 4.24. Using 1-bit RAM chips on 8-bit systems.

4.15 DYNAMIC RAM CHIPS

Dynamic RAM chips are most commonly used with processors like the Zilog Z80, which provide the necessary control signals to allow easy interfacing between the processor and memory chips. The Motorola 6809 does not provide the address bus multiplexing and refresh signals required by dynamic RAM. Whilst these can be produced by either software or by external hardware, it is more usual for M6809 systems to be designed with static RAM. However, for completion of the consideration of the major types of memory systems, the following description of dynamic RAM chips has been included.

Dynamic RAM chips are both cheap and reliable and have a high packing density, i.e. a large number of bits per chip. Each bit is stored as a low or high voltage on the gate capacitance of an MOS transistor cell, and thus, if data is to be held for longer than the self-discharge time of the capacitor, it must be sensed before it is lost and restored to its original voltage level (a process known as memory refresh).

Dynamic RAMs are bit-organized chips, the memory matrix being an $m \times n$ array of 1-bit storage elements. Each time that a row of the array is addressed each cell in that row is simultaneously refreshed, a process that must occur for each row in the matrix at least once every 1 or 2 milliseconds if data is to be maintained. Figure 4.25 lists some typical dynamic RAM chips.

Chip number	Organization
MCM4027	4K×1 bit
MCM4116	16K×1 bit
MK4164	64K×1 bit

Fig. 4.25. Typical dynamic RAM chips.

4.16 THE MCM4116 DYNAMIC RAM CHIP

Figure 4.26 shows the pin assignments for the Motorola MCM4116 16K-bit dynamic RAM chip which is an industry standard 16-pin package.

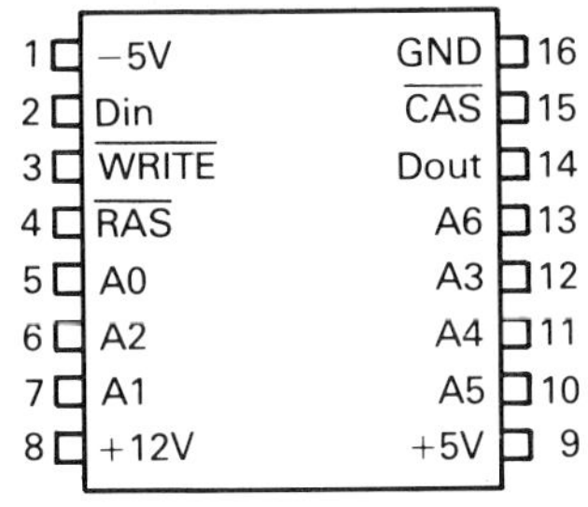

Fig. 4.26. Pin assignments for the MCM4116.

Figure 4.27 shows the internal organization of this chip.

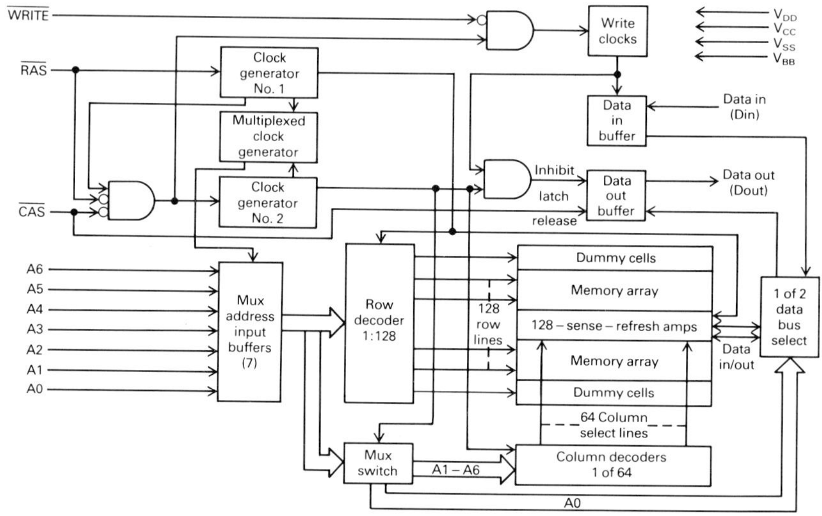

Fig. 4.27. Internal organization of the MCM4116.

This chip has four power supply terminals for +5V, +12V, −5V and GND. The seven address lines A0–A6 are used to supply the required 14-bit address to the 128×128-bit memory matrix. The seven bit row address is latched first, when the Row Address Strobe terminal ($\overline{\text{RAS}}$) goes low, followed by the seven bit column address on a high to low transition of $\overline{\text{CAS}}$. Data supplied on the Din terminal is written to the chip provided that the $\overline{\text{WRITE}}$ terminal is low. Data is read from the chip on the Dout pin if $\overline{\text{WRITE}}$ is high.

The row and column addresses are latched on the falling edges of the respective $\overline{\text{RAS}}$ and $\overline{\text{CAS}}$ pulses provided that they have been present for at least the minimum set-up times (*Tras* and *Tcas* respectively) prior to the transition and are held for at least the minimum hold times (*Trah* and *Tcah*) after it. Provided that the column address strobe occurs within a period *Trcd* of the row address strobe, the data will become available after a period *Tcac* (the access time from $\overline{\text{CAS}}$) and will be maintained for a time *Toff* (the output buffer turn off delay) after the column address strobe is again made inactive (see Fig. 4.28).

During a memory write cycle the data to be written to the selected cell is latched into the on-chip buffer when $\overline{\text{CAS}}$, $\overline{\text{RAS}}$ and $\overline{\text{WRITE}}$ are all active (low). The latter of the $\overline{\text{CAS}}$ and $\overline{\text{WRITE}}$ signals to make its negative transition is therefore the strobe for the Din register enabling several different options for write cycle timing. Figure 4.29 shows a

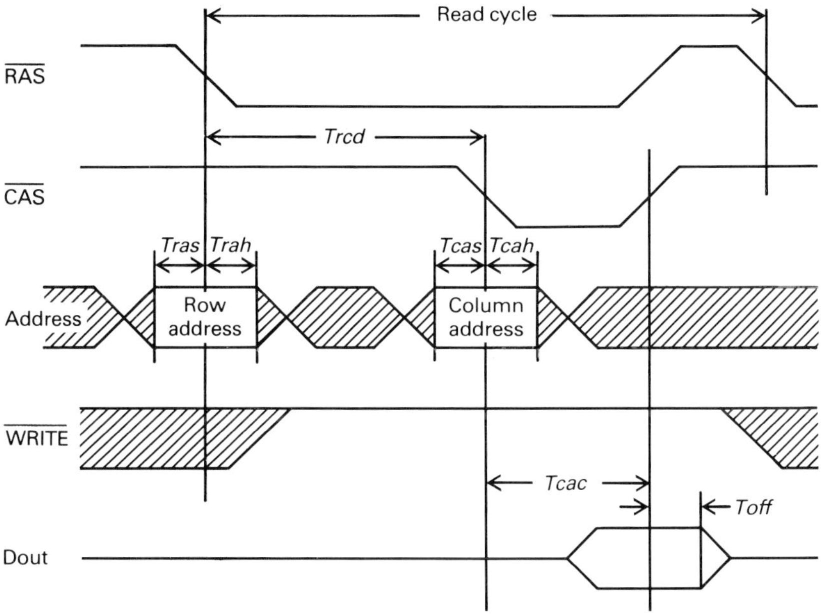

Fig. 4.28. Dynamic RAM read cycle timing diagram.

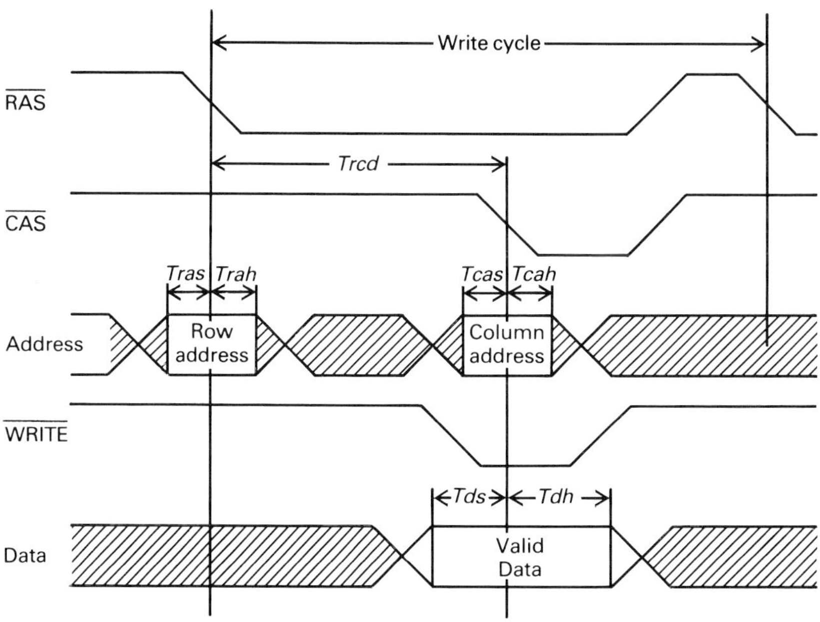

Fig. 4.29. Dynamic RAM write cycle timing diagram.

simplified timing diagram for a memory write cycle in which $\overline{\text{WRITE}}$ is active before $\overline{\text{CAS}}$.

The data must be available on the Din terminal at least *Tds* (the data set-up time) before the falling edge of the $\overline{\text{CAS}}$ pulse and be held for at least *Tdh* (the data hold time) after it. For more detailed timing citeria the reader should consult the manufacturer's data sheets.

Other modes of operation include read/write cycles and page mode in which successive memory operations on different columns of the same row are performed at increased speed.

Refresh is accomplished by performing a memory cycle on each of the 128 row addresses at least once every 2 milliseconds. Whilst normal memory cycles will perform this operation, a special $\overline{\text{RAS}}$ only cycle with a substantial reduction in operating power is usually used. Figure 4.30 shows the timing diagram for a $\overline{\text{RAS}}$ only cycle.

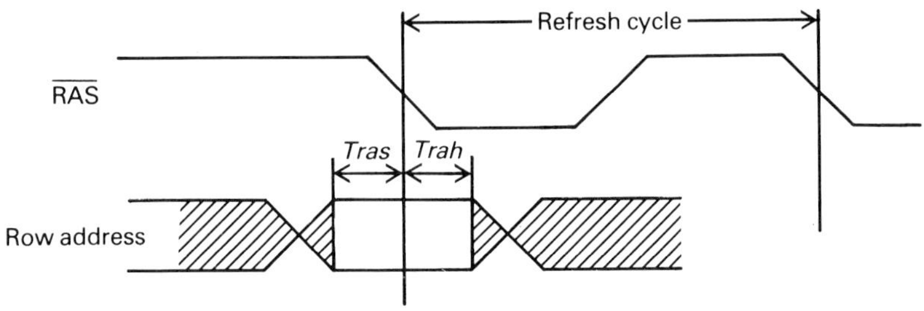

Fig. 4.30. Refresh cycle timing diagram.

This chapter has described the main types of memory chips. The selection of which type and size of chip to use in a particular microcomputer design will be made according to the application, the RAM, ROM and EPROM requirements, and the processor used.

Chapter 5

Input/Output

5.1 INTRODUCTION

Data is transmitted between a processor and a peripheral in either parallel or serial forms depending on the type of peripheral and the type of interface used to connect it to the processor buses. This chapter describes LSI parallel and serial interface chips and gives M6809 examples showing how different input/output devices are connected, and their assembly language driver routines.

5.2 PARALLEL INTERFACES

Parallel interfaces provide the mechanism for connecting several input/output lines directly onto the data bus of a central processor. They are also capable of providing handshaking signals and of allowing interrupts to be sent to the processor. This variety of functions can be provided on a single programmable LSI interface chip with the following features:

1 buffers and latches for the input and output lines,
2 status and control signals for handshaking,
3 interrupt lines for connection to input/output devices,
4 a direct interface with the processor buses,
5 registers that can be programmed from the central processor to specify the function to be performed by the interface.

5.3 THE MOTOROLA MC6821 PIA

The Motorola MC6821 Peripheral Interface Adaptor (PIA) is a typical LSI parallel interface chip. Figure 5.1 shows the pin assignments and Fig. 5.2 the internal organization of the chip.

This chip provides two functionally identical parallel interfaces, referred to as A and B. Each has eight input/output lines (PA0–PA7 and PB0–PB7) and two control lines (CA1, CA2 and CB1, CB2) for connection to external devices. The input/output lines on the A side have CMOS drive capability, whilst those on the B side are TTL-compatible. The direction of data transfer on each of the input/output

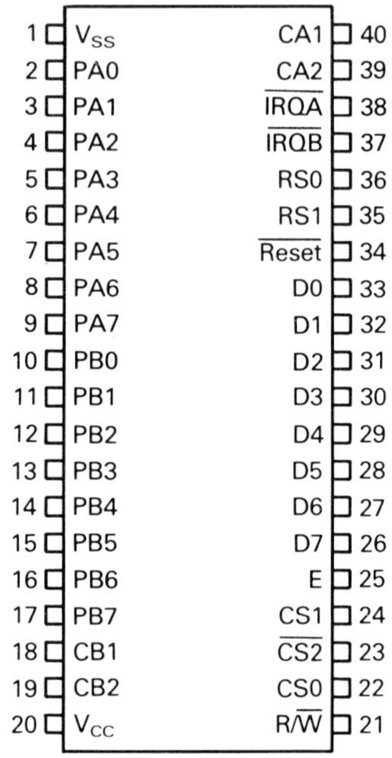

Fig. 5.1. MC6821 pin assignments.

lines is specified by a bit being either cleared or set in the corresponding data direction register (DDRA or DDRB). If the bit is clear the line will be used for input and if it is set for output from the processor to the peripheral. The buffered D0–D7 terminals provide the connections between the interface and the processor's data bus allowing the eight input/output terminals on one port to be read or set simultaneously.

The functions of the control lines CA1, CA2, CB1 and CB2 are determined by the contents of the respective programmable control registers, CRA and CRB. They can be used as interrupt lines to external devices provided that the $\overline{\text{IRQA}}$ and/or $\overline{\text{IRQB}}$ pins have been connected to an interrupt terminal on the processor. In interrupt mode, the corresponding control register in the PIA has to be programmed to enable the required interrupt facility. Alternatively, the control register can be programmed to enable the CA2 and CB2 lines to be used as outputs for handshaking with a peripheral device or to allow them to be set or cleared directly. Figure 5.3 summarizes the functions of the control registers.

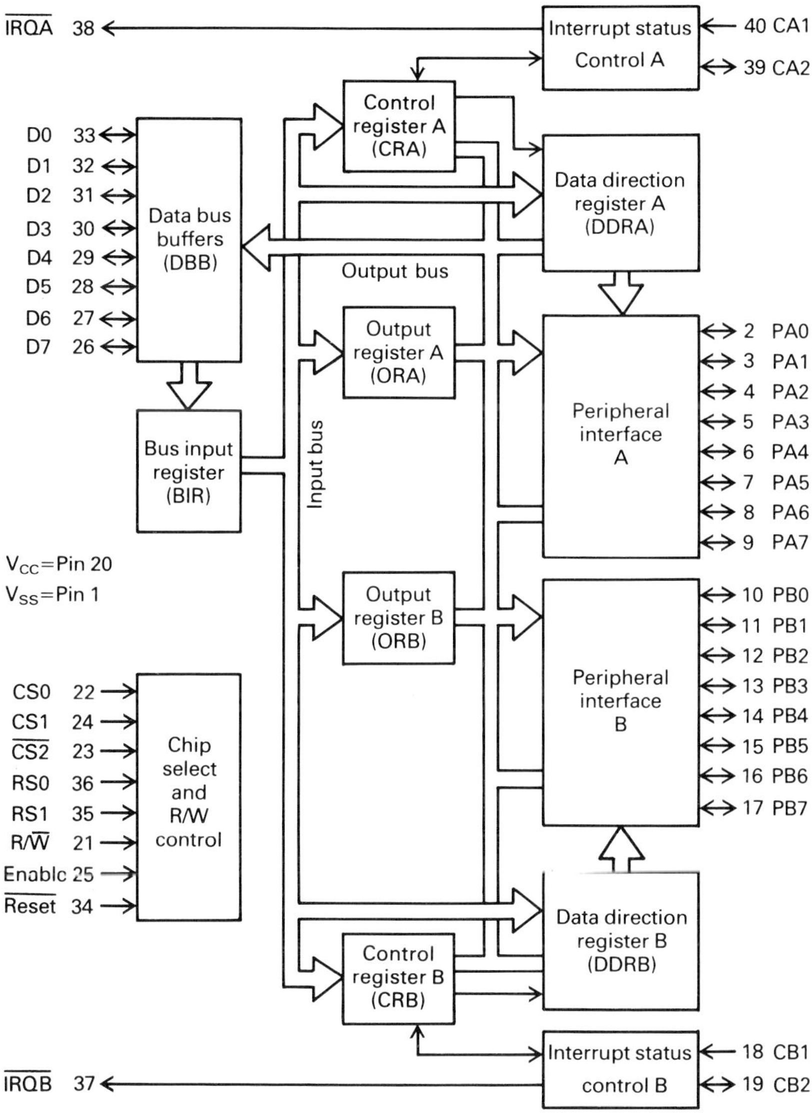

Fig. 5.2. The Motorola MC6821 PIA.

The three input pins, CS0, CS1 and $\overline{CS2}$, are used to select the chip. CS0 and CS1 must be high and $\overline{CS2}$ low for the PIA to be selected. All data transfers are then performed under the control of the Enable (E)

Bit Number

7	6	5	4	3	2	1	0
IRQA1 IRQB1	IRQA2 IRQB2	CA2 control CB2 control			DDRA DDRB	CA1 control CB1 control	
Interrupt flag Set by a transition of CA1 or CB1 Cleared by reading data register	Same as bit 7 with CA2 or CB2 as inputs As handshaking outputs CA2 cleared by reading data register A & CB2 by writing to data register B	0=CA2 or CB2 used as interrupt line	0=bit 6 set by high to low transition of CA2 or CB2 1=bit6 set by low to high transistion	Interrupt enable on IRQA or IRQB 1=enable interrupts	0=DDR access data direction register 1=DR access data register	0=bit 7 set by high to low transition of CA1 or CB1 1=bit 7 set by low to high transition	Interrupt enable on IRQA or IRQB 1=enable interrupts
		1=CA2 or CB2 used as an output	0=Handshake 1=CA2 or CB2 output =bit 3	0=Full 1=Pulse 0 1			

Fig. 5.3. Function of MC6821 PIA control registers.

and read/write (R/$\overline{\text{W}}$) signals. The E terminal provides the timing for the transfer whilst R/$\overline{\text{W}}$ specifies its direction.

The $\overline{\text{Reset}}$ input is used to reset all register bits in the PIA to zero and can be used as a power-on reset and with the master reset under system operation.

The PIA occupies four memory locations, two for the A side and two for the B side. The programmer needs access to three registers for each port, the control register, the peripheral data register and the data

RS1	RS0	Register	CRA2	CRB2
0	0	Peripheral data register A Data direction register A	1 0	X X
0	1	Control register A	X	X
1	0	Peripheral data register B Data direction register B	X X	1 0
1	1	Control register B	X	X

X = don't care

Fig. 5.4. MC6821 register addressing.

direction register. The peripheral data and data direction registers are accessed by the same address, which register is accessed being determined by bit 2 of the corresponding control register. The register select pins RS0 and RS1 are used to determine the register/s being addressed as shown in Fig. 5.4.

5.4 CONNECTING THE MC6821 TO AN M6809 PROCESSOR

The four addresses occupied by the MC6821 are determined by the address decoding performed in selecting the chip.

Consider the case where the chip addresses are given by:

A15	A14	A13	A12–A2	A1	A0	
1	1	0	X	0	0	DRA and DDRA
1	1	0	X	0	1	CRA
1	1	0	X	1	0	DRB and DDRB
1	1	0	X	1	1	CRB

where X = don't care and the system being designed is such that the PIA can be mirrored on the memory map for every combination of the address lines A12–A2. The decoding, in this case, will be minimal and will produce the cheapest solution whilst using up 8K of memory addresses for the PIA. On a small target system requiring only limited memory, the wastage of addressing capability will not be important provided sufficient address space is available for the other system components. Figure 5.5 shows the connections between an M6809

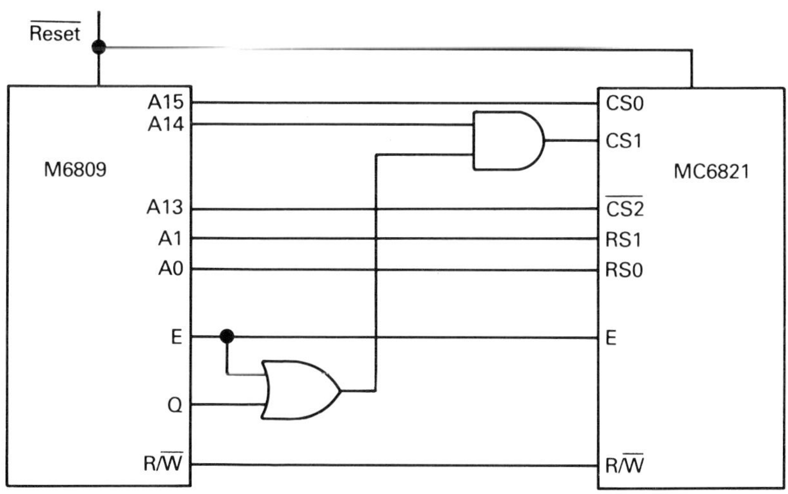

Fig. 5.5. M6809/MC6821 bus connections.

processor an MC6821 PIA at the addresses given above for this type of system.

The valid address signal E+Q is combined with one of the address lines so that the chip is only selected when a stable address is present on the bus.

5.5 INPUT/OUTPUT PROGRAMMING FOR A PIA

The simplest form of input is a switch and of output is a light-emitting diode (LED). Figure 5.6 shows a PIA with eight switches connected as inputs on PA0–PA7 and eight light-emitting diodes as outputs on PB0–PB7.

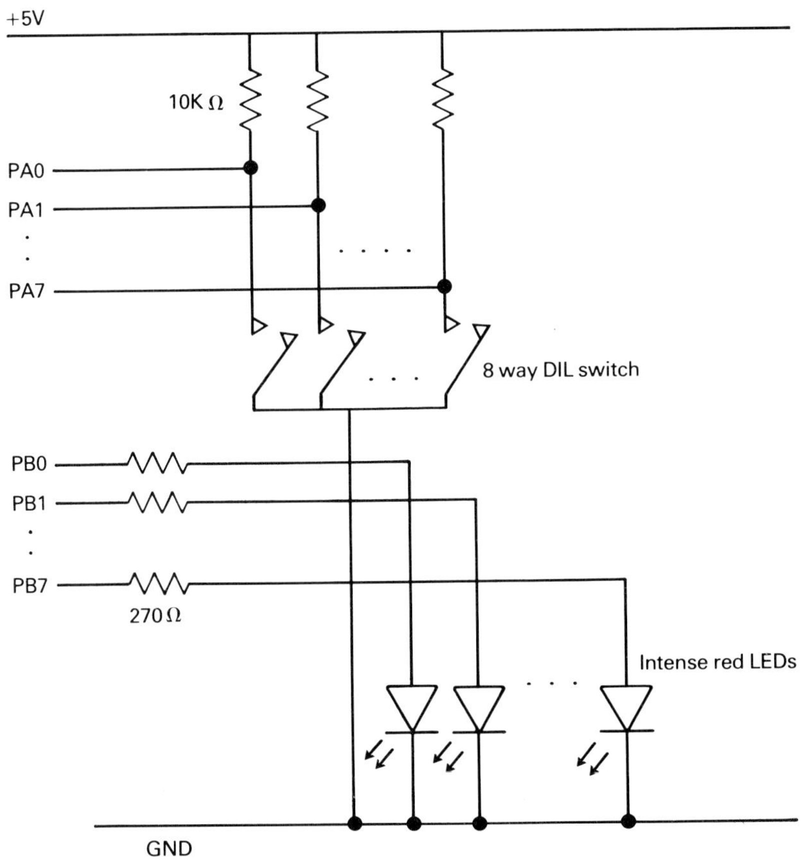

Fig. 5.6. A parallel input/output system.

Program 5.1 continuously reads the switches on the A port and displays their settings on LEDs connected to the B port. The PIA is at addresses F608–F60B.

```
             NAM     PARALLEL I/O
      *PROGRAMMER P.J.THEWLIS
      *23 MARCH 1983
      *PROGRAM READS EIGHT SWITCHES CONNECTED TO THE A SIDE
      *OF A PIA AND DISPLAYS THEM ON EIGHT LEDS CONNECTED TO
      *THE B SIDE OF THE SAME PIA
      *
      *BEGIN INITIALISE PIA
      *      DO FOREVER READ SWITCHES
      *                 OUTPUT TO LIGHTS
      *      END DO FOREVER
      *END
      *
      *PIA ADDRESSES $F608 TO $F60B
      *
             ORG     $800
      PIADR  EQU     $F608
      BEGIN  LDX     #PIADR    BASE ADDRESS OF PIA
             CLR     1,X       CLEAR CRA - ACCESS DDRA
             CLR     0,X       SET ALL BITS OF DDRA TO 0 (INPUT)
             CLR     3,X       CLEAR CRB - ACCESS DDRB
             LDA     #$FF
             STA     2,X       SET ALL BITS OF DDRB TO 1 (OUTPUT)
             LDA     #$04
             STA     1,X       SET CRA2=1 TO ACCESS DRA
             STA     3,X       SET CRB2=1 TO ACCESS DRB
      DOEV   LDA     0,X       READ SWITCHES
             STA     2,X       OUTPUT TO LIGHTS
      ENDEV  JMP     DOEV
             END
```

Program 5.1.

The method described above can be used when interfacing a keyboard, which, in its simplest form is merely a collection of switches which can be connected to a microprocessor by a parallel port. Each switch may be connected directly to an input line or the switches may be arranged as an array with each switch connecting a row to a column. Figure 5.7 shows a typical layout for a hexadecimal keyboard and its connection to the B side of a PIA.

The keyboard is handled as follows.

1 Make the columns outputs and rows inputs.

2 Ground the columns by outputting a 0 on PB4–PB7.

3 Read the rows by reading peripheral data register B. If no switch has been pressed the inputs PB0–PB3 will all be 1 and no further action is needed. If however any key is closed that row will be connected to the corresponding column grounding it and making the input 0.
e.g. If any of the keys C–F are pressed, the value read from the PIA will be 00001110 or $0E.

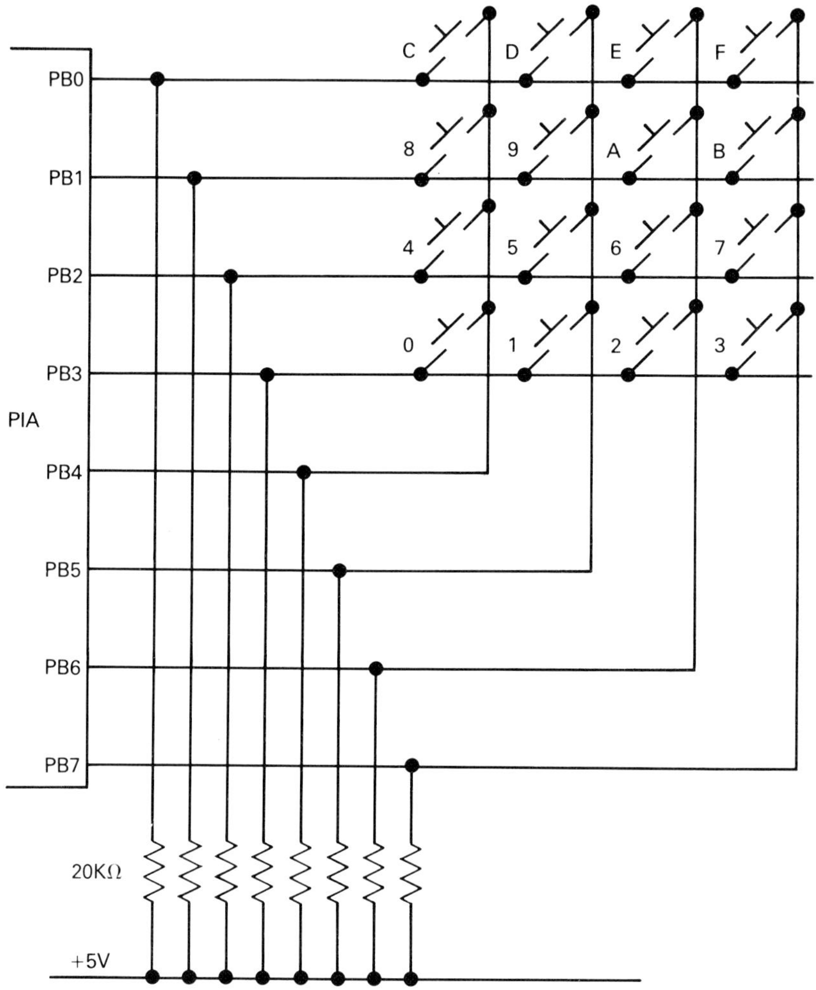

Fig. 5.7. A hexadecimal keyboard.

4 Make the rows outputs and the columns inputs.
5 Ground the rows by outputting a 0 on PB0–PB3 and read the columns by again reading peripheral data register B. The column with the closed key will be grounded.
e.g. If the key D is pressed, the value from the PIA will be 11010000 or \$D0.
6 Adding together the values read for the row and column scans gives a unique code for the key pressed (Fig. 5.8).

Key	Code	Key	Code	Key	Code	Key	Code
C	EE	D	DE	E	BE	F	7E
8	ED	9	DD	A	BD	B	7D
4	EB	5	DB	6	BB	7	7B
0	E7	1	D7	2	B7	3	77

Fig. 5.8. Key codes.

The following subroutine (Program 5.2) scans the hexadecimal keyboard and returns with the hexadecimal value for the key pressed in the A register.

```
        NAM    KEYBOARD
*PROGRAMMER P.J.THEWLIS
*2 APRIL 1984
*SUBROUTINE TO READ A HEXADECIMAL KEYBOARD AND TO RETURN WITH
*THE A REGISTER CONTAINING THE BINARY VALUE OF THE KEY PRESSED.
*IF AN ERROR OCCURS,SUCH AS TWO KEYS BEING PRESSED AT THE SAME
*TIME, THE A REGISTER IS LOADED WITH $FF.
*
*THE KEYBOARD ARRAY HAS ROWS CONNECTED TO PB0 TO PB3 AND COLUMNS
*TO PB4 TO PB7 ON A PIA WHICH IS AT ADDRESSES $F608 TO $F60B.
*
*THE SUBROUTINE USES A DATA TABLE WHICH CONTAINS THE HEXADECIMAL
*VALUE FOR THE INPUT FROM EACH KEY IN ASCENDING KEY VALUE
*
*BEGIN SET PIA FOR COLUMNS AS OUTPUTS AND ROWS AS INPUTS
*      DO  GROUND COLUMNS
*          READ PIA
*          SAVE PIA INPUT (ROWS)
*      WHILE NO KEY CLOSED (KEY CLOSED = A ZERO ON ANY OF PB0 TO PB3)
*      SET PIA FOR ROWS AS OUTPUTS AND COLUMNS AS INPUTS
*      GROUND ROWS
*      READ PIA (COLUMNS)
*      IF KEY NOT CLOSED THEN RESTART SUBROUTINE
*      KEY PATTERN = PIA INPUT (COLUMNS) + PIA INPUT (ROWS)
*      COUNTER = 0
*      TABLE ITEM POINTER = TABLE BASE ADDRESS
*      WHILE TABLE ITEM CONTENTS <> KEY PATTERN DO
*          INCREMENT COUNTER
*          INCREMENT TABLE ITEM POINTER
*      IF COUNTER=10 THEN REGISTER A=$FF
*                    ELSE REGISTER A=COUNTER
*      RETURN
*END
*
        ORG    $800
PIADR   EQU    $F608
PIARO   RMB    01
TABLE   FCB    $E7,$D7,$B7,$77,$EB,$DB,$BB,$7B
        FCB    $ED,$DD,$BD,$7D,$EE,$DE,$BE,$7E
KEYB    PSHS   B          SAVE B REGISTER
KEB1    LDX    #PIADR     INDEX=PIA BASE ADDRESS
        CLR    3,X        CLEAR CRB  ACCESS DDRB
        LDA    #$F0       COLUMNS=OUTPUT ROWS=INPUT
        STA    2,X        SET DDRB
        LDA    #$04
        STA    3,X        SET CRB2=1  ACCESS DRB
        LDA    #$0F
DO1     STA    2,X        GROUND COLUMNS
        LDA    2,X        READ PIA - INPUT ROWS
        STA    PIARO
        CMPA   #$0F       TEST FOR KEY CLOSED
WHILE1  BEQ    DO1        NO KEY CLOSED, KEEP LOOKING
```

```
*KEY CLOSURE DETECTED
              CLR     3,X        CLEAR CRB ACCESS DDRB
              LDA     #$0F       COLUMNS=INPUT ROWS=OUTPUT
              STA     2,X        SET DDRB
              LDA     #$04
              STA     3,X        SET CRB2 TO ACCESS DDRB
              LDA     #$F0
              STA     2,X        GROUND ROWS
              LDB     2,X        READ PIA - INPUT COLUMNS
              CMPB    #$F0       CHECK FOR KEY STILL CLOSED
      IF1     BEQ     KEB1       IF NOT RESTART
              ADDB     PIARO      GENERATE KEY PATTERN
              LDX     #TABLE
              LDA     #$0        COUNTER=0
      WHILE2  CMPB    ,X+        TEST FOR KEY PATTERN
              BEQ     ENDW2      IF KEY PATTERN FOUND THEN EXIT
              INCA               INCREMENT COUNTER
      IF2     CMPA    #$10       TEST FOR END OF TABLE
              BEQ     LFF        ERROR CONDITION
              JMP     WHILE2     KEEP LOOKING
      LFF     LDA     #$FF       SET FLAG
      ENDW2   PULS    B
              RTS                RETURN FROM SUBROUTINE
              END
```

Program 5.2.

5.6 HANDSHAKING

Handshaking is an input/output method which involves providing two control signals, one from the peripheral to the interface and one from the interface to the peripheral. These signals are used to control the timing of the data transfers between the interface and peripheral. This method enables slow and moderate-speed data transfers from peripherals that operate at irregular intervals (asynchronously) to be handled (Fig. 5.9).

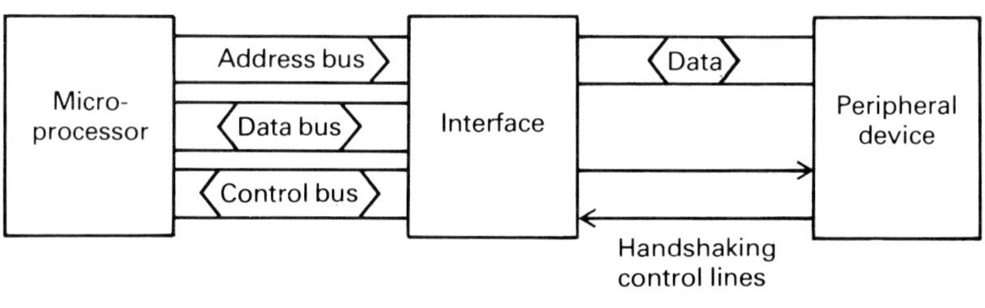

Fig. 5.9. Handshaking.

On data input, the peripheral provides a 'data ready' signal at the same time as the data. Both the data and the 'data ready' signals are latched by the interface until the processor reads them, after which they are cleared. An 'input acknowledge' signal is then sent from the interface to the peripheral, indicating that the data has been read and that the device can send more data.

On data output, the peripheral sends a 'device ready' signal to the interface. The processor detects that the device is ready and writes the data into the interface's data register. The interface makes this data available to the peripheral and at the same time sends it a 'data ready' signal (Strobe). The next 'device ready' signal from the peripheral is used to inform the processor that the data transfer is complete and that more data can be sent to the interface.

5.7 HANDSHAKING AND THE MC6821 PIA

The PIA can be used in handshaking mode with CA1 and/or CB1 as handshaking inputs and CA2 and/or CB2 as handshaking outputs. Port A is usually used when the peripheral is transmitting to the microprocessor, since the CA2 control line is reset by the processor reading data from the A side peripheral data register. Similarly port B is used when the microprocessor is sending data to the peripheral, as the CB2 line is reset by the processor writing data into the B side peripheral data register.

Peripheral to microprocessor transfer

Using the A port for input, bits CRA5, CRA4 and CRA3 of the control register are set to 100 respectively to specify full handshaking. The sequence of events during a peripheral microprocessor transfer is then as follows:

Step 1

The peripheral sends a 'data ready' signal to the PIA via the CA1 line. This sets the IRQA1 flag and informs the microprocessor that data is available (Fig. 5.10).

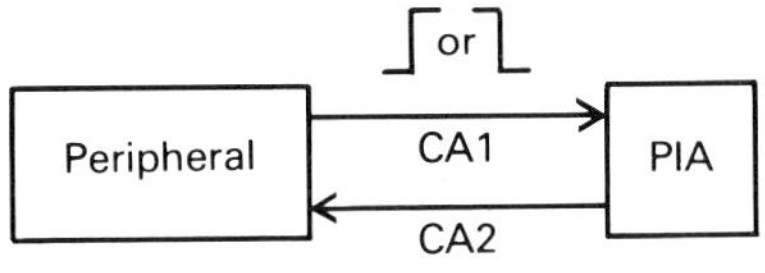

Fig. 5.10.

The type of transition (low to high or high to low) needed to set the IRQA1 flag is determined by bit 1 of control register A (CRA1).

Step 2

When the IRQA1 flag is set to a 1 the CA2 line is set high (1) (Fig. 5.11).

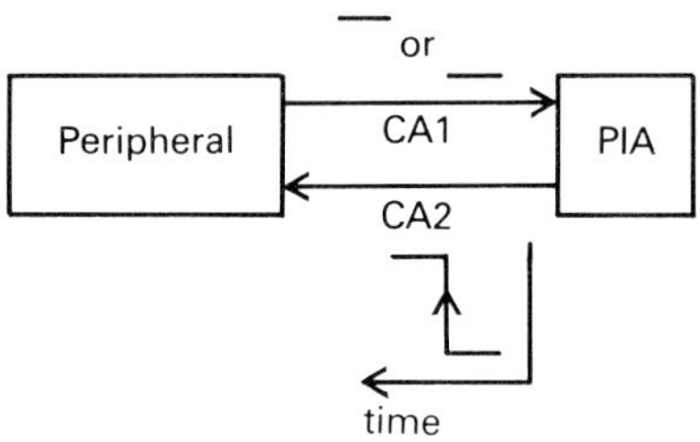

Fig. 5.11.

Step 3

The peripheral resets the CA1 line and holds the data on PA0–PA7.

Step 4

The microprocessor reads the contents of the A side peripheral data register, causing the CA2 line to go low and the IRQA1 flag to be cleared. This 'input acknowledge' signal indicates to the peripheral that the PIA is ready to receive more data (Fig. 5.12).

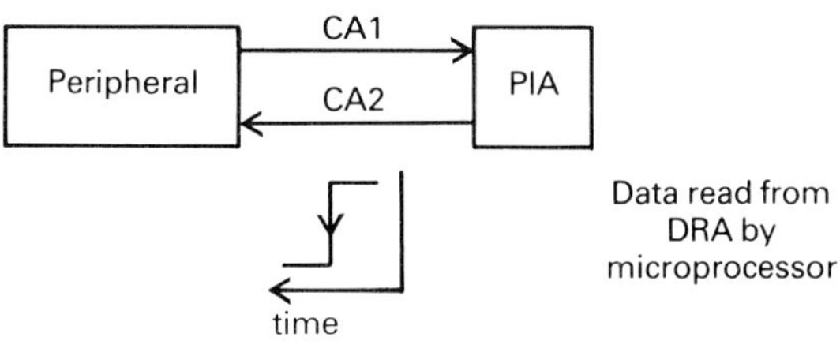

Fig. 5.12.

Program 5.3 polls the IRQA1 flag and reads the data on PA0–PA7 with handshaking when the flag is set. IRQA1 is set by a low to high transition of CA1 and cleared when the data register is read.

```
        NAM    HANDSHAKE
*PROGRAMMER P.J.THEWLIS
*5 APRIL 1984
*PROGRAM USES HANDSHAKING TO READ DATA ON THE A PORT OF A
*PIA. THE DATA IS THEN OUTPUT ON THE B PORT. THE PERIPHERAL
*SIGNALS THAT IT HAS DATA AVAILABLE BY A LOW TO HIGH
*TRANSITION OF THE CA1 LINE.
*
*BEGIN INITIALISE PIA-B SIDE OUTPUT,A SIDE INPUT WITH HANDSHAKING
*       DO FOREVER
*          IF HANDSHAKE FLAG CLEAR THEN CONTINUE
*                                   ELSE READ SWITCHES
*                                        OUTPUT TO LIGHTS
*       END DO FOREVER
*END
*
*PIA ADDRESSES $F608 TO $F60B
*
        ORG    $800
PIADR   EQU    $F608
BEGIN   LDX    #PIADR    BASE ADDRESS OF PIA
        CLR    1,X       CLEAR CRA - ACCESS DDRA
        CLR    0,X       SET ALL BITS OF DDRA TO 0 (INPUT)
        CLR    3,X       CLEAR CRB - ACCESS DDRB
        LDA    #$FF
        STA    2,X       SET ALL BITS OF DDRB TO 1 (OUTPUT)
        LDA    #$04
        STA    3,X       SET CRB2=1 TO ACCESS DRB
        LDA    #$26
        STA    1,X       SET CRA FOR HANDSHAKING & ACCESS DRA
DOEV    LDA    1,X       GET CRA
        BGE    DOEV      WAIT FOR HANDSHAKING FLAG SET
        LDA    0,X       READ A PORT: RESET CRA7
        STA    2,X       OUTPUT ON B PORT
        JMP    DOEV,PCR
        END
```

Program 5.3.

Microprocessor to peripheral transfer

A microprocessor to peripheral transfer can use handshaking to enable the peripheral to control the operation.

Step 1

The peripheral requests data by sending a ‘device ready’ pulse on the CB1 input to set the IRQB1 flag (Fig. 5.13).

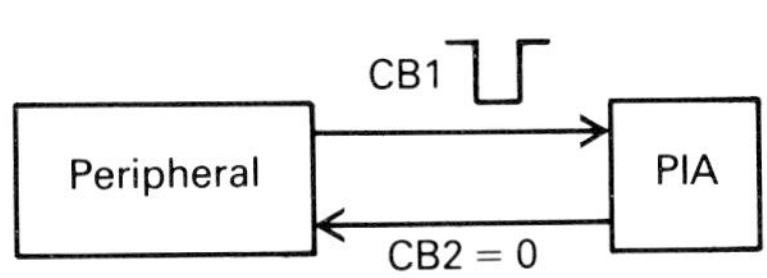

Fig. 5.13.

Step 2

The PIA output line CB2, which was initially low, is set high as IRQB1 is set (Fig. 5.14).

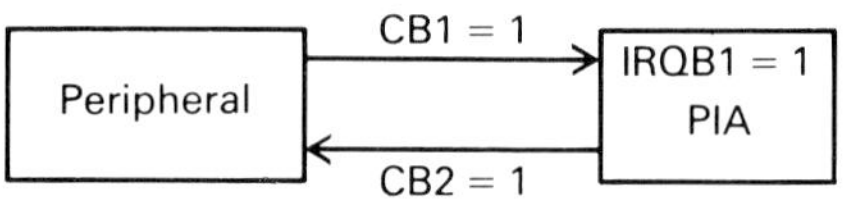

Fig. 5.14.

Step 3

After the microprocessor has written data into the B side peripheral data register, CB2 is cleared providing a 'data ready' signal for the peripheral. IRQB1 is cleared at the same time allowing the peripheral to request further data (Fig. 5.15).

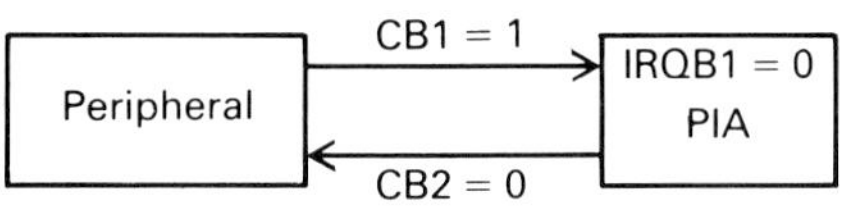

Fig. 5.15.

The following table (Fig. 5.16) gives typical pin connections for a Centronics type parallel printer interface (e.g. Epson MX80).

Pin no.	Signal	Direction	Function
1	$\overline{\text{STROBE}}$	In	Strobe pulse to read data in. Signal normally high. Data read on low.
2–9	Data0–Data7	In	8 bit data.
10	$\overline{\text{ACKNLG}}$	Out	A low pulse indicates that data has been received and printer is ready for more.
11	BUSY	Out	A high indicates printer is busy and cannot receive data. Busy conditions are: (a) Data entry (b) Printing (c) Off-line (d) Printer error
12	PE	Out	A high indicates printer out of paper.
13	SLCT	Out	A high indicates printer selected
14	$\overline{\text{AUTO FEEDXT}}$	In	A low causes the paper to be automatically fed one line after printing

Pin no.	Signal	Direction	Function
15	Not used		
16	GND		Logic ground
17	CHASGND		Printer chassis ground
18	Not Used		
19–30	GND		Return ground signal for pins 1 to 12 respectively
31	$\overline{\text{INIT}}$	In	Low=reset printer to initial state and clear buffer
32	$\overline{\text{ERROR}}$	Out	Low=error for: (a) paper out (b) off-line (c) error state
33	GND		Return ground
34	Not Used		
35	+5V		
36	$\overline{\text{SLCT IN}}$	In	Low=enable data entry. Can be set by internal switch

Fig. 5.16. Printer pin connections (Centronics type interface)

To drive this type of printer in handshaking mode with a PIA the following connections have to be made:

CB1 to $\overline{\text{ACKNLG}}$
CB2 to $\overline{\text{STROBE}}$
PB0–PB7 to Data0–Data7
PIA GND to GND (pin 16)
Pins 19–30 to GND (pin 16)

The characters are transferred to a buffer in the printer which is printed out when a command character such as CR (carriage return), LF (line feed) or VT (vertical tab) is received.

Program 5.4 prints out the message stored in a memory buffer \$801 to \$8FF on a printer with a Centronics type interface connected to the B port of a PIA.

```
            NAM     PRTSTRING
*PROGRAMMER P.J.THEWLIS
*6 APRIL 1984
*PROGRAM TO PRINT THE CHARACTER STRING (<256 CHARACTERS) STARTING
*AT ADDRESS STRG ($0801) AND TERMINATED WITH A CR, LF OR VT.
*THE LENGTH OF THE STRING IS GIVEN IN LEN ($800). THE B SIDE
*OF A PIA ACT AS A CENTRONICS TYPE INTERFACE TO THE PRINTER.
*
*BEGIN SET UP PRINT STRING AND LENGTH
*           INITIALISE PIA B PORT TO OUTPUT WITH HANDSHAKING
*           INITIALISE PRINTER
*           COUNTER=NUMBER OF CHARACTERS
*           IF COUNTER=0 THEN END
*           CHARACTER POINTER = FIRST CHARACTER POSITION
*           DO IF PRINTER BUSY THEN CONTINUE
*                                  ELSE CLEAR ACKNOWLEDGE FLAG
*                                       OUTPUT CHARACTER
*                                       INCREMENT CHARACTER POINTER
*                                       DECREMENT COUNTER
*           WHILE COUNTER>0
*END
*
*PIA ADDRESSES $F608 TO $F60B
*
            ORG     $800
LEN         FCB     10
STRG        FCC     /PRINT    THIS/
            ORG     $A00
BEGIN       LDX     #$F608    PIA BASE ADDRESS
            CLR     3,X       CLEAR CRB2 - ACCESS DDRB
            LDA     #$FF
            STA     2,X       SET ALL BITS OF DDRB=1 (OUTPUT)
            LDA     #$24      PREPARE TO SET BITS 5 AND 2
            STA     3,X       SET BIT 5: FULL HANDSHAKING
*                             SET BIT 2: ACCESS DRB
            LDA     2,X       CLEAR ACKNOWLEDGE FLAG
            LDA     #$0D      CARRIAGE RETURN
            STA     2,X       OUTPUT CR TO INITIALISE PRINTER
            LDA     LEN       COUNTER=NUMBER OF CHARACTERS
            BEQ     ENDW      IF LEN=0 THEN END
            LDY     #STRG     CHARACTER PRINTER=FIRST CHARACTER POSITION
DO          LDB     3,X
            BGT     DO        IF BUSY THEN CONTINUE
            LDB     2,X       CLEAR ACKNOWLEDGE FLAG
            LDB     ,Y+       GET CHARACTER AND INCREMENT POINTER
            STB     2,X       OUTPUT CHARACTER
            DECA
ENDW        BNE     DO
            END
```

Program 5.4.

5.8 INTERRUPTS AND THE PIA

With the $\overline{\text{IRQA}}$ and/or the $\overline{\text{IRQB}}$ output pins of the PIA connected to the processor's $\overline{\text{IRQ}}$ input and with interrupts enabled the PIA can be used in interrupt mode.

The MC6809 processor's IRQ interrupt vector is at memory addresses \$FFF8 and \$FFF9, the contents of which are loaded into the program counter when a low input is received on the $\overline{\text{IRQ}}$ terminal. On development systems this is usually a ROM area, and to enable the programmer to position the IRQ interrupt routine being developed in RAM, the vector points at an extended indirect jump instruction. The operand of this jump is an address which contains the start address for the interrupt service routine (see Fig. 5.17).

Address	Hexa-decimal	Assembly code	Comment
00E2	08 00		Address labelled IRQV
0800			Interrupt service routine
F934	6E 9F 00 E2	JMP[IRQV]	Extended indirect jump
FFF8 FFF9	F9 34		Interrupt vector

Fig. 5.17. Development system entry to IRQ service routine.

The $\overline{\text{IRQA}}$ and $\overline{\text{IRQB}}$ active low interrupt requests can be connected together and to similar $\overline{\text{IRQ}}$ outputs from other support chips to provide a wired-or configuration on the processor's $\overline{\text{IRQ}}$ interrupt terminal. On receipt of an IRQ interrupt, the processor enters the IRQ service routine, polls all the support chips that could have caused the interrupt to determine the source of the request, and enters the correct routine for servicing the interrupting device. Note that on a PIA there are four possible sources from which the interrupt could have originated, namely CA1, CA2, CB1 and CB2, and the polling routine must therefore check CRA6, CRA7, CRB6 and CRB7 of each PIA.

Program 5.5, on receipt of an IRQ interrupt request on CA1, reads eight switches connected to the A port of the same PIA and displays their settings on eight LEDs on the B port.

```
        NAM     INTERRUPT
*PROGRAMMER P.J.THEWLIS
*6 JUNE 1984
*PROGRAM WHICH ON RECEIPT OF AN INTERRUPT (ON PIA TERMINAL CA1)
*READS EIGHT SWITCHES CONNECTED TO THE A SIDE OF THE SAME PIA
*AND DISPLAYS THEM ON EIGHT LEDS CONNECTED TO THE B SIDE OF THE
*SAME PIA.
*
*BACKGROUND ROUTINE
*BEGIN INITIALISE SYSTEM STACK POINTER
*       INITIALISE PIA
*       INITIALISE INTERRUPT VECTOR
*       DO FOREVER
*                ENABLE INTERRUPTS
*                WAIT FOR INTERRUPT
*       END DO FOREVER
*END
*
        ORG     $900
PIADR   EQU     $F608     PIA BASE ADDRESS
IRQVEC  EQU     $00E2     INTERRUPT VECTOR
BEGIN   LDS     #$00A0    INITIALISE SYSTEM STACK
        LDX     #ISERV
        STX     IRQVEC    INITIALISE INTERRUPT VECTOR
        LDX     #PIADR    BASE ADDRESS OF PIA
        CLR     1,X       CLEAR CRA-ACCESS DDRA
        CLR     0,X       SET ALL BITS OF DDRA TO 0 (INPUT)
        CLR     3,X       CLEAR CRB-ACCESS DDRB
        LDA     #$FF
        STA     2,X       SET ALL BITS OF DDRB TO 1 (OUTPUT)
        LDA     #$05      SET CRA2 TO ACCESS DRA AND CRA0 TO ENABLE
        STA     1,X       PIA INTERRUPT (IRQA) TERMINAL
        LDA     #$04
        STA     3,X       SET CRB2 TO ACCESS DRB
DOEV    CWAI    #$EF      CLEAR INTERRUPT FLAG, ENABLE INTERRUPTS & WAIT
        JMP     DOEV
*
*
*INTERRUPT ROUTINE
*BEGIN IF CA1 SET THEN READ SWITCHES
*                         CLEAR INTERRUPT FLAG
*                         OUTPUT TO LEDS
*       RETURN FROM INTERRRUPT
*END
*
        ORG     $800
ISERV   LDX     #PIADR
        LDA     1,X       READ CRA
        LSLA              TEST FOR CA1 INTERRUPT (CRA7=1)
        BCC     BACK      IF NOT RETURN TO BACKGROUND PROGRAM
        LDA     0,X       READ SWITCHES
        STA     2,X       DISPLAY ON LEDS
BACK    RTI               RETURN TO BACKGROUND PROGRAM
        END
```

Program 5.5.

5.9 SERIAL TRANSMISSION

For input, a serial interface is used to convert data received as a stream of bits down a single wire into parallel form for input on the system's data bus. For output, it converts data received from the data bus into the required serial form for transmission to a similar interface in the receiving device. A SIPO (serial in parallel out) shift register forms the basis of the receiving part of the interface and a PISO (parallel in serial out) shift register the basis for the output. The conceptual connection of a VDU to a processor using serial transmission is shown in Fig. 5.18.

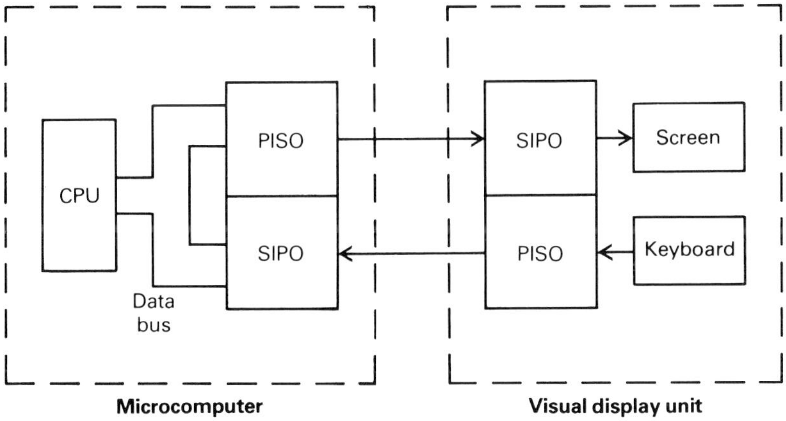

Fig. 5.18. Serial transmission.

Characters are transmitted using one of the widely adopted character codes, such as the 8-bit Extended Binary Coded Decimal Interchange Code or EBCDIC, originated by IBM, or the 7-bit American Standard Code for Information Interchange, or ASCII (see Appendix 1).

In serial transmission, the transmitter and receiver must be exactly synchronized to the same clock frequency. There are two basic methods of achieving this.

1 Sending timing control information with each character which is sent when it becomes available (asynchronous transmission). This method is the normal technique adopted for interfacing terminals and will be covered in detail in the following sections.

2 Sending a synchronization code with each message. This is used by the receiver to synchronize its clock to that of the transmitter (synchronous transmission). This technique is normally used for the high speed transfer of blocks of data and will not be covered in detail in this text.

5.10 ASYNCHRONOUS TRANSMISSION

In asynchronous transmission, one character is sent at a time when it becomes available. The receiving interface must therefore detect when a new character is being sent. To achieve this, the interconnecting line is normally held high (Mark) when no information is being transferred, and a start bit of level 0 is sent before the 8 data bits of the character itself. The receiving interface thus has a clear change from a 1 to a 0 to inform it that a character is being sent.

The interface must then sample each of the data bits and must therefore know for how long each bit is going to be on the line before the next is transmitted. The duration of each bit depends on the clock frequency, a characteristic known in data transmission as the baud rate. In this case it is equivalent to the number of bits per second that are being sent. The receiver and transmitter must both be set to the same baud rate before data can be transferred between them. There are a limited number of standard baud rates which have been agreed internationally, and these are 110, 300, 600, 1200, 2400, 4800 and 9600 baud.

Once the baud rate has been set, the length of time that each pulse is on the line is fixed. For example at 300 baud, each bit has a duration of 3.3 milliseconds, and as soon as the start bit has been received, the receiving interface circuitry samples the line once every 3.3 milliseconds to see if a 0 or a 1 is being sent.

Finally one more bit is added at the end of each character. This is known as the 'stop' bit and gives the interface unit time to process completely the character that has just been received before the next character arrives. Thus a total of 10 bits are used for each character (Fig. 5.19), so that at 300 baud 30 characters are transmitted every second. Originally, asynchronous teletypes worked at 110 baud. At this transmission rate two stop bits are used to give additional response time and 10 characters are transmitted per second.

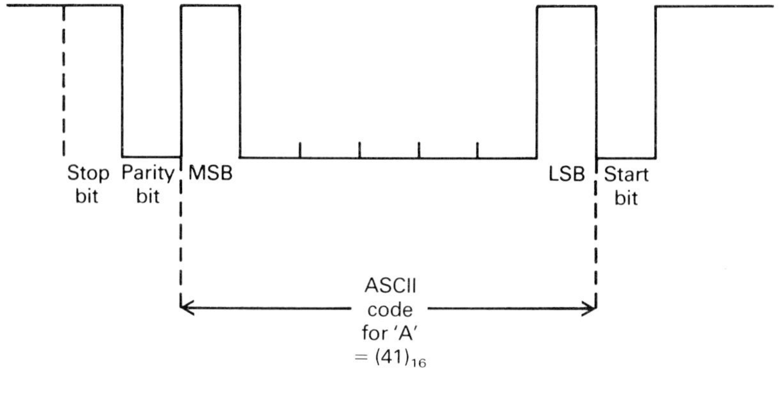

Fig. 5.19. A complete character.

When digital signals are transmitted over a single line, it is possible to read erroneous values due to noise on the line. To minimize this, a sampling technique can be used to determine the validity of the start bit. After a valid start bit has been detected, each bit in the character is sampled at approximately its centre rather than at the beginning or end. This minimizes the effect of noise and makes allowance for any small variations that may occur between the timing circuits of the transmitting and receiving interfaces.

Sampling is accomplished by using an external clock of a higher frequency than that of the required baud rate (16, 32 and 64 times baud rate are often used). The incoming signal is sampled on the rising edge of the clock pulse, and with a clock frequency of 16 times baud rate, nine consecutive samples of zero must be obtained before a valid start bit has been detected. The character's data bits are then read on each 16th rising edge after that (see Fig. 5.20).

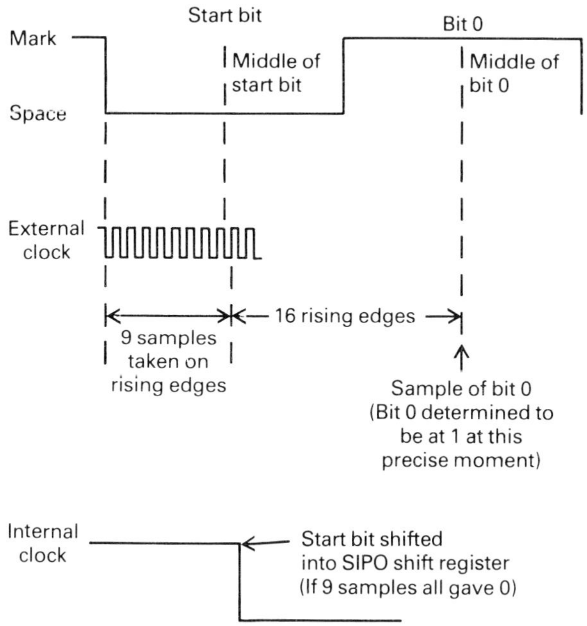

Fig. 5.20. Sampling.

Since the samples for the start bit (and the single sample for each of the data bits) are taken at precise moments in time, a read error will only occur if noise is present at exactly one of these times (see Fig. 5.21).

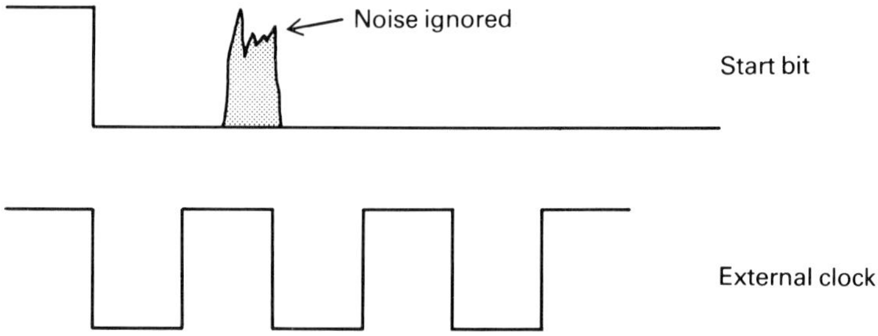

Fig. 5.21. Noise immunity.

5.11 THE MOTOROLA MC6850 ACIA

The Motorola Asynchronous Communications Interface Adaptor (ACIA) is a typical 24-pin LSI asynchronous serial interface chip. Figure 5.22 shows the pin assignments for the chip.

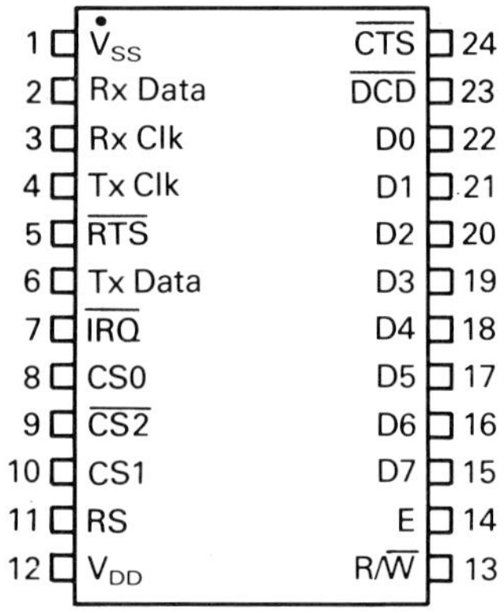

Fig. 5.22. MC6850 pin assignments.

The ACIA chip interfaces directly with the system's data bus (D0–D7) and provides TTL level serial input (Rx Data) and output (Tx Data) from SIPO and PISO shift registers. Each register has its own clock input (Rx Clk and Tx Clk respectively), allowing different baud rates to be used for input and output.

Figure 5.23 shows a block diagram of the ACIA which has four registers each of which can be addressed by the processor. The Status and Received Data registers are read only, whilst the Control and Transmit Data registers are write only. These four registers occupy two

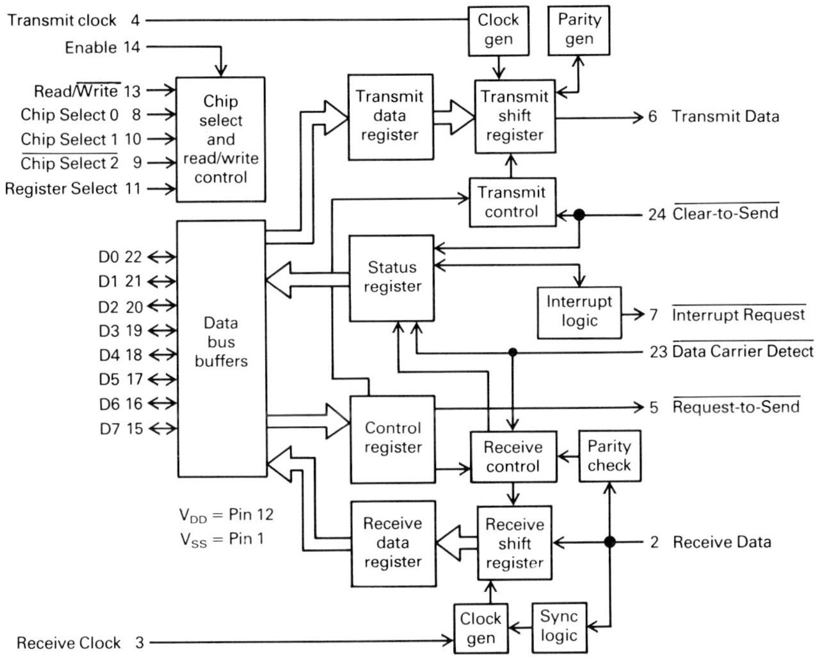

Fig. 5.23. The Motorola MC6850 ACIA.

addresses, the Status and Control registers occupying one location and the Received and Transmit Data registers the second. The pair of registers selected depends on the level of the RS (register select) input and the register within the pair is specified by the R/$\overline{\text{W}}$ input signal. Thus a read from the address for the Status and Control registers will read the Status register, whilst a write to the same address will write to the Control register. (See Fig. 5.24).

The three input pins CS0, CS1 and $\overline{\text{CS2}}$ are used to select the chip. CS0 and CS1 must be high and $\overline{\text{CS2}}$ low for the ACIA to be selected. All

		RS	R/$\overline{\text{W}}$ (1 = Read)
Status register	Read only	0	1
Received data	Read only	1	1
Control register	Write only	0	0
Transmit data	Write only	1	0

Control signals used to select register

Fig. 5.24. ACIA registers.

data transfers are then performed under the control of the Enable (E) input which enables the input/output buffers to the data bus and clocks data to and from the ACIA.

Serial data being transmitted over telephone lines must be sent from the serial interface to a modem which converts the data into a suitable acoustic form for transmission. Similarly data being received over a telephone line has to be converted by the modem before it can be received by the serial interface. (See Fig. 5.25).

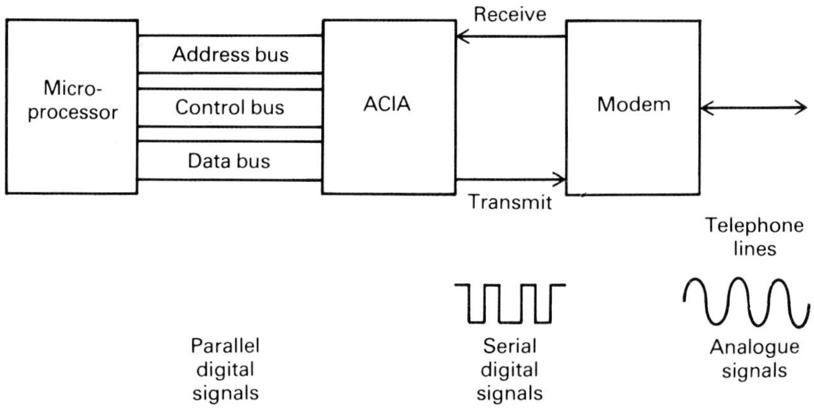

Fig. 5.25. Modem control.

The ACIA has three signals which are used for handshaking and modem control.

$\overline{\text{CTS}}$ (Clear to send). A low input on this terminal informs the ACIA that the modem is ready for more data.

$\overline{\text{RTS}}$ (Request to send). A low on this output enables the processor to control a peripheral or modem via the data bus. When connected to a modem's Data Terminal Ready input, it is used to enable the modem.

$\overline{\text{DCD}}$ (Data carrier detect). This input provides automatic control over the receiving end of a modem. When interrupts are enabled, a low to high transition of the signal on this terminal interrupts the processor, indicating a loss of carrier signal on the modem.

The ACIA can also be used in interrupt mode with its $\overline{\text{IRQ}}$ output pin connected to one of the processor's interrupt lines. A low on this output will then cause the processor to be interrupted provided that interrupts have been enabled.

The status register

The status of the ACIA is indicated at any time by the eight flags in the read only status register (Fig. 5.26).

7	6	5	4	3	2	1	0
IRQ	PE	ROV	FE	$\overline{\text{CTS}}$	$\overline{\text{DCD}}$	TDRE	RDRF

Fig. 5.26. ACIA status register.

RDRF=1 when the received data register is full. The IRQ flag is also set and remains set until the data in the received data register is read by the processor.

=0 when the received data has been read. A high signal on $\overline{\text{DCD}}$ will also cause this flag to be low, indicating no connection over the transmission line. Note therefore, if the $\overline{\text{DCD}}$ line is not being used, it should be tied to ground.

TDRE=1 when the transmit data register is empty and more data can be transferred from the processor to the ACIA. The IRQ flag is also set and remains so until further data is written into the transmit data register.

=0 when the transmit data register contains data ready for transmission. A high signal on $\overline{\text{CTS}}$ will also cause this flag to be low indicating that the modem is busy. Note therefore, if the $\overline{\text{CTS}}$ line is not being used, it should be tied to ground.

$\overline{\text{DCD}}$=1 when there is no carrier from the modem. The IRQ flag is also set and remains so until the processor reads both the status and received data registers. The RDRF flag is also held at 0. Note therefore, if $\overline{\text{DCD}}$ line is not being used, it should be tied to ground.

=0 when the modem is receiving a carrier signal.

$\overline{\text{CTS}}$=1 when the modem is not ready to receive data (indicated by the $\overline{\text{CTS}}$ signal from the modem being high).

=0 when the modem is ready (i.e. the line from modem is low).

FE=1 when the received data is not properly framed with the required start and stop bits.

=0 when the received data is correctly framed.

ROV=1 The Receiver Overrun flag indicates that data has been lost. It is set when one or more characters are received without the previous one being read from the received data register. The flag is reset after data is read.

=0 when there has been no loss of data.

PE=1 when there is a parity error on the received data. The flag is reset when data is read.

=0 when there is no parity error.

IRQ=1 when there is an interrupt request. The flag is cleared by either reading the received data register or writing to the transmit data register.

=0 when there is no interrupt request.

The control register

The control register has four main functions, to specify the division of the clock frequency, to determine the data format to be used, to control the $\overline{RTS}$ line and to enable/disable interrupts. (See Fig. 5.27.)

7	6	5	4	3	2	1	0
↑ Interrupt enable	Transmitter control		Word select			Counter divide	

Fig. 5.27. MC6850 ACIA control register.

Bits 0 and 1 (Fig. 5.28) are used to specify the division ratio for both the transmitter and receiver clocks. They also provide the master reset function, which initializes the transmitter and receiver and clears all the status register bits, except for $\overline{CTS}$ and $\overline{DCD}$ which are fixed by their respective external signals.

Bit 1	Bit 0	Function
0	0	Divide by 1
0	1	Divide by 16
1	0	Divide by 64
1	1	Master reset

Fig. 5.28. Counter divide bits.

Bits 2, 3 and 4 (Fig. 5.29) are used to specify the data format being used and the framing for the data bits.

Bit 4	Bit 3	Bit 2	Number of data bits	Parity	Number of stop bits
0	0	0	7	Even	2
0	0	1	7	Odd	2
0	1	0	7	Even	1
0	1	1	7	Odd	1
1	0	0	8	No	2
1	0	1	8	No	1
1	1	0	8	Even	1
1	1	1	8	Odd	1

Fig. 5.29. Word select bits.

Bits 5 and 6 (Fig. 5.30) provide control over the level being sent on the $\overline{\text{RTS}}$ line and allow the interrupt facility to be enabled/disabled from the Transmit Data Register Empty condition. They can also be used to send a 'Break' signal on the transmit data line to interrupt a remote system.

Bit 6	Bit 5	$\overline{\text{RTS}}$	Transmitting Interrupt	
0	0	Low	Disabled	Request to establish communications channel
0	1	Low	Enabled	Channel established, enable interrupts on TDRE
1	0	High	Disabled	Turn off channel
1	1	Low	Disabled	Transmit Break to interrupt remote device

Fig. 5.30. Transmitter control bits.

Setting bit 7, Receiver Interrupt Enable, enables interrupts caused by the Received Data Register being full or by a low to high transition of $\overline{\text{DCD}}$.

5.12 CONNECTING THE MC6850 TO AN M6809 PROCESSOR

The two addresses occupied by the MC6850 are determined by the address decoding performed in selecting the chip.

Consider the case where the chip addresses are given by:

A15	A14	A13	A12–A1	A0	
1	0	1	X	0	Status and Control registers
1	0	1	X	1	Receive and Transmit Data registers

where X = don't care and the system being designed is such that the ACIA can be mirrored on the memory map for every combination of the address lines A12–A1. The connections between the M6809 and an ACIA at the addresses given above are shown as part of the circuit diagram Fig. 5.31.

The valid address signal E+Q is combined with one of the address lines used in selecting the chip to ensure that the chip is only selected when a stable address is on the bus.

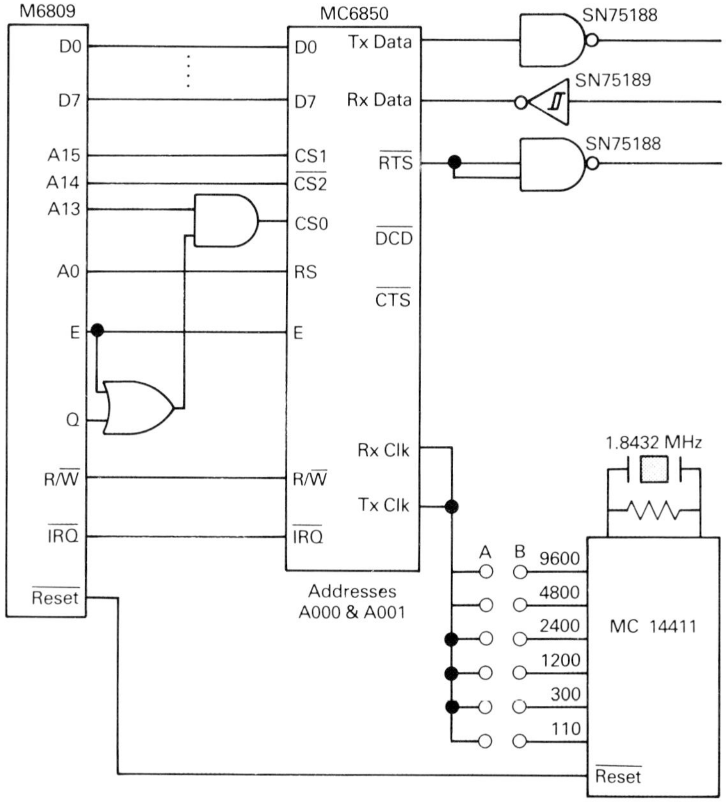

Fig. 5.31. RS232-C type serial interface.

5.13 INPUT/OUTPUT PROGRAMMING FOR AN ACIA

The most common use of an ACIA is in connecting an asynchronous serial terminal, such as a VDU, to a microcomputer system.

Figure 5.31 shows a simple RS232-C type serial interface using an MC14411 Baud Rate Generator chip to provide the Rx Clk and Tx Clk signals. The speed of the clock signal is chosen by inserting a jumper connection between any pair of the points A and B.

The standard signal levels for an RS232-C interface are −3 to −12V for a 1 or 'Mark', and +3 to +12V for a 0 or 'Space'. The interface shown in Fig. 5.31 uses an SN75188 Quad line driver chip and an SN75189 Quad line receiver chip to convert the TTL level outputs of the ACIA to the required levels and to interface it to the data terminal.

```
            NAM     SREAD
 *PROGRAMMER P.J.THEWLIS
 *24 JULY 1984
 *PROGRAM REPEATEDLY READS A CHARACTER FROM THE KEYBOARD OF A
 *VDU AND DISPLAYS IT ON THE SCREEN.
 *
 *BEGIN RESET ACIA
 *          CONFIGURE ACIA
 *          DO FOREVER
 *                 WHILE RECEIVED DATA REG FULL FLAG = 0 DO NOTHING
 *                 READ A CHARACTER
 *                 WHILE TRANSMIT DATA REG EMPTY FLAG = 0 DO NOTHING
 *                 SEND A CHARACTER
 *          END DO FOREVER
 *END
 *
 *ACIA ADDRESSES $F7FE AND $F7FF
 *
            ORG     $800
 ACIAS      EQU     $F7FE
 ACIAD      EQU     ACIAS+1
 DATA       EQU     $900
            LDA     #03
            STA     ACIAS    MASTER RESET
            LDA     #$15     8 BIT, NO PARITY, 1 STOP BIT
            STA     ACIAS
 WHL1       LDA     ACIAS    ACIA STATUS REGISTER
            LSRA             MOVE RDRF FLAG TO CARRY
            BCC     WHL1     WAIT FOR FLAG SET
            LDA     ACIAD    READ CHARACTER
            STA     DATA
 WHL2       LDA     ACIAS    LOAD STATUS REGISTER
            ANDA    #$02     CHECK TDRE FLAG
            BEQ     WHL2     IF ZERO WAIT
            LDA     DATA
            STA     ACIAD    SEND CHARACTER
            BRA     WHL1     END DO FOREVER LOOP
            END
```

Program 5.6.

Program 5.6, which accepts characters from the keyboard of a VDU and echoes them to the screen, illustrates the type of driver routine used with an ACIA.

5.14 COMBINED MEMORY AND INPUT/OUTPUT SYSTEMS

Most microcomputers use the same buses for both memory and input/output transfers. There are two widely adopted methods for distinguishing between input/output and memory transfers:

1 isolated input/output,

2 memory mapped input/output.

Isolated input/output

In isolated input/output, separate decoders are used for memory and input/output address decoding. The processor has a bus line which specifies whether the address on the address bus is for memory or input/output and which is used to enable the appropriate decoders (see Fig. 5.32).

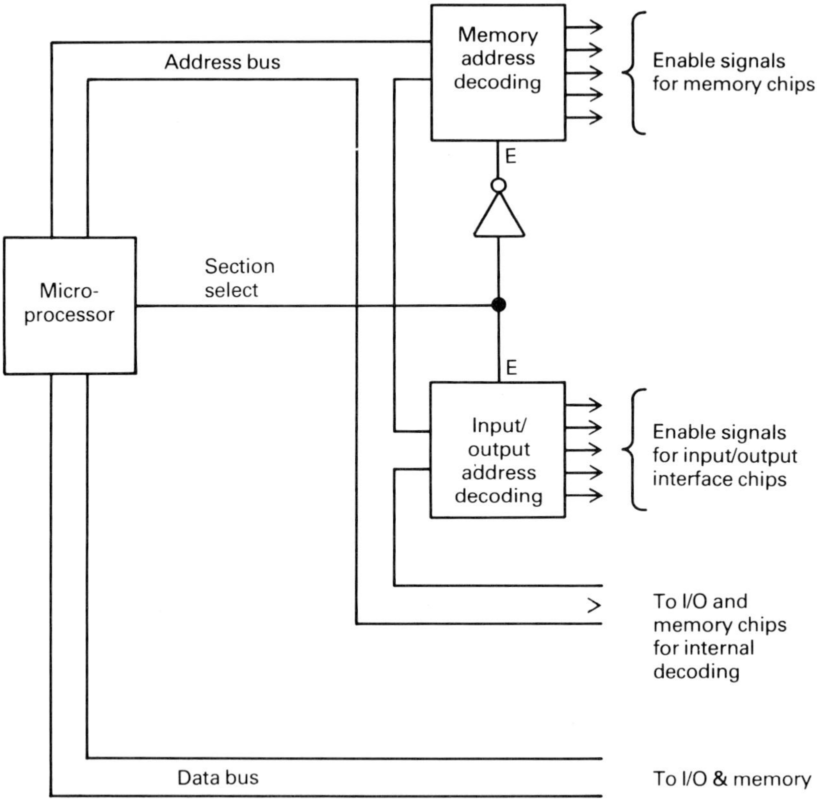

Fig. 5.32. Isolated input/output.

A microprocessor with isolated input/output has different instructions for input/output and memory reference. If the input/output instructions set the section select control line high (1), then it will be set low by any memory reference instruction. Thus a specific numerical address can apply to either a memory location or an input/output port, depending on the instruction that placed it on the bus. Input/output addresses are usually short, 8 bits allowing sufficient ports and leading to shorter instruction formats. Figure 5.33 shows an outline memory map for an isolated input/output system with a 16-bit address bus, the 8 least significant bits of which are used for input/output addressing.

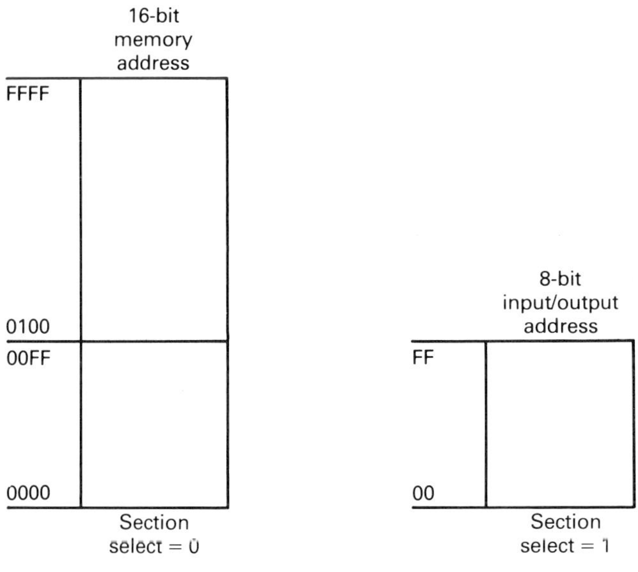

Fig. 5.33. Memory map for an isolated input/output system.

The Zilog Z80 addressing system is similar to the one shown above, but with separate control lines for selecting memory or input/output address decoding circuitry. Thus the Z80 processor is capable of accessing up to 64K bytes of memory and 256 input/output port addresses.

Memory-mapped input/output

On a memory-mapped input/output system, some of the most significant address bus lines are decoded to provide the chip enables for memory chips or input/output ports alike (see Fig. 5.34).

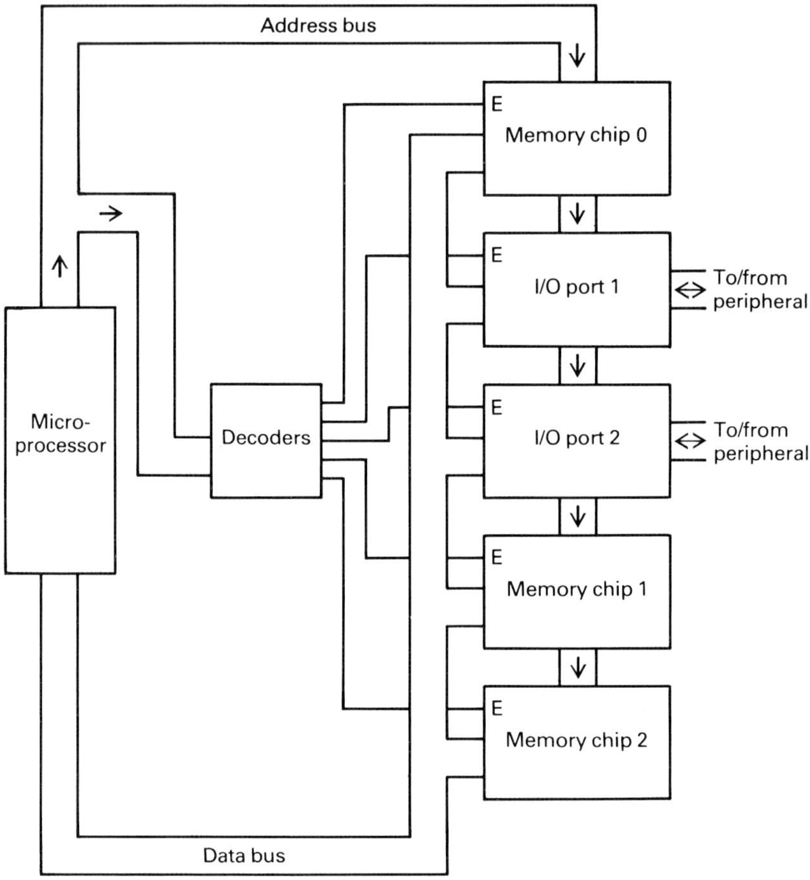

Fig. 5.34. A memory-mapped input/output system.

Any instruction that operates on data in memory will therefore equally operate on data held in registers in an input/output port, and the only way to recognize an input/output port is by its address. Figure 5.35 shows an outline memory map for such a system with a 16-bit address bus and two input/output ports each with four addressable registers. The port addresses are not significant but used only to show that the input/output ports on this type of system reside within the memory addressing capability of the processor.

The Motorola M6809 has memory-mapped input/output. Any memory reference instruction also operates on registers within the input/output ports which occupy space within the 64K bytes address range of the processor.

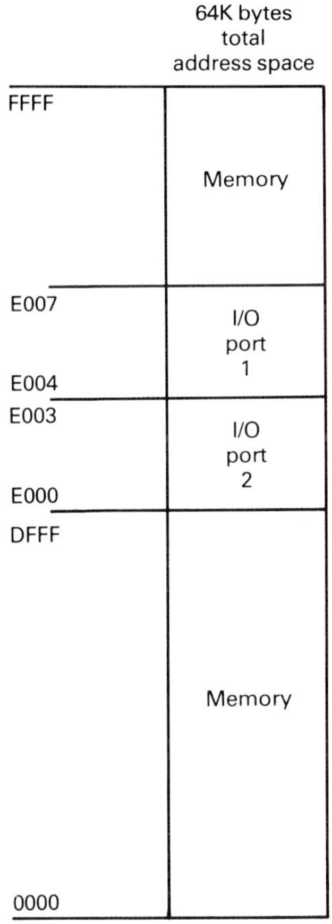

Fig. 5.35. Memory map for a memory-mapped input/output system.

5.15 AN EXAMPLE M6809 SINGLE BOARD MICROCOMPUTER SYSTEM

The following M6809-based single board computer uses three MCM68316 2K-byte ROM chips to store a 3.5K background program entered through the RESET vector, and two 1K interrupt routines entered through the IRQ and FIRQ interrupts. The firmware also requires storage for 128 single length integer variables and a systems stack of up to 128 bytes. Two MCM6810 128-byte static RAM chips are used for this purpose. The system is to be used as an industrial controller, the control interface being a PIA. An ACIA is also included for serial communications with either a terminal or a host computer.

A typical memory map for this system is shown in Fig. 5.36.

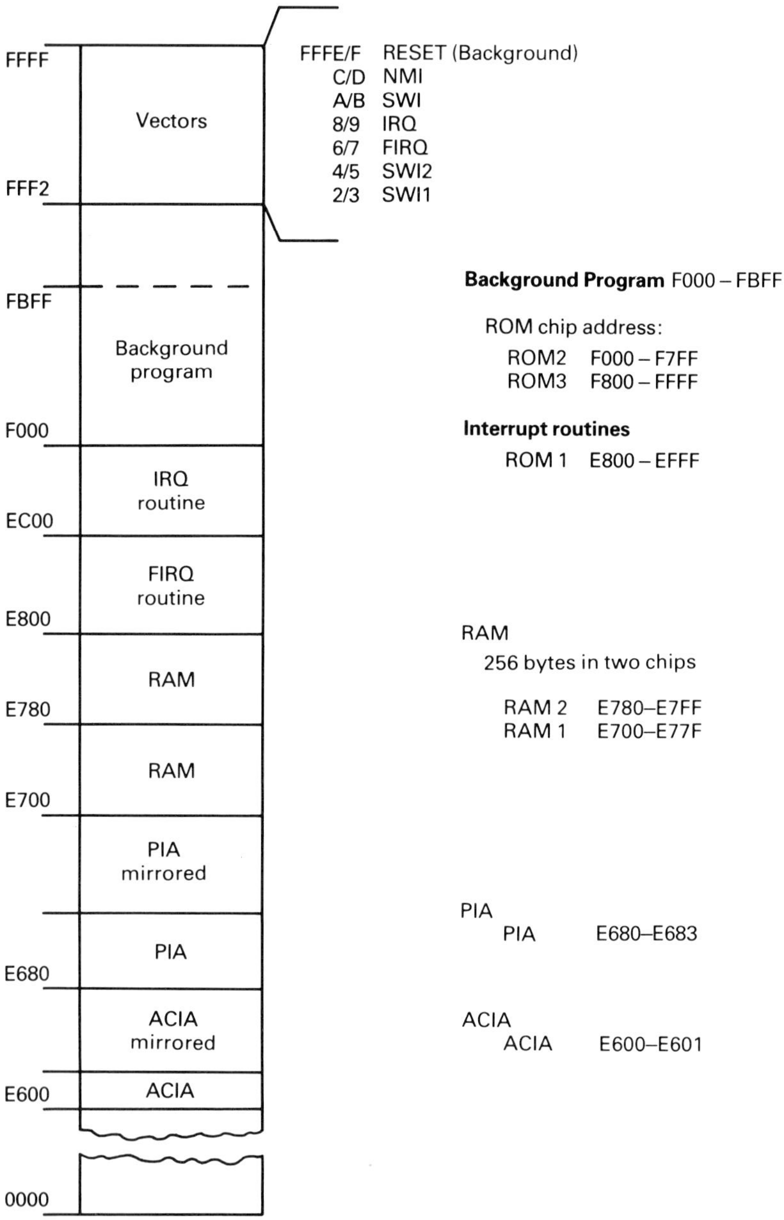

Fig. 5.36. System memory map.

The address decoding for a system using three 3:8 decoders is given in Fig. 5.37.

		A15	A14	A13	A12	A11	A10	A9	A8	A7	A6	---	A0
ROM 3	F800–FFFF	1	1	1	1	1	X	–	–	–	–	–	X
ROM 2	F000–F7FF	1	1	1	1	0	X	–	–	–	–	–	X
ROM 1	E800–EFFF	1	1	1	0	1	X	–	–	–	–	–	X
RAM 2	E780–E7FF	1	1	1	0	0	1	1	1	1	X	---	X
RAM 1	E700–E77F	1	1	1	0	0	1	1	1	0	X	---	X
PIA	E680–E683	1	1	1	0	0	1	1	0	1	X	---	X
ACIA	E600–E601	1	1	1	0	0	1	1	0	0	X		X
		3:8 Decoder			3:8 Decoder			3:8 Decoder					

Fig. 5.37. Address decoding.

The ROM and RAM addresses are fully decoded and therefore each logical address refers to a unique physical memory location. The addresses for both the ACIA and the PIA are, however, only partially decoded, causing each physical device to be mirrored in logical address space (E600–E67F for the ACIA and E680–E6FF for the PIA). Figure 5.38 shows the address decoding circuitry for this system.

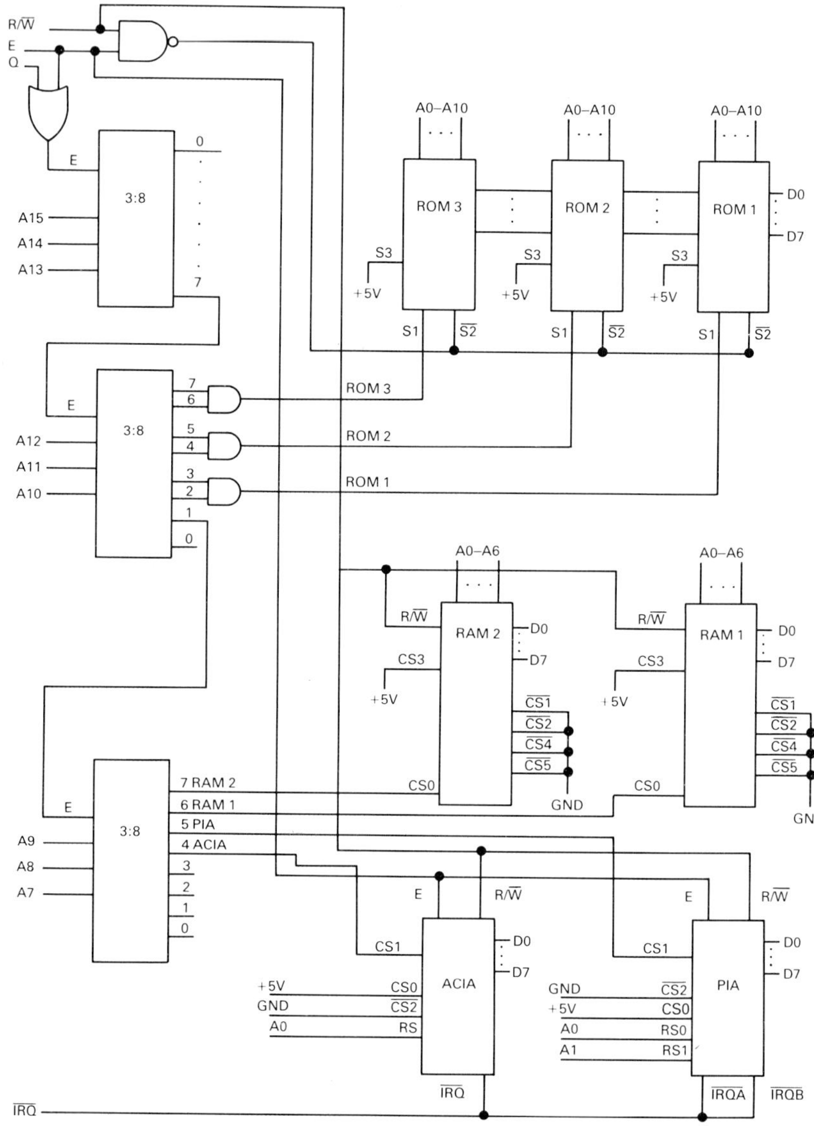

Fig. 5.38. Address decoding circuitry.

Chapter 6

Real-Time Applications

6.1 INTRODUCTION

This chapter introduces the reader to the use of microcomputers in a control environment. Digital sequencers, in which the microcomputer inputs and outputs are digital signals, are described and their application as the controller for a simple automatic washing machine considered. In common with many control applications, this requires the generation of accurate timings, and both hardware and software methods for giving accurately timed periods are developed. Finally, analogue systems are described. Interface hardware and software driver routines for the input and output of analogue signals are described and applications in regulatory control outlined to give an overall view of interfacing techniques used in real-time applications areas.

6.2 SEQUENCERS

Perhaps the simplest form of microcomputer control system is one in which a number of digital outputs, derived from a PIA, are used to switch motors on and off, or to open and close valves on the industrial plant or machinery under control. These digitally controlled devices may be activated in a preset sequence with each step in the sequence existing for a predetermined period of time or until a given input condition occurs. In the simplest forms of sequencer the input conditions are also digital signals, derived from switches and sensors on the plant and input to the controller via a PIA.

An everyday example of a conditional sequencer is an automatic washing machine controller. Figure 6.1 lists the logical inputs and outputs for such a controller of a simplified single-programme washing machine.

Logical output	Controlled device
0	Hot water control valve
1	Cold water control valve
2	Water heater
3	Tub motor – wash/rinse speed
4	Tub motor – spin speed
5	Pump motor
6	Door lock
Logical input	
0	On/off switch
1	Water level – tub full
2	Water thermostat – temperature reached

Fig. 6.1. Washing machine controller inputs and outputs.

The steps in the programme to be performed by the washing machine are given in Fig. 6.2.

	Step no	Action
	1	Wait until machine switched on
Wash	2	Lock door & fill with hot water until full
	3	Heat water until required temperature reached
	4	Wash for 10 minutes
	5	Empty for 30 seconds.
3 rinses	6	Fill with cold water until full
	7	Rinse for 5 minutes
	8	Empty for 30 seconds
	9–14	Repeat 6, 7, 8 twice more
	15	Spin for 2 minutes
	16	Wait for 30 seconds
	17	Unlock door

Fig. 6.2. Washing machine programme steps.

The sequencer can be implemented in hardware consisting of an M6809 processor, ROM or EPROM for the control program, RAM for stacks and variable storage and a PIA for input/output. The B port of the PIA is used for the control outputs and the A port for the digital inputs.

The control program uses two state tables, one for the digital outputs for each state and the second for the condition which, when true, signifies the completion of the action for that state and the start of that

State no.	Output table							Condition table						
	Controlled device							Digital I/P			Delays			
	0	1	2	3	4	5	6	0	1	2	10m	5m	2m	30s
1	0	0	0	0	0	0	0	1	0	0	0	0	0	0
2	1	0	0	0	0	0	1	1	1	0	0	0	0	0
3	0	0	1	0	0	0	1	1	1	1	0	0	0	0
4	0	0	0	1	0	0	1	1	1	0	1	0	0	0
5	0	0	0	0	0	1	1	1	0	0	0	0	0	1
6	0	1	0	0	0	0	1	1	1	0	0	0	0	0
7	0	0	0	1	0	0	1	1	1	0	0	1	0	0
8	0	0	0	0	0	1	1	1	0	0	0	0	0	1
9–14	Repeat 6, 7, 8, twice more													
15	0	0	0	0	1	1	1	1	0	0	0	0	1	0
16	0	0	0	0	0	0	1	1	0	0	0	0	0	1
17	0	0	0	0	0	0	0	1	0	0	0	0	0	0

Fig. 6.3. Washing machine controller state tables.

for the next. Figure 6.3 shows the state tables for the washing programme described above.

The pseudo-code for the sequencer control program is :

```
begin
      initialize PIA
      initialize state table pointer
      while state table pointer <= end of table do
            read digital inputs
            while digital inputs <> condition do
                  if delay specified then wait specified period
                          else wait for required input condition
            endwhile
            increment state table pointer
      endwhile
endprogram
```

The only major difficulty in implementing this control program is in accurately producing the specified time delays. Two main methods are available:

1 a software solution using accurately timed program loops, or

2 a hardware solution using additional circuits to generate interrupts at precisely defined intervals.

The generation of accurate time periods is essential in many control applications and an example implementation of each of the above methods, on an M6809 system, is described fully in the following sections.

6.3 PROGRAMMED DELAY LOOPS AND THE M6809

An M6809 processor with a 4 MHz clock oscillator has an internal clock frequency of 1 MHz. Machine code instructions take one or more internal cycles to be executed, each cycle being 1×10^{-6} seconds, and thus a loop, or nested loops, can be written to introduce delays.

The subroutine in Program 6.1 uses nested loops to produce a delay of approximately one second.

```
       NAM    SEC      ONE SECOND DELAY
*
*THIS SUBROUTINE PRODUCES AN APPROXIMATELY ONE SECOND DELAY
*
*BEGIN
*      SAVE ALL REGISTERS USED
*      TENTH SECOND COUNTER=0
*      REPEAT WAIT 1/10TH SECOND
*             INCREMENT TENTH SECOND COUNTER
*      UNTIL TENTH SECOND COUNTER = 10
*      RESTORE REGISTERS
*END                                             NO OF   NO OF
*                                                CYCLES  TIMES
*
       ORG    $900
DELAY  PSHU   B,X      SAVE REGISTERS              8       1
       LDB    #10                                  2       1
DELY1  LDX    #N       COUNT FOR 1/10TH SEC        3       10
DELY2  LEAX   -1,X     COUNT DOWN FOR 1/10TH SEC   5       10N
       BNE    DELY2                                3       10N
       DECB            10 X 1/10TH SEC = 1 SEC     2       10
       BNE    DELY1                                3       10
       PULU   B,X      RESTORE REGISTERS           8       1
       RTS                                         5       1
```

Program 6.1.

The inner loop uses a 16-bit counter to produce a 0.1-second delay whilst the outer loop repeats this operation 10 times to give an approximately 1-second delay. The value of the 0.1-second counter, N, is given by

Number of cycles/second = 1,000,000

$$103 + 80N = 1{,}000{,}000$$

and thus $N = 999{,}897/80$

or

$$N = 12{,}499 \text{ or } \$30D3 \text{ approximately.}$$

In practice, when calculating the required count for the delay loop, the number of cycles used in the calling routine must be included if the delay is to be accurate.

An alternative method for producing accurately timed periods is to use external hardware to generate interrupts at precisely defined intervals.

6.4 THE MC6840 PROGRAMMABLE TIMER

The hardware implementation of timer loops can be achieved using a programmable counter-timer like the MC6840. The chip is programmed to interrupt the processor at regular intervals, the interrupt being generated when an internal counter, which is being decremented by each clock pulse, reaches zero. The counter is then automatically reset to an initial value stored in the on-chip latches during the initialization process.

Figure 6.4 below shows the pin assignments for the Motorola MC6840 Programmable Timer Module (PTM).

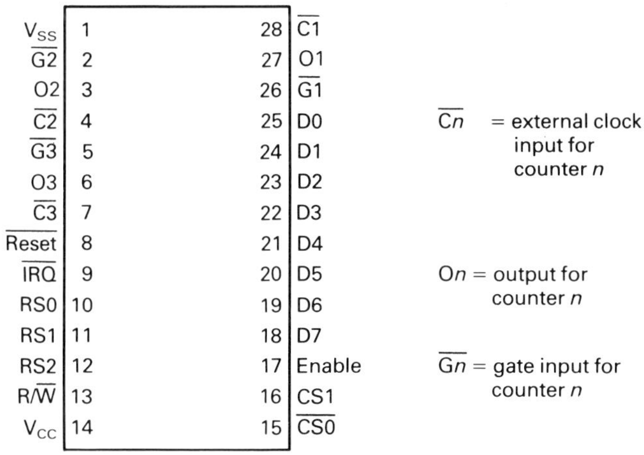

Fig. 6.4. Pin assignments for the MC6840 PTM.

The chip has three independently programmable 16-bit timers which are accessed in much the same way as memory.

Each timer consists of a 16-bit counter, an associated 16-bit latch and a control register. The latch is first loaded with an initial value which is transferred to the counter where it is decremented by either an external clock, supplied on the C*n* terminal, or by the sytem clock, supplied on the Enable terminal. When a counter reaches its selected end condition (chosen from one of several predetermined conditions specified in the counter's control register), its interrupt flag in the chip's status register is set and the counter is either halted or recycled. The interrupt flags can be either polled by the processor or, with interrupts enabled, used to generate a processor interrupt request via the $\overline{\text{IRQ}}$ terminal.

The MC6840 interfaces directly with the processor bus as follows.

1 The direction of data transfer on the bidirectional data bus D0 to D7 is controlled by the signal on the R/$\overline{\text{W}}$ terminal and its timing by the clock signal on the Enable pin.

2 The chip has two select pins $\overline{\text{CS0}}$ and CS1. $\overline{\text{CS0}}$ must be low and CS1 high for the chip to be selected.

3 The $\overline{\text{IRQ}}$, active low interrupt request can be tied together with similar $\overline{\text{IRQ}}$ outputs from other support chips to provide a wired-or configuration on the processor's interrupt request terminal.

4 A low input on the external $\overline{\text{Reset}}$ terminal causes the following initial conditions to be set:

all counter latches to their maximum value;

all control register bits low except bit 0 of the control register for counter 1 (CR10) which is set high (internal reset);

all counters preset to the contents of the latches;

all counter outputs reset and counter clocks disabled;

all status register bits cleared.

5 The register select lines, RS0, RS1 and RS2, are used to specify the register being addressed. Since all the registers are either read-only or write-only, a read-only and a write-only register can share the same address. The direction of the transfer taking place (signalled by the R/$\overline{\text{W}}$ bus line) is then used to select which of the pair of registers at the given address is being accessed (see Fig. 6.5).

RS2	RS1	RS0	Write (R/$\overline{\text{W}}$=0)	Read (R/$\overline{\text{W}}$=1)
0	0	0	If CR20=0 CR3 If CR20=1 CR1	
0	0	1	CR2	Status register
0	1	0	MSB buffer register	Timer 1 MSB counter
0	1	1	LSB timer 1 latches	LSB buffer register
1	0	0	MSB buffer register	Timer 2 MSB counter
1	0	1	LSB timer 2 latches	LSB buffer register
1	1	0	MSB buffer register	Timer 3 MSB counter
1	1	1	LSB timer 3 latches	LSB buffer register

Fig. 6.5. PTM register selection.

As the chip uses an 8-bit data bus to load and read 16-bit registers, data is transferred in two operations, a byte at a time. When loading a 16-bit counter latch, the most significant byte (MSB) is loaded into the MSB buffer register by the first operation, and the least significant byte (LSB) into the counter's LSB latches by the second. The data from the

MSB buffer register is automatically transferred to the MSB latches of timer *n* when the Write LSB To Timer *n* Latches command is performed.

The MSB buffer register has three addresses for the same 8-bit buffer register, enabling a single Store 16-Bit Register instruction, such as STX (which first transfers the MSB to the selected address and then the LSB to the selected address + 1), to be used to load the counter latches.

Similarly, when reading the contents of registers, a Read Timer *n* MSB Counter instruction will read the most significant byte of the

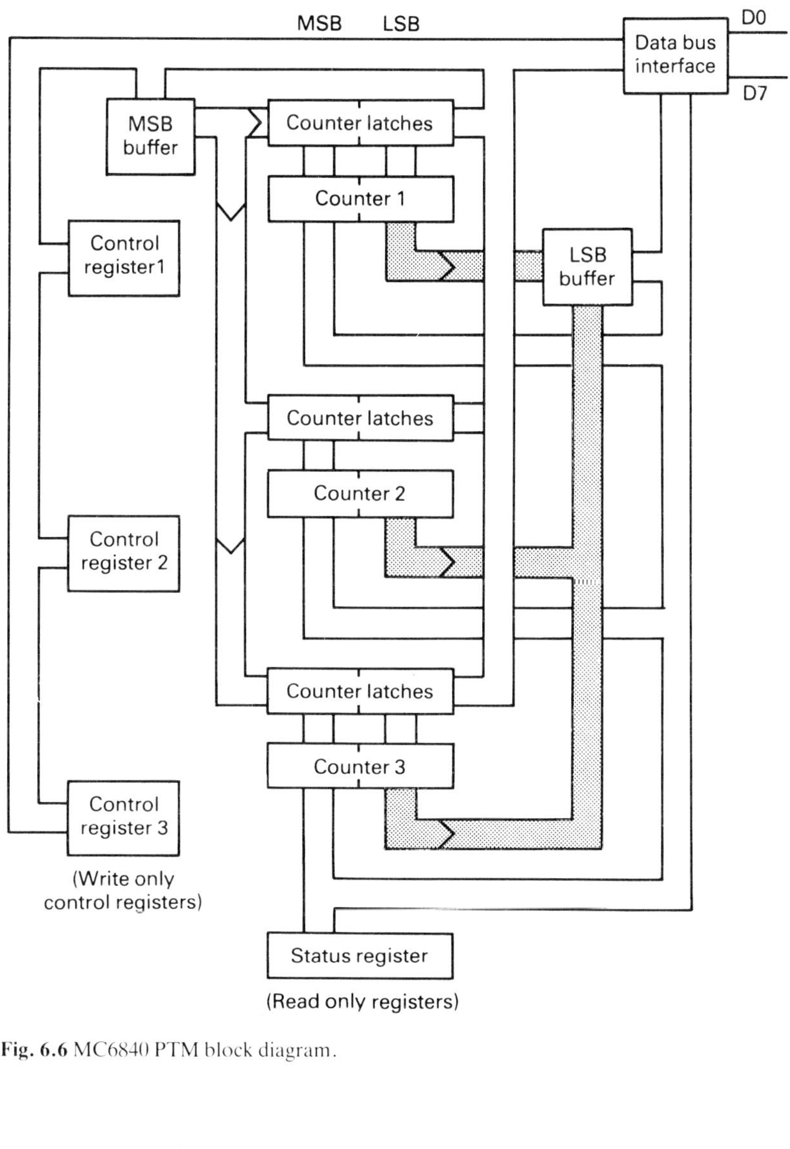

Fig. 6.6 MC6840 PTM block diagram.

counter and cause the LSB to be loaded into the LSB buffer register which can be read by the next instruction. A single 16-Bit Register Load instruction, such as LDX, will therefore read the full counter contents into the selected register.

Figure 6.6 shows a block diagram for the internal organization of registers in the MC6840 PTM.

Control registers

Figure 6.7 shows the functions of the three control registers CR1, CR2 and CR3. Bits 1–7 operate identically for all three registers, but bit 0 has different functions dependent on the register.

7	6	5 4 3	2	1	0
0=Output disabled 1=Output enabled	0=IRQ disabled 1=IRQ enabled	Operating modes See below	0=16-bit counting mode 1=dual 8-bit counting mode. (L+1) *(M+1) counts	0=Use external clock on *Cn* 1=Use system clock on Enable	See below

Fig. 6.7. Control register functions.

Bit 0 functions

Figure 6.8 summarizes the function of bit 0 for each fo the three control registers.

Control register	0	1
CR1	All counters start	Preset for all counters from latches
CR2	Access CR3	Access CR1
CR3	Timer clock = Input	Timer clock =Input/8

Fig. 6.8. Bit 0 functons.

Timer outputs

The timer can also be programmed so that the outputs, O1, O2 and O3 produce a defined waveform in either Continuous or Single-shot modes.

The form of the output is chosen by selecting either '16-bit' or 'Dual 8-bit' operating modes with bit 2 of the corresponding control register. (See Fig. 6.9.)

Bit no. 5	4	3	Operating mode	
0	0	0	Continuous	Counter initialized by G*n* or CR10=1 or Reset or a Write Timer Latches command
0	1	0	Continuous	Counter initialized by G*n* or CR10=1 or Reset
1	0	0	Single-shot	Counter initialized by G*n* or CR10=1 or Reset or a Write Timer Latches command
1	1	0	Single-shot	Counter initialized by G*n* or CR10=1 or Reset

Fig. 6.9. Selection of continuous and single-shot modes.

Output waveforms

Both 16-bit Continuous and Single-shot modes produce a square wave, whilst Dual 8-bit Continuous and Single-Shot modes produce a variable duty cycle pulse as shown in Fig. 6.10.

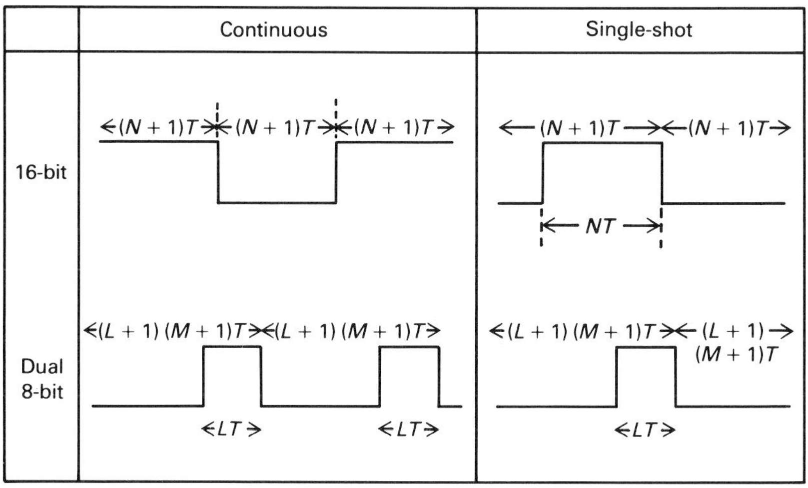

Fig. 6.10. Continuous and single-shot modes.

Timer interval modes

Two timer interval modes are provided for applications requiring more flexible methods of counter initialization or interrupt generation. Using these methods, interrupts are generated by comparing the frequency or pulse width of a signal applied on the counter Gate terminal ($\overline{Gn}$) with the frequency or period of the counter (Fig. 6.11).

Bit no.			Mode	Condition for interrupt
5	4	3		
0	0	1	Frequency	Gate input frequency > counter frequency
1	0	1	Frequency	Gate input frequency < counter frequency
0	1	1	Pulse width	Gate pulse width < counter period
1	1	1	Pulse width	Gate pulse width > counter period

Fig. 6.11. Timer interval modes.

For full details the reader should consult the MC6840 data sheet.

Status register

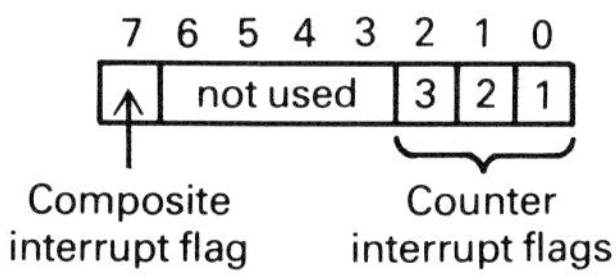

Fig. 6.12. Status register

Only four bits of the status register (Fig. 6.12) are used, the three least significant bits being the interrupt flags for the individual timers and bit 7 being a composite interrupt flag. Bit 7 is set when any of the individual flags are set, provided that bit 6 of the corresponding control register is a 1 (interrupts are enabled).

The interrupt flags are cleared by:

1 an external reset (reset terminal low);
2 an internal reset (bit CR10=1);
3 a read status register, read timer counter sequence;
4 a write to timer instruction;
5 initializing the counter.

The first three methods clear all flags, whilst the last two clear only the flag for the selected counter.

6.5 A REAL-TIME CLOCK USING AN MC6840 PTM

The following program uses a programmable counter timer chip to produce a real-time clock which is updated every second and shows a convenient method for producing accurate timings on a microcomputer system (see Fig. 6.13).

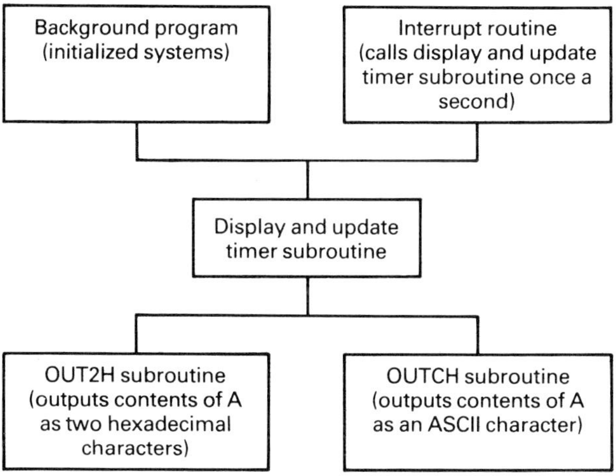

Fig. 6.13. Structure of real-time clock program.

The background program initializes the system and calls the display and update timer subroutine, which displays the initial timer value (0000), increments it, and then enters an endless loop with interrupts enabled.

The PTM causes regular interrupts which are counted by the interrupt routine and which are used to call the display and update counter subroutine once a second. If the MC6840 is being used with a system's clock generated by a 4 MHz M6809 processor, the clock used by the PTM will be at 1 MHz and the counters will be decremented 1,000,000 times a second. Since the counters are 16 bits, the maximum interval between interrupts is 65.536 milliseconds and a 1-second delay can be produced by counting 20 interrupts at 50-millisecond intervals.

The display and update counter subroutine calls two further subroutines which are assumed to be in the system's monitor (see Chapter 7). These routines provide the communications with the system's terminal on which the time is to be displayed and which is driven via an ACIA. The first (OUT2H) outputs the contents of the A register as two hexadecimal characters and the second (OUTCH) outputs the contents of the same register as an ASCII character. In the simple example in Program 6.2, time is displayed as a four-digit hexadecimal number.

```
        NAM    CLOCK
*PROGRAMMER P.J.THEWLIS
*30 JULY 1984
*PROGRAM TO PRODUCE A REAL TIME CLOCK USING A COUNTER TIMER.
*THE CLOCK IS DISPLAYED ON A VDU SCREEN IN HEXADECIMAL AND
*UPDATED EVERY SECOND
*
*BACKGROUND INITIALISATION ROUTINE
*BEGIN INITIALISE SYSTEM STACK POINTER
*       INITIALISE INTERRUPT VECTOR
*       INTERRUPT COUNTER = 0
*       TIMER OUTPUT = 0
*       LOAD BUFFER OF COUNTER 1 WITH TIME INTERVAL
*       DISPLAY TIME OUTPUT
*       START COUNTER
*       DO FOREVER ENABLE INTERRUPTS
*                  WAIT FOR INTERRUPT
*       END DO FOREVER
*END
*
        ORG    $800
CR1     EQU    $F600     CONTROL REGISTER 1
CR2     EQU    $F601     CONTROL REGISTER 2
BUF1    EQU    $F602     BUFFER FOR TIMER 1
STATUS  EQU    $F601     STATUS REGISTER
INTVEC  EQU    $00E2     ADDRESS OF INTERRUPT VECTOR
TIME    EQU    $840      CLOCK VALUE
ICOUNT  EQU    $842      INTERRUPT COUNTER
BACK    LDS    #$00A0    INITIALISE SYSTEM STACK
        LDX    INTER     SET INTERRUPT VECTOR TO START ADDRESS OF
        STX    INTVEC    INTERRUPT ROUTINE
        LDA    #20
        STA    ICOUNT    SET INTERRUPT COUNTER
        CLR    TIME
        CLR    TIME+1    SET CLOCK OUTPUT TO ZERO
        LDA    #01       SELECT CONTROL REGISTER 1 BY SETTING
        STA    CR2       BIT 0 OF CONTROL REGISTER 2 TO ZERO
        LDX    #50000
        STX    BUF1      SET 50ms TIME INTERVAL
        LDA    #$43      SET TIMER TO BUFFER PRESET CR10 = 0
*                        USE SYSTEM CLOCK           CR11 = 1
        STA    CR1       16 BIT COUNTING MODE       CR12 = 0
*                        CONTINUOUS MODE        CR13,4,5 = 0
*                        ENABLE INTERRUPTS          CR16 = 1
*                        OUTPUT OFF                 CR17 = 0
        JSR    DISP
        LDA    #$42
        STA    CR1       START COUNTERS
DOEV    CWAI   #$EF      CLEAR INTERRUPT FLAG,ENABLE INTERRUPTS & WAIT
        JMP    DOEV
*
*
*
* DISPLAY ROUTINE
*BEGIN OUTPUT CARRIAGE RETURN
*       OUTPUT TIME
*       INCREMENT TIME
*       RETURN
*END
*
*THIS SUBROUTINE CALLS TWO MONITOR SUBROUTINES
*OUTAS - OUTPUTS AN ASCII CHARACTER FROM THE A REGISTER
*OUT2H - OUTPUTS THE CONTENTS OF THE A REGISTER AS 2 HEX CHARACTERS
*
        ORG    $850
OUTAS   EQU    $F800
OUT2H   EQU    $F80C
DISP    PSHS   A,X       SAVE REGISTERS
        LDA    #$0D      CARRIAGE RETURN
        JSR    OUTAS
        LDA    TIME      MOST SIGNIFICANT BYTE
```

```
        JSR     OUT2H
        LDA     TIME+1    LEAST SIGNIFICANT BYTE
        JSR     OUT2H
        LDX     TIME
        LEAX    1,X       INCREMENT TIME
        STX     TIME
        PULS    A,X       RESTORE REGISTERS
        RTS
*
*
*
*FOREGROUND (INTERRUPT) ROUTINE
*BEGIN CLEAR INTERRUPTS
*       INCREMENT INTERRUPT COUNTER
*       IF INTERRUPT COUNTER<20 THEN RETURN
*                                ELSE CALL DISPLAY ROUTINE
*                                     INTERRUPT COUNTER = 0
*       RETURN FROM INTERRUPT
*END
*
        ORG     $900
INTER   LDA     STATUS    CLEAR INTERRUPTS
        LDX     BUF1      BY DUMMY READS
        INC     ICOUNT    INCREMENT INTERRUPT COUNTER
        LDA     ICOUNT
        CMPA    #20       TEST FOR 1 SEC
        BLT     ENDF      IF 1 SEC NOT ELAPSED THEN EXIT
        JSR     DISP      IF 1 SEC ELAPSED THEN OUTPUT TIME
        CLR     ICOUNT    CLEAR INTERRUPT COUNTER
ENDF    RTI
        END
```

Program 6.2.

6.6 ANALOGUE SIGNALS

In many real-time control applications, a microprocessor system has to accept and produce continuously varying analogue signals. The circuitry needed to interface these signals is based on the parallel interface described in Chapter 5 with additional hardware being included to convert the analogue signals to or from binary for input or output.

The following sections of this chapter describe the hardware used to produce these interfaces and give examples of their respective driver routines.

6.7 DIGITAL TO ANALOGUE CONVERTERS

To produce an analogue output (Fig. 6.14), the digital value from the microprocessor is fed via a parallel interface to a digital to analogue converter (DAC) which converts the digital input into a voltage or current. The analogue signal from the DAC is then amplified before being output to external devices.

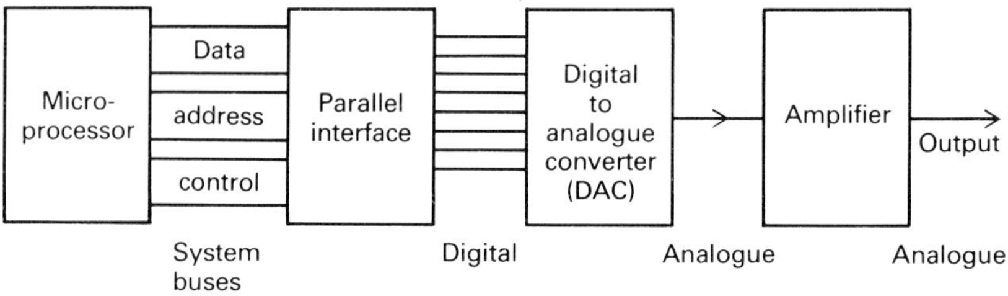

Fig. 6.14. Analogue outputs.

The level of the ouput from the DAC is proportional to the binary value of the input word. The chip can be considered as being a form of multiplier circuit the operation of which is expressed by the equation

$$V_{out} = D \times V_{ref}$$

where V_{out} = the output voltage,
D = the digital input (treated as a fraction), and
V_{ref} = the analogue reference voltage.

The configuration of the amplifier on the output of the DAC can be used to give an interface which operates in either unipolar mode to produce outputs between 0 and V_{max} or in bipolar mode giving outputs between V'_{min} and V'_{max} (see Fig. 6.15).

Digital word	Unipolar	Bipolar
11111111	$V_{max} = V_{ref}(1-2^{-8})$	$V'_{max} = V_{ref}(1-2^{-7})$
10000000	$0.5 \times V_{ref}$	0
00000000	0	$V'_{min} = -V_{ref}$

Fig. 6.15. Unipolar and bipolar output ranges.

Operational amplifiers (inverting mode)

The simplest form of DAC is the binary weighted resistor type. Before considering its operation, however, the effects of the output amplifier have to be considered. Figure 6.16 shows a typical unipolar configuration with the operational amplifier operating in an inverting configuration.

An ideal operational amplifier has the following DC characteristics:

1 infinite open loop gain,
2 infinite input resistance,
3 zero output resistance.

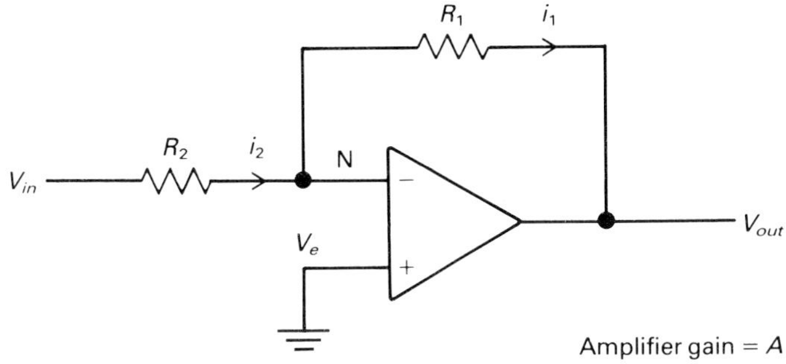

Fig. 6.16. Operational amplifier (inverting mode).

The output voltage is given by:

$$V_{out} = AV_e$$

and thus

$$V_e = \frac{V_{out}}{A}$$

If V_{out} is to have a maximum value of say 10 volts, then since by definition the gain of the amplifier (A) is very large.

$$V_e \approx 0$$

Thus the node N is effectively at earth, and since the amplifier has infinite input resistance, Kirchhoff's first law gives

$$i_1 = i_2$$

By Ohm's Law

$$i_1 = \frac{V_e - V_{out}}{R_1} \quad \text{and} \quad i_2 = \frac{V_{in} - V_e}{R_2}$$

Hence

$$\frac{V_e - V_{out}}{R_1} = \frac{V_{in} - V_e}{R_2}$$

and since $V_e \approx 0$

$$V_{out} = -\frac{R_1}{R_2}V_{in} \qquad \textbf{Eq. A}$$

The binary weighted resistor D to A converter

Figure 6.17 shows a binary weighted resistor digital to analogue converter with the output amplifier operating in inverting mode.

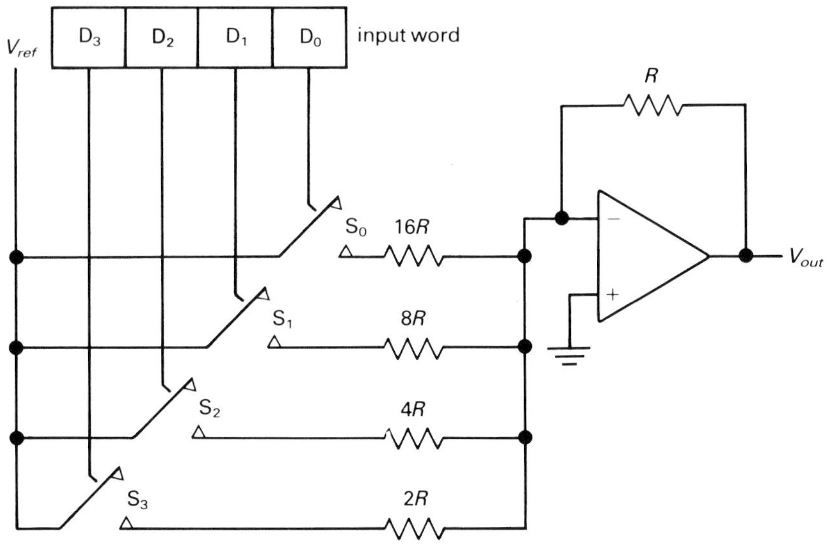

Fig. 6.17. A binary weighted resistor DAC.

With $D_0=1$ in the input word, S_0 is closed and from Equation A

$$V_{out} = -\frac{R}{16R}V_{ref} = -\frac{1}{16}V_{ref}$$

With $D_1 = 1$, S_1 is closed and

$$V_{out} = -\frac{R}{8R}V_{ref} = -\frac{1}{8}V_{ref}$$

With both D_0 and $D_1=1$, the $16R$ and $8R$ resistors are in parallel giving

$$V_{out} = -\frac{3R}{16R}V_{ref} = -\frac{3}{16}V_{ref}$$

(See Appendix 2 for the combination of resistors in series and parallel.)

Similarly for any other combination of switches closed, it can be shown that the output voltage is proportional to the digital input. The maximum output produced when all the switches are closed is

$$V_{out} = -\frac{15}{16}V_{ref}$$

Thus the digital input word is converted into an analogue voltage V_{out} in the range 0 to $-(1-2^{-n})V_{ref}$ where n is the number of bits in the input word. Whilst it is possible to construct reasonably accurate 4-bit converters using this method, as the number of bits increases it becomes both difficult and expensive to produce the range of resistors to the accuracies required. Most commercially available devices, therefore, are based on the R–$2R$ ladder network described below and shown in Fig. 6.18.

The *R*–2*R* ladder network

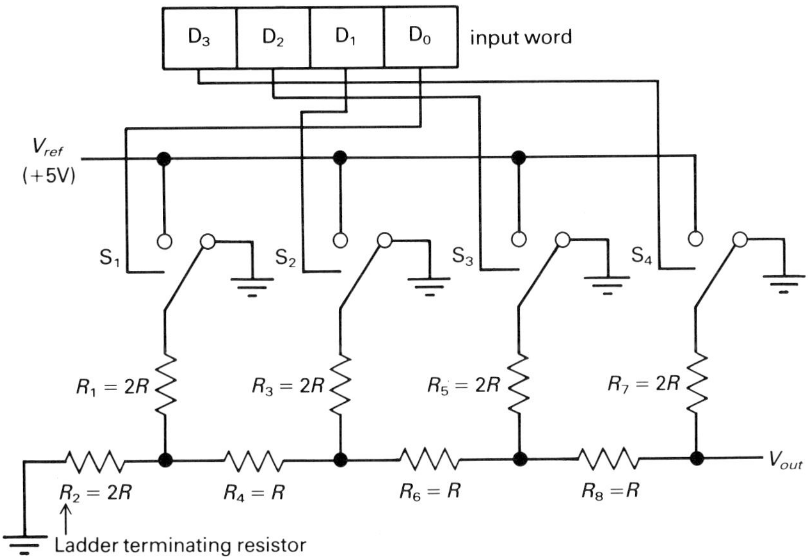

Fig. 6.18. An *R*–2*R* resistor ladder DAC.

The following example shows the method for proving that the output V_{out} is proportional to the value of the input word.

Assume that $D_3=1$ switching S_4 to V_{ref}. R_1 and R_2 are in parallel to ground giving a combined resistance $R_{12} = R$. The circuit then reduces as shown in Fig. 6.19.

R_{12} and R_4 are in series to ground giving a combined resistance $R_{124}=2R$.

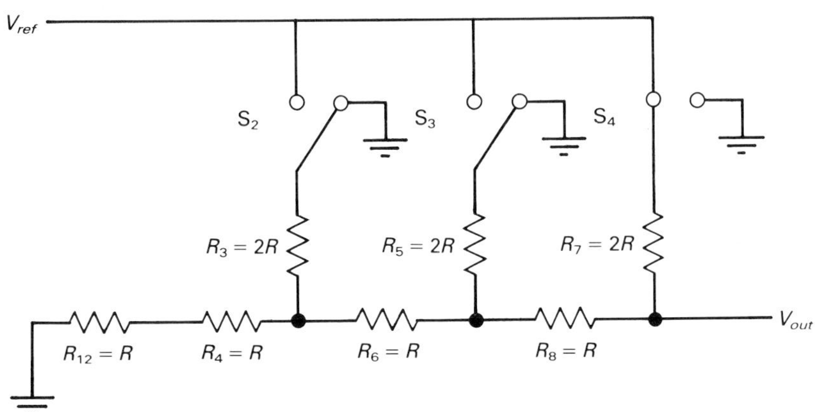

Fig. 6.19.

Applying the same procedure to S_2 and S_3 the circuit reduces as shown in Fig. 6.20.

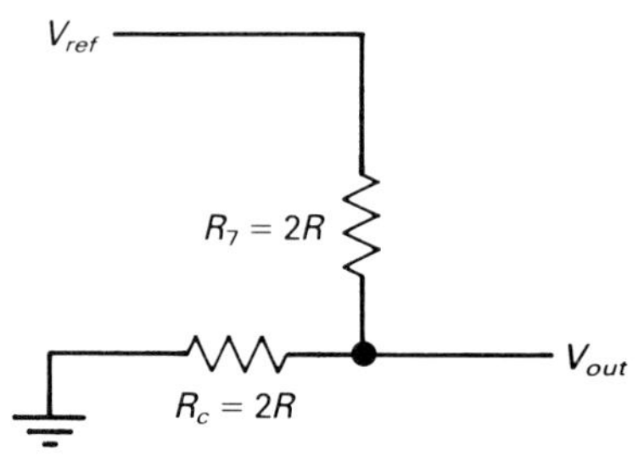

and $V_{out} = \dfrac{2R}{2R + 2R} V_{ref} = \frac{1}{2} V_{ref}$

Fig. 6.20.

By using this method of analysis with different combinations of the input word, it can be shown that the output $V_{out} = (d/2^n)V_{ref}$ where d=the integer value of the input word and n=the number of bits.

Operational amplifiers (non-inverting mode)

The output from the $R-2R$ ladder network is amplified before being sent to the plant or device being controlled. The following operational amplifier circuit can be used to give an output of the same polarity as the reference voltage V_{ref} applied to the R–$2R$ network.

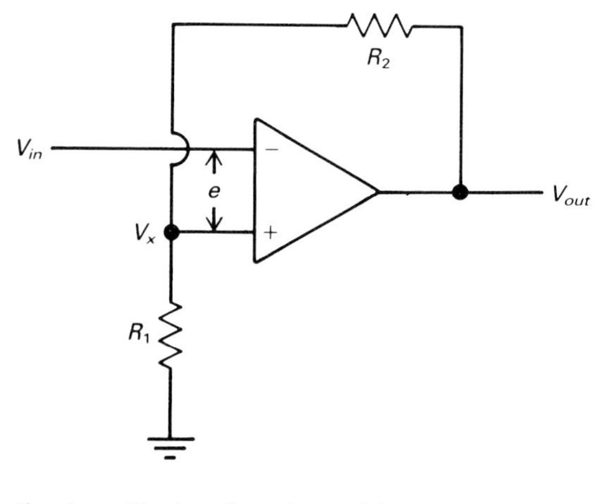

Fig. 6.21. Operational amplifier (non-inverting mode).

$$V_{out} = A \times e$$

and hence

$$e = \frac{V_{out}}{A}$$

Since V_{out} is small (10 volts) and A is very large

$$e \approx 0$$

and since

$$e = V_{in} - V_x$$
$$V_{in} \approx V_x$$

However, since the amplifier has infinite input resistance,

$$V_x = \frac{R_1}{R_1 + R_2} V_{out}$$

and therefore

$$V_{out} = \frac{R_1 + R_2}{R_1} V_{in}$$

6.8 THE FERRANTI ZN428 8-BIT DAC

The ZN428 is an 8-bit DAC converter with input latches and an optional 2.56V internal reference voltage which may be substituted by an external reference. Figure 6.22 shows the pin assignments for this chip.

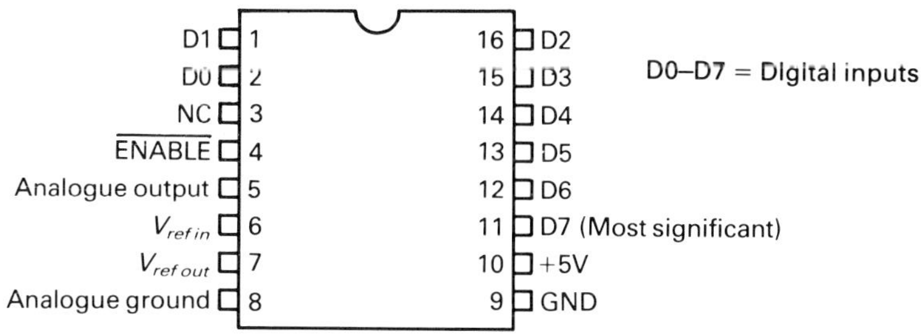

Fig. 6.22. Ferranti ZN428 pin assignments.

Figure 6.23 shows the internal organization of this chip which is based on the *R*–2*R* ladder network. The data latch is transparent when the $\overline{\text{ENABLE}}$ terminal is low and the data is held when it is high.

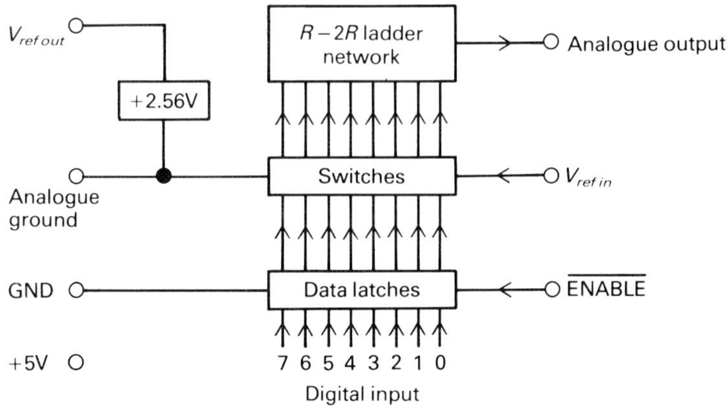

Fig. 6.23. Internal organization of the Ferranti ZN428 DAC.

A DAC is interfaced to a microcomputer by a parallel interface. Figure 6.24 shows the Ferranti ZN428 DAC interfaced to an M6809 system by an MC6821 PIA.

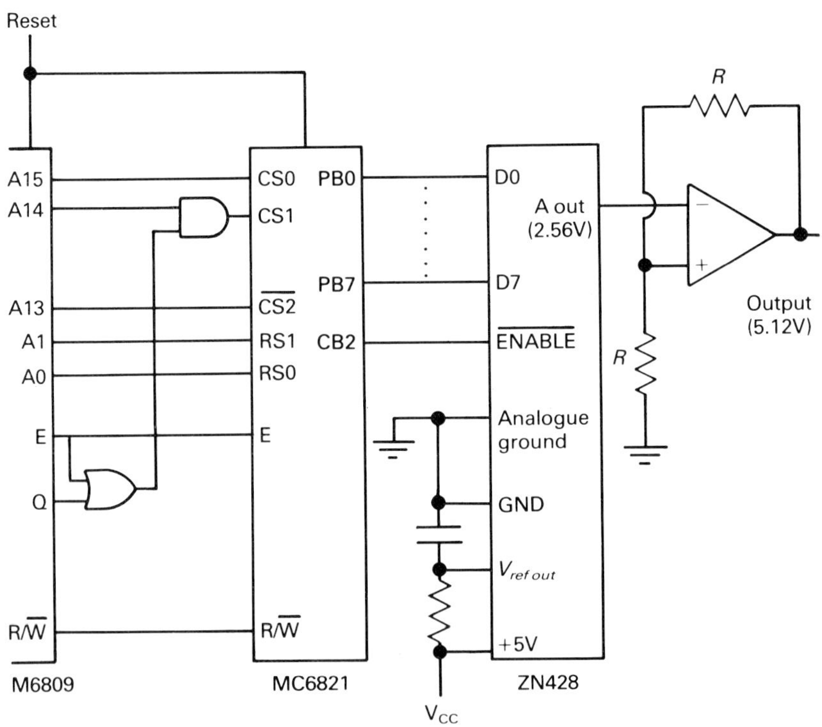

Fig. 6.24. A DAC interface using the ZN428.

In the unipolar configuration shown in Fig. 6.24, the ZN428, which is driven from the B side of the PIA, uses its internal 2.56V reference voltage. The operational amplifier amplifies the converter output by a factor of 2 to give a system output in the range 0–5.12 volts. The CB2 terminal of the PIA, which is connected to the $\overline{\text{ENABLE}}$ input of the converter, has to be driven low to make the converter's input latches transparent and enable the data on PB0–PB7 to be loaded.

Program 6.3 sends the value held in the memory location DATA to a DAC connected to the B side of a PIA which resides at addresses $F608 to $F60B.

```
        NAM     DTOA
*PROGRAMMER P.J.THEWLIS
*7 SEPTEMBER 1984
*PROGRAM TO OUTPUT THE VALUE HELD IN MEMORY LOCATION
*$900 VIA A D TO A CONVERTER ATTAVHED TO THE B SIDE
*OF A PIA AT ADDRESSES $F608 TO $F60B
*
*BEGIN INITIALISE PIA
*       OUTPUT VALUE FROM DATA
*END
*
        ORG     $800
PIADR   EQU     $F608
DATA    EQU     $0900
        LDX     #PIADR    LOAD X REGISTER WITH PIA BASE ADDRESS
        CLR     3,X       ACCESS B SIDE DATA DIRECTION REGISTER
        LDA     #$FF      B SIDE AS OUTPUTS
        STA     2,X       STORE IN B SIDE DATA DIRECTION REGISTER
        LDA     #$34      CRB2=1 FOR ACCESS TO DATA REGISTER
*                         CRB4=CRB5=1 & CRB3=0 TO MAKE CB2 O/P =0
        STA     3,X       STORE IN B SIDE CONTROL REGISTER
        LDA     DATA
        STA     2,X       OUTPUT DATA
        END
```

Program 6.3.

Operational amplifiers (bipolar configuration)

To produce a bipolar D to A converter the operational amplifier is used in the configuration shown in Fig. 6.25.

The differential input

$$e = \frac{V_{out}}{A}$$

Since V_{out} is comparatively small whilst A is almost infinite

$$e = V_{in} - V_x \approx 0$$

and

$$V_x = V_{in}$$

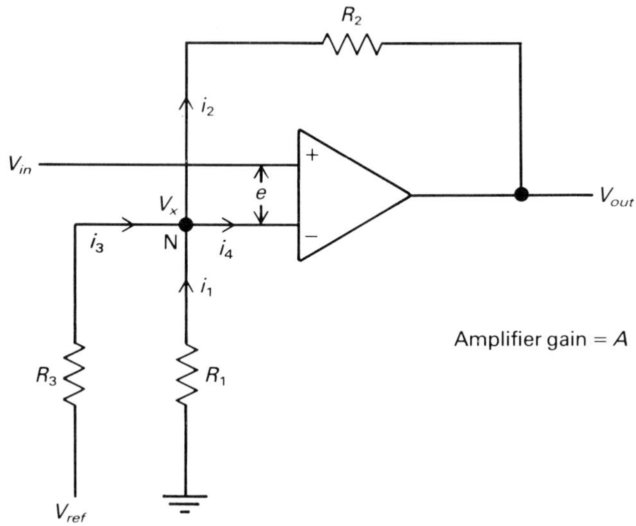

Fig. 6.25. Operational amplifier (bipolar configuration).

At node N

$$i_2 + i_4 = i_1 + i_3$$

An operational amplifier has an almost infinite input resistance and hence

$$i_4 \approx 0$$

and thus

$$i_2 = i_1 + i_3$$

Applying Ohm's Law

$$\frac{V_{in} - V_{out}}{R_2} = -\frac{V_{in}}{R_1} + \frac{V_{ref} - V_{in}}{R_3} \quad \text{(using } V_x = V_{in}\text{)}$$

and thus

$$V_{out} = R_2\left(\frac{1}{R_1} + \frac{1}{R_2} + \frac{1}{R_3}\right) V_{in} - \frac{R_2}{R_3} V_{ref}$$

For $R_1 = R_2 = 2R$ and $R_3 = R$

$$V_{out} = 2(2V_{in} - V_{ref})$$

Thus when $V_{in} = 0$ $\quad V_{out} = -2V_{ref}$

when $V_{in} = \dfrac{V_{ref}}{R_2}$ $\quad V_{out} = 0$

and when $V_{in} = V_{ref}$ $\quad V_{out} = 2V_{ref}$

which is a bipolar configuration with a gain of 2.

6.9 ANALOGUE TO DIGITAL CONVERTERS

To enable analogue signals to be input to a microcomputer system, they first have to be converted into digital form. An analogue to digital converter (ADC) chip will perform this function, its digital output being interfaced to the microcomputer by parallel interface.

The analogue signal to the ADC, which is derived from the plant or device being monitored, has to be converted to the correct form and level before being input. An amplifier circuit similar to those described for the DAC interfaces is commonly used for this purpose. (See Fig. 6.26).

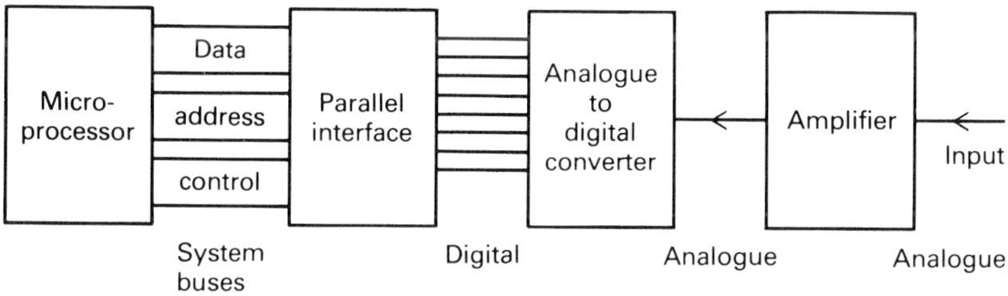

Fig. 6.26. Analogue input.

There are four main types of ADCs, counter-comparator, dual ramp, successive approximation and parallel. The majority of those designed for use with microcomputer systems are of the successive approximation type and are easily interfaced to the system.

Successive approximation converters

All analogue to digital converters are based on digital to analogue converters. In successive approximation converters the output from a DAC is compared with the analogue input. The digital value input to the DAC is then changed depending on the result. Figure 6.27 shows the organization of an 8-bit successive approximation ADC.

When the start pulse is applied to the control section the shift register is cleared and the clock pulse gated in.

On the first clock pulse, the most significant bit of the shift register is set to 1. The input to the DAC is therefore 10000000. The analogue input is compared with the DAC output and, if it is greater, the most significant bit of the shift register output (D7) is latched to 1. If the DAC output is less than the analogue input. D7 is reset to 0 and latched.

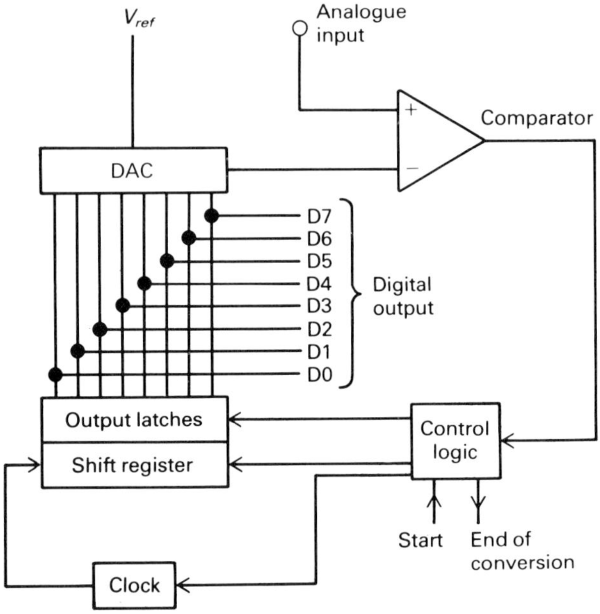

Fig. 6.27. A successive approximation ADC.

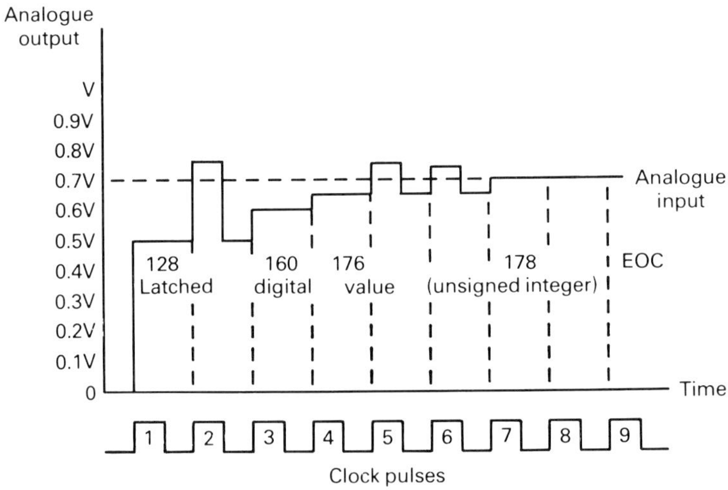

Fig. 6.28. Operation of successive approximation ADC.

On the second clock pulse, bit D6 is set to 1 and the comparison and latching procedure repeated. If the analogue input is still greater than the DAC output, the latches will be set to 11000000 with D7 and D6 latched. If it is less, the latches will be set to 10000000 with D7 and D6 latched.

The process is repeated for D5 in the next clock cycle and for D4 to D0 in the next five cycles.

On the ninth clock pulse, the shift register will overflow and this becomes the End of Conversion (EOC) pulse which both signals that the digital output is ready and stops the conversion process. (See Fig. 6.28.)

This type of converter is reasonably fast, requiring only $n+1$ clock pulses to complete the conversion, where n is the number of bits in the resultant output.

6.10 THE FERRANTI ZN427 8-BIT ADC

The Ferranti ZN427 is an 8-bit successive approximation ADC with tri-state outputs. It is designed to work with any negative supply voltage in the range −3 to −30 volts depending on the value of an external resistor connected between R_{ext} pin and the negative supply. Figure 6.29 shows the pin configuration for this 18-pin chip.

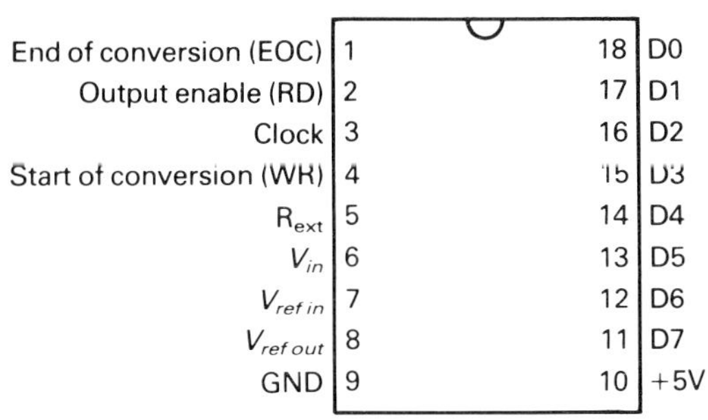

Fig. 6.29. Pin assignments for the Ferranti ZN427.

This chip is based on an $R-2R$ ladder network and like the ZN428 has an internal 2.56V reference. Figure 6.30 shows the internal structure for this chip.

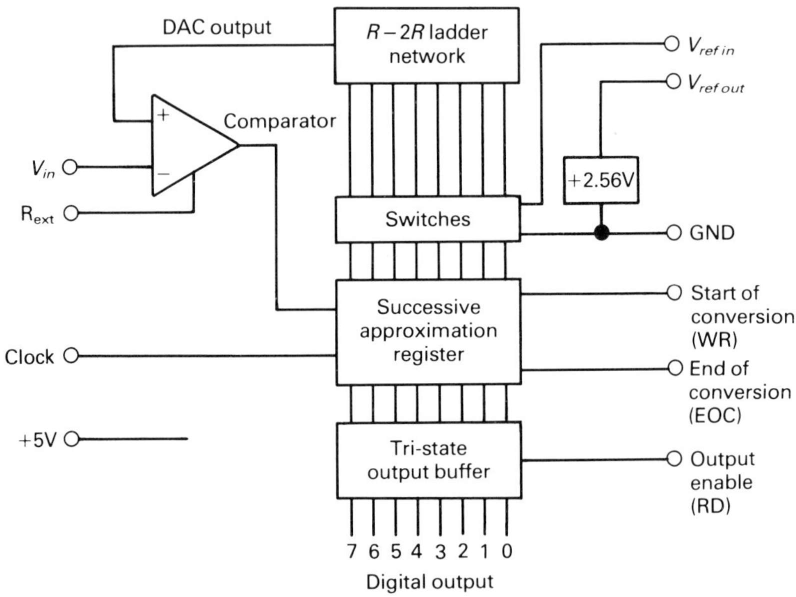

Fig. 6.30. Internal organization of the Ferranti ZN427 ADC.

An ADC is interfaced to a microcomputer by a parallel interface. Figure 6.32 shows the Ferranti ZN427 ADC converter interfaced to an M6809 system by an MC6821 PIA.

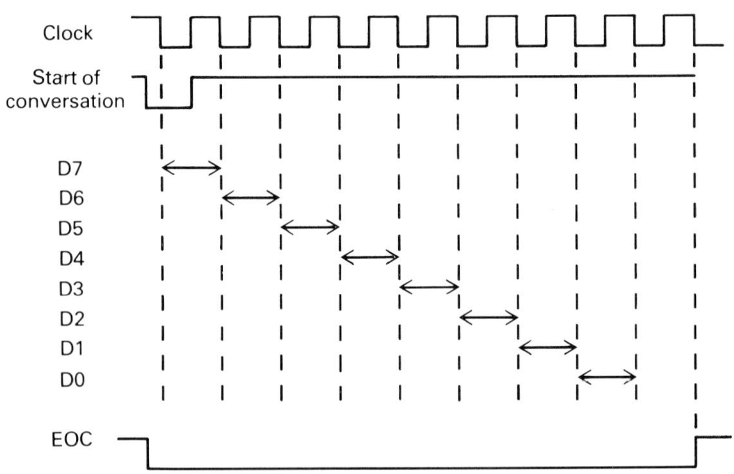

Fig. 6.31. Timing diagram for ADC interface.

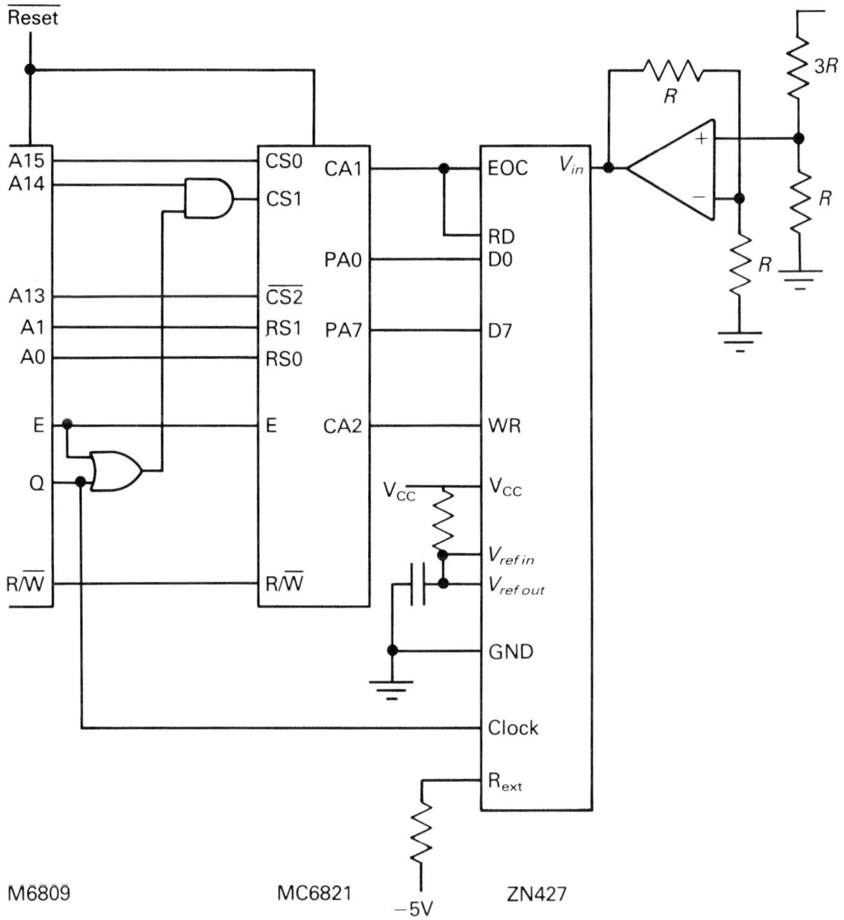

Fig. 6.32. An ADC interface using the ZN427.

In the unipolar configuration shown in Fig. 6.32 the ZN427 is connected to the A side of the PIA. The WR input (Start of Conversion) is driven from the CA2 terminal of the PIA. Conversion starts after this terminal is driven low and then high. End of conversion is signalled by a low to high transition of the EOC terminal which is connected to CA1 of the PIA. Figure 6.31 shows a timing diagram for this interface.

Program 6.4 reads a value from an ADC connected to the A side of PIA which resides at addresses \$F608 to \$F60B.

```
        NAM     ATOD
*PROGRAMMER P.J.THEWLIS
*7 SEPTEMBER 1984
*PROGRAM TO READ A VALUE FROM AN A TO D CONVERTER
*CONNECTED TO THE A PORT OF A PIA AT ADDRESSES
*$F608 TO $F60B.
*
*BEGIN INITIALISE PIA A SIDE AS INPUT. WITH CA2=1 MAKE
*                     CA2=0  AND THEN 1 TO START CONVERSION
*       WHILE CA1=0 DO NOTHING
*       READ AND STORE VALUE FROM A TO D
*END
*
        ORG     $800
PIADR   EQU     $F608
RES     EQU     $0900
        LDX     #PIADR   LOAD X WITH PIA BASE ADDRESS
        LDA     #$3A     CA2=1 & ACCESS DATA DIRECTION REGISTER A
        STA     1,X
        CLR     0,X      MAKE A SIDE INPUT
        LDA     #$36     CA2=0
        STA     1,X
        LDA     #$3E     CA2=1
        STA     1,X
WHILE   LDA     1,X      READ CONTROL REGISTER A
        TSTA
        BGE     WHILE    IF CA1=0 DO NOTHING
        LDA     0,X      GET DATA
        STA     RES
        END
```

Program 6.4.

6.11 APPLICATIONS IN REGULATORY CONTROL

In regulatory control, process parameters are maintained at, or made to go to, a desired level (within specified limits of error). Figure 6.33 shows a process with a single output parameter which is to be controlled.

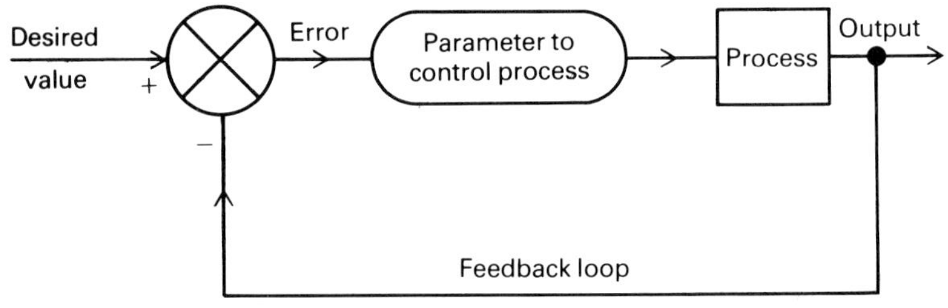

Fig. 6.33. Closed loop control.

The process is controlled using closed loop control in which the output parameter is measured, fed back for comparison with the desired value, and the difference, or error, used to control the process by changing its input conditions.

One of the most simple and commonly used regulatory control systems is an on–off temperature control system (or thermostat) for a boiler (Fig. 6.34).

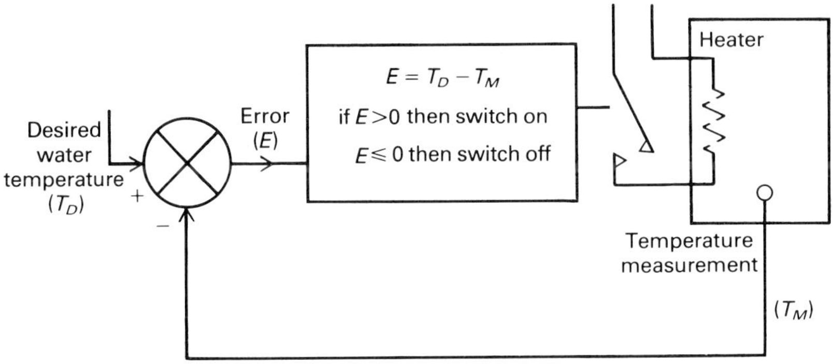

Fig. 6.34. Temperature control for a boiler.

The temperature of the water in the boiler (T_M) is measured, fed back and compared with the desired temperature (T_D). The error E is used to control a switch which enables or disables power to the heater in the boiler, the heater being switched on if the measured temperature is less than the desired temperature.

In most control systems, the process inputs are analogue variables, and the controlling device, or actuator, can be varied continously by the control system to set the levels of the inputs. There are many possible control strategies in this type of regulatory control, the following three being the most common:

1 proportional control, in which the input level to the process is proportional to the error between the measured variable and its desired value;

2 integral control, in which the input level is proportional to the integral of the error between the measured variable and its desired value;

3 derivative control, in which the input level is proportional to the derivative, or rate of change, of the error.

Two or more of these strategies are frequently combined to optimize the response of the process to changes in the desired value of the output.

Three-term control (or PID control) combines the proportional, integral and derivative strategies in a single control equation which gives the input level $x(t)$ as:

$$x(t) = K_1E + K_2 \int E dt + K_3 \frac{dE}{dt}$$

where K_1 = the proportional gain
K_2 = the integral gain
K_3 = the derivative gain
E = the error (desired value − measured value)

This control algorithm can be shared by many different closed loops, each of which has values for the constants K_1, K_2 and K_3 which optimize the response of that loop.

Almost all industrial processes have many closed loops in their control systems. Each loop may have its own unique control equation or set of parameters for a shared equation such as that shown above. These equations will form the control strategy which may be implemented on equipment ranging from a single computer system to individual microcomputer controllers with analogue input and output on each loop.

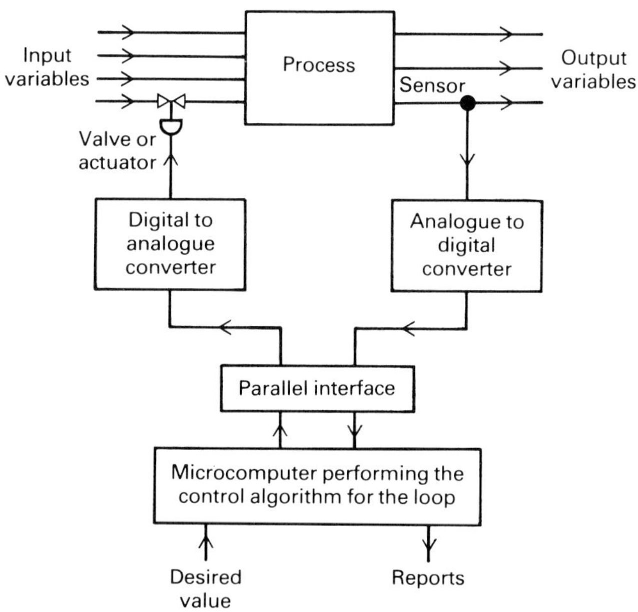

Fig. 6.35. Process control system (single loop).

Figure 6.35 shows a single control loop on such a multi-microcomputer process control system.

The desired value or set-point for each controller may be input directly, on a keyboard, by the operator or may be supplied over a data link from a centralized supervisory computer system which may include, or be linked to, production control and scheduling systems (Fig. 6.36).

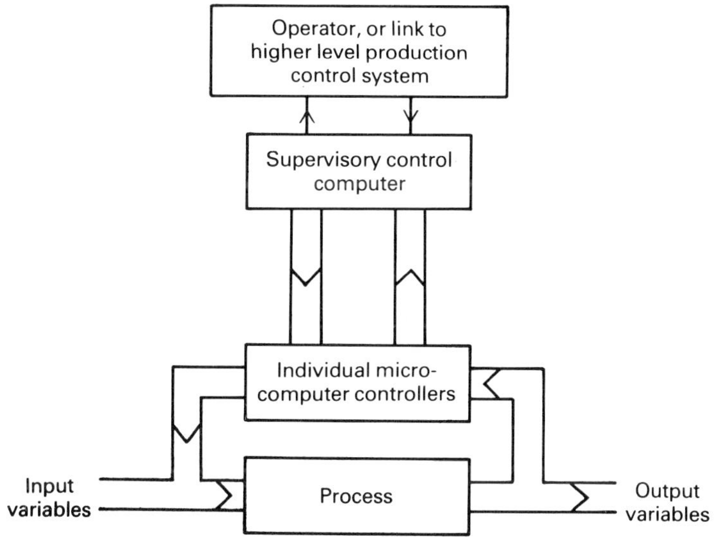

Fig. 6.36. Supervisory control system.

Chapter 7

Systems' Monitors

7.1 INTRODUCTION

To aid in the development of systems requiring only limited software and input/output facilities, many manufacturers offer a ready-made single-board microcomputer system similar to those already described. These systems usually consist of a processor, RAM, interface chips, sockets for the user to insert EPROMs or ROMs containing applications software and a program in ROM, supplied by the manufacturer and known as the system's monitor.

The system's monitor, on this type of microcomputer, enables the user to load, modify and run machine code, or in some instances assembly language programs, via the system's terminal. On larger systems, such as those with twin floppy disks, the system's monitor is called at start-up and used to load the operating system.

This chapter briefly outlines a system's monitor for an M6809 single-board microcomputer with a serially driven VDU acting as the system's input/output terminal. Typical functions provided by such a monitor are described, and examples of the type of subroutines which are available to the programmer are given.

7.2 MONITOR FACILITIES

Typical facilities provided by a system's monitor include the following.

1 Block Memory Display (B). This displays in hexadecimal the contents of a block of memory between the start and end addresses specified by the programmer.

2 Go To Subroutine (G). This function is used to execute programs or to test subroutines by performing a Jump to Subroutine at the address specified. Programs run in this way should, therefore, be terminated by a Return instruction to transfrer control back to the system's monitor on completion of execution.

3 Help (H). The help command causes a list of monitor facilities, with a brief description of each, to be produced on the system's terminal.

4 Insert Breakpoint (I). This causes an SWI instruction to be stored at the specified address and for the operation code, which was at that address, to be stored in the breakpoint table. The breakpoint table consists of a list of operation codes and their addresses in the program.
5 Memory Display And Modify (M). This facility enables the programmer to examine and modify the contents of memory locations starting from the specified address. It provides the mechanism for loading and modifying machine code programs, usually in hexadecimal format, from the system consol.
6 Remove Breakpoint (R) from the specified address, replaces the breakpoint (SWI instruction) at the address with the operation code which was stored in the breakpoint table when the breakpoint was inserted.
7 View And Modify Registers (V). This facility enables the programmer to examine and change the contents of any of the processor's registers.

Many other facilities are often included in a system's monitor but the seven given above provide a working subset and are commonly found in most monitors.

7.3 MONITOR STRUCTURE

A system's monitor should be, but is not always, a structured program. It provides the basic level of user interaction with the system, giving control over the basic operations of the microcomputer. The monitor will perform basic input/output operations, particularly with the system's terminal, and can therefore, if properly structured and documented provide the low-level programmer with many useful subroutines which can be called from applications programs.

The main monitor program

The monitor structure described below consists of a main program from which all other functions are called as subroutines. The main program, which consists of an initialization section followed by an endless loop to control input/output and call the command subroutines, is entered through the reset vector at addresses $FFFE and $FFFF.

```
begin inhibit interrupts
      initialize system stack
      initialize input/output interfaces
      de-activate breakpoints
      initialize SWI vector to breakpoints subroutine
      initialize other interrupt vectors to monitor start address
      do forever output carriage return, line feed
                 display prompt
                 read keyboard
                 if key=B, G, H, I, M, R or V then call
                                                    command subroutine
      end do forever
end
```

Carriage return, line feed subroutine

The carriage return (CR), line feed (LF) characters are output by the CRLF subroutine which loads the ASCII code for CR into the A register, calls the OUTCH subroutine to output an ASCII character and then repeats the process for the LF character (Program 7.1).

```
*CRLF SUBROUTINE
*
CRLF    PSHS   A        SAVE A REGISTER
        LDA    #$0D     CARRIAGE RETURN
        LBSR   OUTCH
        LDA    #$0A     LINE FEED
        LBSR   OUTCH
        PULS   A,PC     RESTORE A & RETURN
*
*
*OUTCH SUBROUTINE
*
*BEGIN SAVE REGISTERS
*       WHILE ACIA BUSY DO-NOTHING
*       TRANSMIT CHARACTER IN A
*       RESTORE REGISTERS & RETURN
*END
*
*
OUTCH   PSHS   B        SAVE B REGISTER
OUTCH1  LDB    ACIAS    GET ACIA STATUS REGISTER
        ANDB   #$02     TDR EMPTY?
        BEQ    OUTCH1   NO - WAIT
        STA    ACIAD    TRANSMIT CHARACTER IN A REG
        PULS   B,PC     RESTORE B & RETURN
```

Program 7.1.

The prompt (*) is also produced by using the OUTCH subroutine to transmit the ASCII code for the prompt from the A register.

Read a key subroutine

The read a key subroutine (INCH) is a small subroutine which interrogates the keyboard and waits for a key to be pressed (Program 7.2).

```
*INCH SUBROUTINE
*
*BEGIN WHILE ACIA RDR EMPTY WAIT
*      READ CHARACTER INTO A REGISTER
*      RETURN
*END
*
*
INCH   LDA    ACIAS     GET ACIA STATUS REGISTER
       ASRA             RDR=1 CHARACTER RECEIVED
       BCC    INCH      NO THEN WAIT
       LDA    ACIAD     GET CHARACTER
       RTS
```

Program 7.2.

Command processing routines

The block memory display subroutine, the pseudo-code for which is given below, is a typical example of a command processing subroutine. It is entered in response to a B command input from the system terminal.

The routine asks the user to input the start and end addresses of the block of memory to be displayed, and then lists the contents of each memory location in hexadecimal form in a headed table.

```
begin pointer = start address of "START ADDRESS" string
      call outstring subroutine (OUTSTR)
      call read address subroutine (INADR) to get start address
      pointer = start address of "END ADDRESS" string
      call outstring subroutine (OUTSTR)
      call read address subroutine (INADR) to get end address
      call carriage return, line feed subroutine (CRLF)
      round down start address to NNN0
      round up end address to NNNF
      pointer = start address of table heading string
      call outstring subroutine (OUTSTR)
      line address = block start address
      while line address < end address do
            output line address (call OUT2H twice)
```

```
            for counter = 0 to 15 do
                  output contents of line address + counter (OUT2H)
                  output space (OUTCH)
            line address = line address+16
            output carriage return, line feed (CRLF)
            if line address = 0000 then return
      return
end
```

The routine uses several subroutines. Listings for the output routines are given below.

The OUTSTR subroutine (Program 7.3) displays a string of ASCII characters on the system's terminal. The characters are stored in memory and terminated by an EOT ($04) character. The start address of the string is supplied in the X index register which is used as a character pointer in the subroutine. It is assumed that each ASCII string is terminated by carriage return,line feed if the next input/output operation is to be on the next line.

```
*OUTSTR SUBROUTINE
*
*DISPLAYS, ON THE SYSTEM TERMINAL, A STRING OF ASCII
*CHARACTERS STORED IN MEMORY AND TERMINATED BY AN EOT ($04)
*CHARACTER. THE START ADDRESS OF THE STRING IS SUPPLIED IN THE
*X REGISTER WHICH IS USED AS THE CHARACTER POINTER.
*
*BEGIN SAVE REGISTER
*      WHILE CHARACTER <> EOT DO
*             GET CHARACTER POINTED TO BY X REGISTER
*             INCREMENT X REGISTER
*             PRINT CHARACTER
*      RESTORE REGISTER
*      RETURN
*END
*
OUTSTR PSHS   A        SAVE A REGISTER
OUTST1 LDA    ,X+      GET CHARACTER, INCREMENT POINTER
       CMPA   #$04     IF CHARACTER = EOT ...
       BEQ    ENDST    THEN END
       LBSR   OUTCH    ELSE OUTPUT IT
       BRA    OUTST1
ENDST  PULS   A
       RTS
```

Program 7.3.

The OUT2H subroutine (Program 7.4) outputs the contents of the A register as two hexadecimal digits.

```
*OUT2H SUBROUTINE
*
*SUBROUTINE OUTPUTS THE CONTENTS OF THE A REGISTER AS
*TWO HEXADECIMAL DIGITS
*
*BEGIN PUSH REGISTER A
*      MOVE MOST SIGNIFICANT NIBBLE INTO LEAST SIGNIFICANT NIBBLE
*      CONVERT & OUTPUT LEAST SIGNIFICANT NIBBLE IN ASCII
*      PULL A REGISTER TO RESTORE IT
*      CONVERT & OUTPUT LEAST SIGNIFICANT NIBBLE IN ASCII
*END
*
OUT2H  PSHS   A        SAVE A
       LSRA            )
       LSRA            )  GET MOST SIGNIFICANT NIBBLE
       LSRA            )  INTO LEAST SIGNIFICANT NIBBLE
       LSRA            )
       BSR    OUTHX    OUTPUT LEAST SIGNIFICANT NIBBLE
       PULS   A        RESTORE A
*
*FALL INTO OUTHX (CONVERT AND OUTPUT LEAST SIGNIFICANT NIBBLE)
*
OUTHX  AND    #$0F     ISOLATE LEAST SIGNIFICANT NIBBLE
       ADDA   #$30     0 TO 9 TO ASCII ($30 TO $39)
       CMPA   #$39     WAS IT > $39 ?
       BLS    OUTHX1   NO - CHARACTER WAS NUMERIC
       ADDA   #$07     A TO F TO ASCII ($41 TO $46)
OUTHX1 LBSR   OUTCH    OUTPUT CHARACTER
       RTS
```

Program 7.4.

Figure 7.1 shows the typical structure for a system's monitor based on the simple example described in this chapter.

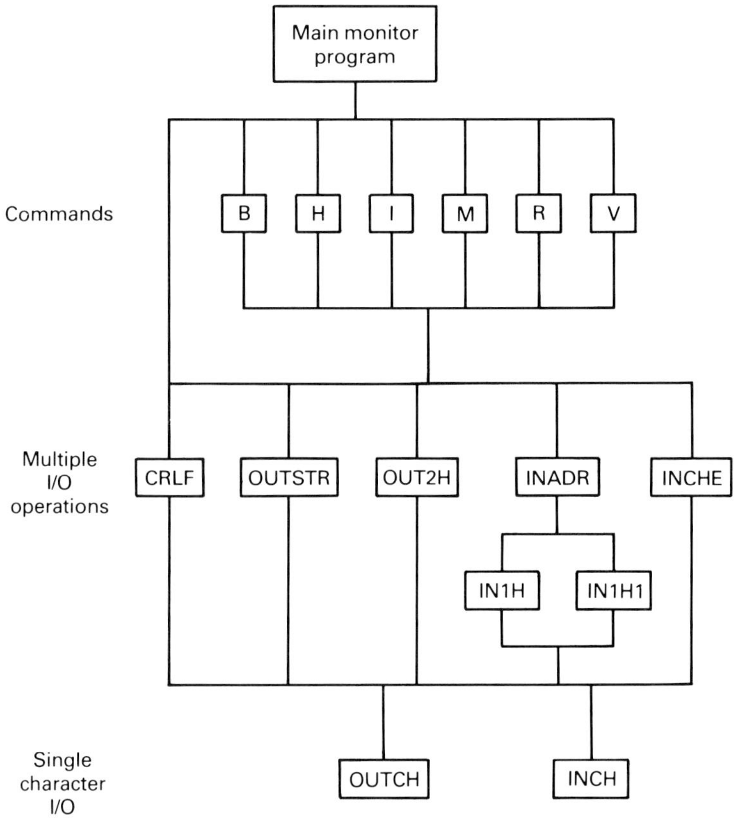

INADR Inputs a 16-bit address,
IN1H Inputs 1 hexadecimal character to the LSN of A,
IN1H1 Add 1 hexadecimal character to the MSN of A,
INCHE Input and echo an ASCII character.

Note: IN1H and IN1H1 also check for any special characters.

Fig. 7.1. Structure of a simple monitor.

Bibliography

Bishop, R. *Basic Microprocessors and the 6800* (Editions Mengis, 1981).

Carr, J. J. *Digital Interfacing with an Analog World* (Tab Books, 1978).

Epson. *MX-80 Operation Manual* (Epson Shinshu Seiki Co., 1981).

Ferranti. *Microprocessor Interfacing Using the ZN427/ZN428 Data Converters* – Applications Report (Ferranti Semiconductors, June 1979).

Halsall, F. & Lister, F.P. *Microprocessor Fundamentals* (Pitman, 1980).

Hitachi. *Semiconductor Data Book* (Hitachi, 1982).

Leventhal, L.A. *Introduction to microprocessors: Software, Hardware, Programming* (Prentice-Hall, 1978).

Leventhal, L.A. *6809 Assembly Language Programming* (Osborne/McGraw-Hill, 1981).

Mostek. *Memory Data Book and Designer's Guide* (Mostek Corporation, 1980).

Motorola. *Microcomputer Components* (Motorola Semiconductors, 1979).

Motorola. *Memory Products* (Motorola Semiconductors, 1979).

Motorola. *Microcomputer Forum*—a collection of articles and data sheets (Motorola Semiconductors, 1980).

Motorola. *MC6809E*—Data Sheet (Motorola Semiconductors, 1980).

Motorola. *Macro Assemblers Reference Manual* (Motorola Inc., 1979).

Thewlis, P.J. & Foxon, B.N.T. *From Logic to Computers* (Blackwell Scientific Publications, 1983).

Appendix 1

ASCII and EBCDIC Codes

ASCII code

Numeric identification bits	Zone identification							
3210	000	001	010	011	100	101	110	111
0000	NULL	DC0	b̸	0	@	P		p
0001	SOM	DC1	!	1	A	Q	a	q
0010	EOA	DC2	"	2	B	R	b	r
0011	EOM	DC3	#	3	C	S	c	s
0100	EOT	DC4	$	4	D	T	d	t
0101	WRU	ERR	%	5	E	U	e	u
0110	RU	SYNC	&	6	F	V	f	v
0111	BELL	LEM	'	7	G	W	g	w
1000	BKSP	S0	(	8	H	X	h	x
1001	HT	S1	)	9	I	Y	i	y
1010	LF	S2	*	:	J	Z	j	z
1011	VT	S3	+	;	K	[	k	{
1100	FF	S4	,	<	L	\	l	|
1101	CR	S5	–	=	M	]	m	}
1110	SO	S6	.	>	N	↑	n	ESC
1111	SI	S7	/	?	O	←	o	DEL

NULL, Null/Idle
SOM, Start of message
EOA, End of address
EOM, End of message
ROT, End of transmission
WRU, 'Who are you?'
RU, 'Are you. . .?'
BELL, Audible signal

BKSP, Backspace
HT, Horizontal tab
LF, Line feed
VT, Vertical tab
FF, From feed
CR, Carriage return
SO, Shift out
SI, Shift in

DC0–DC4, Device control
ERR, Error
SYNC, Synchronous idle
LEM, Logical end of media
S0–S7, Separator information
b̸, Blank
ESC, Escape
DEL, Delete/Idle

Format

7	6	5	4	3	2	1	0

Bit 7 = Parity.

EBCDIC code

Bit positions 3210	Bit positions 7654: 0000	0001	0010	0011	0100	0101	0110	0111	1000	1001	1010	1011	1100	1101	1110	1111
0000	NULL				SP	&	–									0
0001							/		a	j			A	J		1
0010									b	k	s		B	K	S	2
0011									c	l	t		C	L	T	3
0100	PF	RES	BYP	PN					d	m	u		D	M	U	4
0101	HT	NL	LF	RS					e	n	v		E	N	V	5
0110	LC	BS	EOB	UC					f	o	w		F	O	W	6
0111	DEL	IL	PRE	EOT					g	p	x		G	P	X	7
1000									h	q	y		H	Q	Y	8
1001									i	r	z		I	R	Z	9
1010			SM		¢	!		:								
1011					.	$	,	#								
1100					<	*	%	@								
1101					(	)	–	'								
1110					+	;	>	=								
1111					|	—	?	"								

NULL, Null/Idle
PF, Punch off
HT, Horizontal tab
LC, Lower case
DEL, Delete
RES, Restore
NL, New line
BS, Backspace
IL, Idle
BYP, Bypass
LF, Line feed
EOB, End of block
PRE, Prefix
SM, Set mode
PN, Punch on
RS, Reader stop
UC, Upper case
EOT, End of transmission
SP, Space

Format

7	6	5	4	3	2	1	0

Appendix 2

Electrical Principles

This Appendix contains a brief description of the electrical principles used in the main body of the book. It is intended for readers without a detailed knowledge of electronics and contains only enough detail to enable them to follow the main text.

2.1 OHM'S LAW

The fundamental relationship between voltage, current and resistance which forms the basis of all electrical circuits is known as Ohm's Law and is usually expressed as:

$$\underset{\text{(volts)}}{\text{Voltage}} = \underset{\text{(amps)}}{\text{Current}} \times \underset{\text{(ohms)}}{\text{Resistance}}$$

or

$$V = I \times R$$

For example, if a voltage of 10 volts is applied to a circuit with a load resistance of 500 ohms (Fig. A.1), then the current flowing is given by:

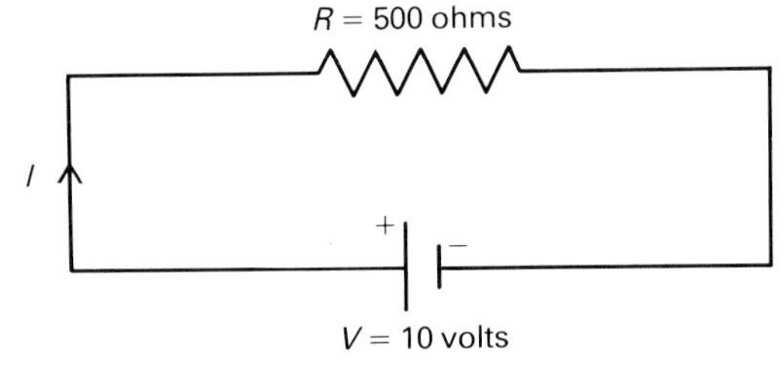

Fig. A.1. A single resistance.

$$I = \frac{V}{R} = \frac{10}{500} = 0.02 \text{ amps } (= 20 \text{ milliamps})$$

2.2 RESISTORS IN SERIES AND PARALLEL

There are two ways in which the components of an electrical circuit can be connected: in series or in parallel.

In series

When connected in series, the current passes through one component before moving to the next. Ohm's law can be used to calculate the current flowing in the circuit by dividing the applied voltage by the total resistance of the circuit. See the example circuit given in Fig. A.2.

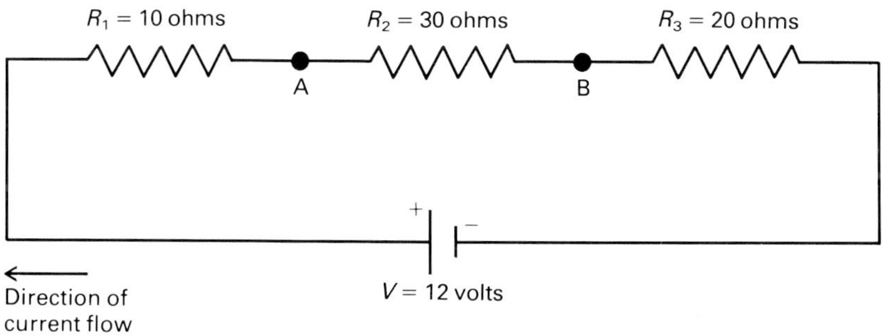

Fig. A.2. Resistors in series.

The total resistance (R_t) = $R_1 + R_2 + R_3$ ohms

$$R_t = 10 + 30 + 20 = 60 \text{ ohms}$$

and the current flowing is given by

$$I = \frac{V}{R_t} = \frac{12}{60} = 0.2 \text{ amps } (= 200 \text{ milliamps})$$

The voltage drop across resistance R_1 is

$$V_1 = I \times R_1 = 0.2 \times 10 = 2 \text{ volts}$$

so that the voltage at A is 12 − 2 = 10 volts.
The voltage drop across resistance R_2 is

$$V_2 = I \times R_2 = 0.2 \times 30 = 6 \text{ volts}$$

so that the voltage at point B is 4 volts.

In parallel

When connected in parallel, the resistors are effectively linked side by side and the supplied voltage is applied across each, as shown in Fig. A.3.

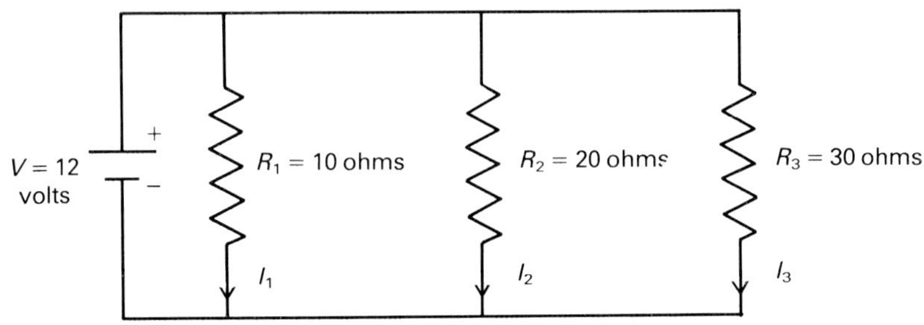

Fig. A.3. Resistors in parallel.

$$\text{The current through } R_1 (I_1) = \frac{V}{R_1} = \frac{12}{10} = 1.2 \text{ amps}$$

$$\text{The current through } R_2 (I_2) = \frac{V}{R_2} = \frac{12}{20} = 0.6 \text{ amps}$$

$$\text{The current through } R_3 (I_3) = \frac{V}{R_3} = \frac{12}{30} = 0.4 \text{ amps}$$

The total current (I_t) is therefore $1.2 + 0.6 + 0.4 = 2.2$ amps

$$\text{or } I_t = \frac{V}{R_1} + \frac{V}{R_2} + \frac{V}{R_3} = V \times \left(\frac{1}{R_1} + \frac{1}{R_2} + \frac{1}{R_3} \right) = V \times \frac{1}{R_t}$$

Thus the combined resistance of resistors in parallel can be calculated using the formula:

$$\frac{1}{R_t} = \frac{1}{R_1} + \frac{1}{R_2} + \frac{1}{R_3}$$

2.3 KIRCHHOFF'S LAWS

An electrical circuit may be made up of many components connected together in complex ways. Each point at which three or more components are connected together is known as a node and each connection between nodes is called a branch. A closed circuit formed by three or more branches is known as a loop. Figure A.4 shows a circuit with four nodes and three loops.

Kirchhoff's Laws are used to calculate the currents flowing in the various branches of complex circuits like the one shown in Fig. A.4.

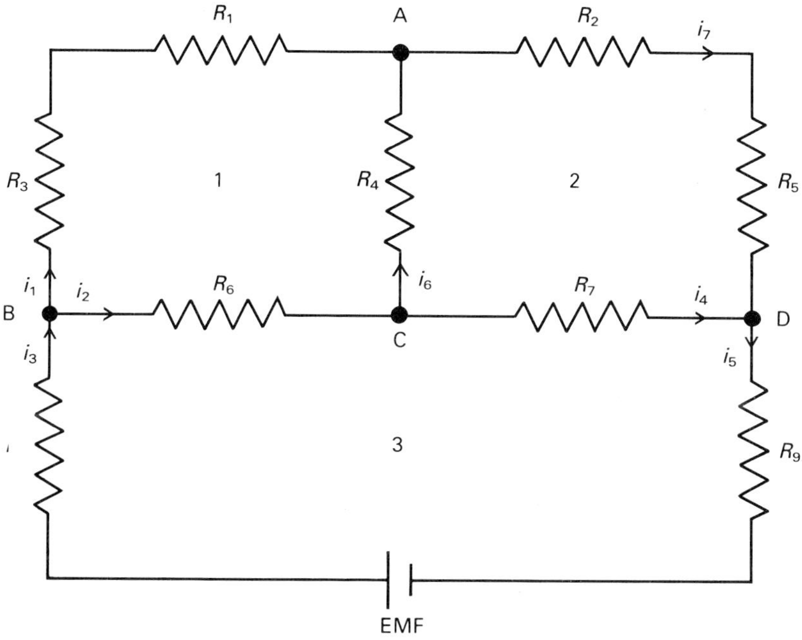

Fig. A.4. An Electrical Circuit (with 4 node & 3 loops).

Kirchhoff's First Law

At each node, the sum of the currents flowing into the node is equal to the sum of those leaving it.

At node B in Fig. A.4, therefore,

$$i_3 = i_1 + i_2$$

Kirchhoff's Second Law

In each circuit loop, the sum of the products of resistance and current in each branch is equal to the algebraic sum of the electromotive forces (EMFs) in the circuit.

For loop 3 in the circuit shown in Fig. A.4,

$$\text{EMF} = i_3R_8 + i_2R_6 + i_4R_7 + i_5R_9$$

For loop 1 some of the currents are not flowing in the same clockwise direction as they are for loop 3, and for loop 1 Kirchhoff's Second Law gives

$$0 = i_1R_3 + i_1R_1 - i_6R_4 - i_2R_6$$

since the total EMF in this loop is zero.

Appendix 3

Programming Aid

Instruction	Forms	Addressing Modes															Description	5	3	2	1	0
		Immediate			Direct			Indexed			Extended			Inherent								
		Op	~	#	Op	~	#	Op	~	#	Op	~	#	Op	~	#		H	N	Z	V	C
ABX														3A	3	1	B + X → X (Unsigned)	•	•	•	•	•
ADC	ADCA	89	2	2	99	4	2	A9	4 +	2 +	B9	5	3				A + M + C → A	↕	↕	↕	↕	↕
	ADCB	C9	2	2	D9	4	2	E9	4 +	2 +	F9	5	3				B + M + C → B	↕	↕	↕	↕	↕
ADD	ADDA	8B	2	2	9B	4	2	AB	4 +	2 +	BB	5	3				A + M → A	↕	↕	↕	↕	↕
	ADDB	CB	2	2	DB	4	2	EB	4 +	2 +	FB	5	3				B + M → B	↕	↕	↕	↕	↕
	ADDD	C3	4	3	D3	6	2	E3	6 +	2 +	F3	7	3				D + M:M + 1 → D	•	↕	↕	↕	↕
AND	ANDA	84	2	2	94	4	2	A4	4 +	2 +	B4	5	3				A Λ M → A	•	↕	↕	0	•
	ANDB	C4	2	2	D4	4	2	E4	4 +	2 +	F4	5	3				B Λ M → B	•	↕	↕	0	•
	ANDCC	1C	3	2													CC Λ IMM → CC					7
ASL	ASLA													48	2	1	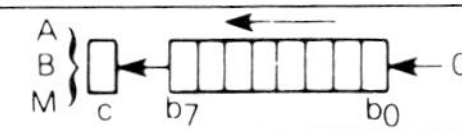	8	↕	↕	↕	↕
	ASLB													58	2	1		8	↕	↕	↕	↕
	ASL				08	6	2	68	6 +	2 +	78	7	3					8	↕	↕	↕	↕
ASR	ASRA													47	2	1	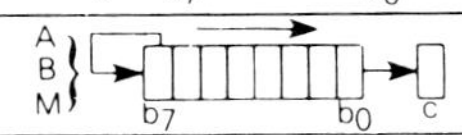	8	↕	↕	•	↕
	ASRB													57	2	1		8	↕	↕	•	↕
	ASR				07	6	2	67	6 +	2 +	77	7	3					8	↕	↕	•	↕
BIT	BITA	85	2	2	95	4	2	A5	4 +	2 +	B5	5	3				Bit Test A (M Λ A)	•	↕	↕	0	•
	BITB	C5	2	2	D5	4	2	E5	4 +	2 +	F5	5	3				Bit Test B (M Λ B)	•	↕	↕	0	•
CLR	CLRA													4F	2	1	0 → A	•	0	1	0	0
	CLRB													5F	2	1	0 → B	•	0	1	0	0
	CLR				0F	6	2	6F	6 +	2 +	7F	7	3				0 → M	•	0	1	0	0
CMP	CMPA	81	2	2	91	4	2	A1	4 +	2 +	B1	5	3				Compare M from A	8	↕	↕	↕	↕
	CMPB	C1	2	2	D1	4	2	E1	4 +	2 +	F1	5	3				Compare M from B	8	↕	↕	↕	↕
	CMPD	10	5	4	10	7	3	10	7 +	3 +	10	8	4				Compare M:M + 1 from D	•	↕	↕	↕	↕
		83			93			A3			B3											
	CMPS	11	5	4	11	7	3	11	7 +	3 +	11	8	4				Compare M:M + 1 from S	•	↕	↕	↕	↕
		8C			9C			AC			BC											
	CMPU	11	5	4	11	7	3	11	7 +	3 +	11	8	4				Compare M:M + 1 from U	•	↕	↕	↕	↕
		83			93			A3			B3											
	CMPX	8C	4	3	9C	6	2	AC	6 +	2 +	BC	7	3				Compare M:M + 1 from X	•	↕	↕	↕	↕
	CMPY	10	5	4	10	7	3	10	7 +	3 +	10	8	4				Compare M:M + 1 from Y	•	↕	↕	↕	↕
		8C			9C			AC			BC											

COM	COMA													43	2	1	$\overline{A} \to A$	•	↕	↕	0	1
	COMB													53	2	1	$\overline{B} \to B$	•	↕	↕	0	1
	COM				03	6	2	63	6+	2+	73	7	3				$\overline{M} \to M$	•	↕	↕	0	1
CWAI		3C	20	2										3C	20	2	CC Λ IMM → CC Wait for Interrupt					7
DAA														19	2	1	Decimal Adjust A	•	↕	↕	0	↕
DEC	DECA													4A	2	1	A − 1 → A	•	↕	↕	↕	•
	DECB													5A	2	1	B − 1 → B	•	↕	↕	↕	•
	DEC				0A	6	2	6A	6+	2+	7A	7	3				M − 1 → M	•	↕	↕	↕	•
EOR	EORA	88	2	2	98	4	2	A8	4+	2+	B8	5	3				A ∀ M → A	•	↕	↕	0	•
	EORB	C8	2	2	D8	4	2	E8	4+	2+	F8	5	3				B ∀ M → B	•	↕	↕	0	•
EXG	R1, R2													1E	7	2	R1 ↔ R2[2]	•	•	•	•	•
INC	INCA													4C	2	1	A + 1 → A	•	↕	↕	↕	•
	INCB													5C	2	1	B + 1 → B	•	↕	↕	↕	•
	INC				0C	6	2	6C	6+	2+	7C	7	3				M + 1 → M	•	↕	↕	↕	•
JMP					0E	3	2	6E	3+	2+	7E	4	3				$EA^3 \to PC$	•	•	•	•	•
JSR					9D	7	2	AD	7+	2+	BD	8	3				Jump to Subroutine	•	•	•	•	•
LD	LDA	86	2	2	96	4	2	A6	4+	2+	B6	5	3				M → A	•	↕	↕	0	•
	LDB	C6	2	2	D6	4	2	E6	4+	2+	F6	5	3				M → B	•	↕	↕	0	•
	LDD	CC	3	3	DC	5	2	EC	5+	2+	FC	6	3				M:M + 1 → D	•	↕	↕	0	•
	LDS	10 CE	4	4	10 DE	6	3	10 EE	6+	3+	10 FE	7	4				M:M + 1 → S	•	↕	↕	0	•
	LDU	CE	3	3	DE	5	2	EE	5+	2+	FE	6	3				M:M + 1 → U	•	↕	↕	0	•
	LDX	8E	3	3	9E	5	2	AE	5+	2+	BE	6	3				M:M + 1 → X	•	↕	↕	0	•
	LDY	10 8E	4	4	10 9E	6	3	10 AE	6+	3+	10 BE	7	4				M:M + 1 → Y	•	↕	↕	0	•
LEA	LEAS							32	4+	2+							$EA^3 \to S$	•	•	•	•	•
	LEAU							33	4+	2+							$EA^3 \to U$	•	•	•	•	•
	LEAX							30	4+	2+							$EA^3 \to X$	•	•	↕	•	•
	LEAY							31	4+	2+							$EA^3 \to Y$	•	•	↕	•	•

Legend:

OP	Operation Code (Hexadecimal)	M	Complement of M	↕	Test and set if true, cleared otherwise
~	Number of MPU Cycles	→	Transfer Into	•	Not Affected
#	Number of Program Bytes	H	Half-carry (from bit 3)	CC	Condition Code Register
+	Arithmetic Plus	N	Negative (sign bit)	:	Concatenation
−	Arithmetic Minus	Z	Zero (byte)	V	Logical or
•	Multiply	V	Overflow, 2's complement	Λ	Logical and
		C	Carry from bit 7	∀	Logical Exclusive or

Instruction	Forms	Immediate Op	Immediate ~	Immediate #	Direct Op	Direct ~	Direct #	Indexed[1] Op	Indexed[1] ~	Indexed[1] #	Extended Op	Extended ~	Extended #	Inherent Op	Inherent ~	Inherent #	Description	5 H	3 N	2 Z	1 V	0 C
LSL	LSLA													48	2	1	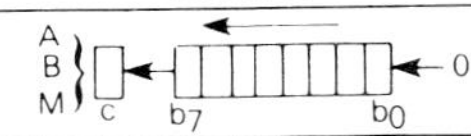	•	↕	↕	↕	↕
	LSLB													58	2	1		•	↕	↕	↕	↕
	LSL				08	6	2	68	6 +	2 +	78	7	3					•	↕	↕	↕	↕
LSR	LSRA													44	2	1	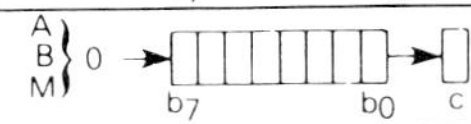	•	0	↕	•	↕
	LSRB													54	2	1		•	0	↕	•	↕
	LSR				04	6	2	64	6 +	2 +	74	7	3					•	0	↕	•	↕
MUL														3D	11	1	A × B → D (Unsigned)	•	•	↕	•	9
NEG	NEGA													40	2	1	$\overline{A}$ + 1 → A	8	↕	↕	↕	↕
	NEGB													50	2	1	$\overline{B}$ + 1 → B	8	↕	↕	↕	↕
	NEG				00	6	2	60	6 +	2 +	70	7	3				$\overline{M}$ + 1 → M	8	↕	↕	↕	↕
NOP														12	2	1	No Operation	•	•	•	•	•
OR	ORA	8A	2	2	9A	4	2	AA	4 +	2 +	BA	5	3				A V M → A	•	↕	↕	0	•
	ORB	CA	2	2	DA	4	2	EA	4 +	2 +	FA	5	3				B V M → B	•	↕	↕	0	•
	ORCC	1A	3	2													CC V IMM → CC				7	
PSH	PSHS	34	5 + [4]	2													Push Registers on S Stack	•	•	•	•	•
	PSHU	36	5 + [4]	2													Push Registers on U Stack	•	•	•	•	•
PUL	PULS	35	5 + [4]	2													Pull Registers from S Stack	•	•	•	•	•
	PULU	37	5 + [4]	2													Pull Registers from U Stack	•	•	•	•	•
ROL	ROLA													49	2	1	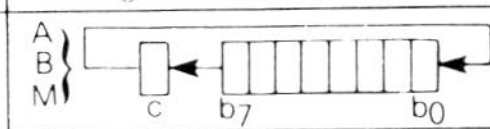	•	↕	↕	↕	↕
	ROLB													59	2	1		•	↕	↕	↕	↕
	ROL				09	6	2	69	6 +	2 +	79	7	3					•	↕	↕	↕	↕
ROR	RORA													46	2	1	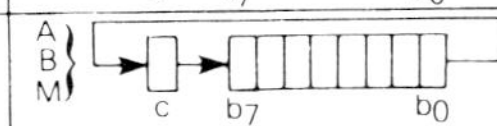	•	↕	↕	•	↕
	RORB													56	2	1		•	↕	↕	•	↕
	ROR				06	6	2	66	6 +	2 +	76	7	3					•	↕	↕	•	↕
RTI														3B	6/15	1	Return From Interrupt					7
RTS														39	5	1	Return from Subroutine	•	•	•	•	•
SBC	SBCA	82	2	2	92	4	2	A2	4 +	2 +	B2	5	3				A − M − C → A	8	↕	↕	↕	↕
	SBCB	C2	2	2	D2	4	2	E2	4 +	2 +	F2	5	3				B − M − C → B	8	↕	↕	↕	↕
SEX														1D	2	1	Sign Extend B into A	•	↕	↕	0	•

ST	STA				97	4	2	A7	4+	2+	B7	5	3				A→M	•	↕	↕	0	•
	STB				D7	4	2	E7	4+	2+	F7	5	3				B→M	•	↕	↕	0	•
	STD				DD	5	2	ED	5+	2+	FD	6	3				D→M:M+1	•	↕	↕	0	•
	STS				10 DF	6	3	10 EF	6+	3+	10 FF	7	4				S→M:M+1	•	↕	↕	0	•
	STU				DF	5	2	EF	5+	2+	FF	6	3				U→M:M+1	•	↕	↕	0	•
	STX				9F	5	2	AF	5+	2+	BF	6	3				X→M:M+1	•	↕	↕	0	•
	STY				10 9F	6	3	10 AF	6+	3+	10 BF	7	4				Y→M:M+1	•	↕	↕	0	•
SUB	SUBA	80	2	2	90	4	2	A0	4+	2+	B0	5	3				A − M→A	8	↕	↕	↕	↕
	SUBB	C0	2	2	D0	4	2	E0	4+	2+	F0	5	3				B − M→B	8	↕	↕	↕	↕
	SUBD	83	4	3	93	6	2	A3	6+	2+	B3	7	3				D − M:M+1→D	•	↕	↕	↕	↕
SWI	SWI[6]													3F	19	1	Software Interrupt 1	•	•	•	•	•
	SWI[6]													10 3F	20	2	Software Interrupt 2	•	•	•	•	•
	SWI[6]													11 3F	20	1	Software Interrupt 3	•	•	•	•	•
SYNC														13	≥2	1	Synchronize to Interrupt	•	•	•	•	•
TFR	R1, R2													1F	7	2	R1→R2[2]	•	•	•	•	•
TST	TSTA													4D	2	1	Test A	•	↕	↕	0	•
	TSTB													5D	2	1	Test B	•	↕	↕	0	•
	TST				0D	6	2	6D	6+	2+	7D	7	3				Test M	•	↕	↕	0	•

Notes:

1. This column gives a base cycle and byte count. To obtain total count, add the values obtained from the INDEXED ADDRESSING MODE table.
2. R1 and R2 may be any pair of 8 bit or any pair of 16 bit registers.
   The 8 bit registers are: A, B, CC, DP
   The 16 bit registers are: X, Y, U, S, D, PC
3. EA is the effective address.
4. The PSH and PUL instructions require 5 cycles plus 1 cycle for each **byte** pushed or pulled.
5. 5(6) means: 5 cycles if branch not taken, 6 cycles if taken (Branch instructions).
6. SWI sets I and F bits. SWI2 and SWI3 do not affect I and F.
7. Conditions Codes set as a direct result of the instruction.
8. Value of half-carry flag is undefined.
9. Special Case — Carry set if b7 is SET.

Branch Instructions

Instruction	Forms	Addressing Mode Relative OP	~5	#	Description	5 H	3 N	2 Z	1 V	0 C
BCC	BCC	24	3	2	Branch C = 0	•	•	•	•	•
	LBCC	10 24	5(6)	4	Long Branch C = 0	•	•	•	•	•
BCS	BCS	25	3	2	Branch C = 1	•	•	•	•	•
	LBCS	10 25	5(6)	4	Long Branch C = 1	•	•	•	•	•
BEQ	BEQ	27	3	2	Branch Z = 0	•	•	•	•	•
	LBEQ	10 27	5(6)	4	Long Branch Z = 0	•	•	•	•	•
BGE	BGE	2C	3	2	Branch ≥ Zero	•	•	•	•	•
	LBGE	10 2C	5(6)	4	Long Branch ≥ Zero	•	•	•	•	•
BGT	BGT	2E	3	2	Branch > Zero	•	•	•	•	•
	LBGT	10 2E	5(6)	4	Long Branch > Zero	•	•	•	•	•
BHI	BHI	22	3	2	Branch Higher	•	•	•	•	•
	LBHI	10 22	5(6)	4	Long Branch Higher	•	•	•	•	•
BHS	BHS	24	3	2	Branch Higher or Same	•	•	•	•	•
	LBHS	10 24	5(6)	4	Long Branch Higher or Same	•	•	•	•	•
BLE	BLE	2F	3	2	Branch ≤ Zero	•	•	•	•	•
	LBLE	10 2F	5(6)	4	Long Branch ≤ Zero	•	•	•	•	•
BLO	BLO	25	3	2	Branch lower	•	•	•	•	•
	LBLO	10 25	5(6)	4	Long Branch Lower	•	•	•	•	•
BLS	BLS	23	3	2	Branch Lower or Same	•	•	•	•	•
	LBLS	10 23	5(6)	4	Long Branch Lower or Same	•	•	•	•	•
BLT	BLT	2D	3	2	Branch < Zero	•	•	•	•	•
	LRLT	10 2D	5(6)	4	Long Branch < Zero	•	•	•	•	•
BMI	BMI	2B	3	2	Branch Minus	•	•	•	•	•
	LBMI	10 2B	5(6)	4	Long Branch Minus	•	•	•	•	•
BNE	BNE	26	3	2	Branch Z ≠ 0	•	•	•	•	•
	LBNE	10 26	5(6)	4	Long Branch Z ≠ 0	•	•	•	•	•
BPL	BPL	2A	3	2	Branch Plus	•	•	•	•	•
	LBPL	10 2A	5(6)	4	Long Branch Plus	•	•	•	•	•
BRA	BRA	20	3	2	Branch Always	•	•	•	•	•
	LBRA	16	5	3	Long Branch Always	•	•	•	•	•
BRN	BRN	21	3	2	Branch Never	•	•	•	•	•
	LBRN	10 21	5	4	Long Branch Never	•	•	•	•	•
BSR	BSR	8D	7	2	Branch to Subroutine	•	•	•	•	•
	LBSR	17	9	3	Long Branch to Subroutine	•	•	•	•	•
BVC	BVC	28	3	2	Branch V = 0	•	•	•	•	•
	LBVC	10 28	5(6)	4	Long Branch V = 0	•	•	•	•	•
BVS	BVS	29	3	2	Branch V = 1	•	•	•	•	•
	LBVS	10 29	5(6)	4	Long Branch V = 1	•	•	•	•	•

SIMPLE BRANCHES

	OP	~	#
BRA	20	3	2
LBRA	16	5	3
BRN	21	3	2
LBRN	1021	5	4
BSR	8D	7	2
LBSR	17	9	3

SIMPLE CONDITIONAL BRANCHES (Notes 1-4)

Test	True	OP	False	OP
N = 1	BMI	2B	BPL	2A
Z = 1	BEQ	27	BNE	26
V = 1	BVS	29	BVC	28
C = 1	BCS	25	BCC	24

SIGNED CONDITIONAL BRANCHES (Notes 1-4)

Test	True	OP	False	OP
r > m	BGT	2E	BLE	2F
r ≥ m	BGE	2C	BLT	2D
r = m	BEQ	27	BNE	26
r ≤ m	BLE	2F	EGT	2E
r < m	BLT	2D	EGE	2C

UNSIGNED CONDITIONAL BRANCHES (Notes 1-4)

Test	True	OP	False	OP
r > m	BHI	22	BLS	23
r ≥ m	BHS	24	BLO	25
r = m	BEQ	27	BNE	26
r ≤ m	BLS	23	BHI	22
r < m	BLO	25	BHS	24

Notes:

1. All conditional branches have both short and long variations.
2. All short branches are 2 bytes and require 3 cycles.
3. All conditional long branches are formed by prefixing the short branch opcode with $10 and using a 16-bit destination offset.
4. All conditional long branches require 4 bytes and 6 cycles if the branch is taken or 5 cycles if the branch is not taken.

INDEXED ADDRESSING MODE TABLE

Type	Forms	Non Indirect				Indirect			
		Assembler Form	Postbyte OP Code	$\overset{+}{\sim}$	$\overset{+}{\#}$	Assembler Form	Postbyte OP Code	$\overset{+}{\sim}$	$\overset{+}{\#}$
Constant Offset From R	No Offset	,R	1RR00100	0	0	[,R]	1RR10100	3	0
(2's Complement Offsets)	5 Bit Offset	n, R	0RRnnnnn	1	0	defaults to 8-bit			
	8 Bit Offset	n, R	1RR01000	1	1	[n, R]	1RR11000	4	1
	16 Bit Offset	n, R	1RR01001	4	2	[n, R]	1RR11001	7	2
Accumulator Offset From R	A Register Offset	A, R	1RR00110	1	0	[A, R]	1RR10110	4	0
(2's Complement Offsets)	B Register Offset	B, R	1RR00101	1	0	[B, R]	1RR10101	4	0
	D Register Offset	D, R	1RR01011	4	0	[D, R]	1RR11011	7	0
Auto Increment/Decrement R	Increment By 1	,R+	1RR00000	2	0	not allowed			
	Increment By 2	,R++	1RR00001	3	0	[,R++]	1RR10001	6	0
	Decrement By 1	,−R	1RR00010	2	0	not allowed			
	Decrement By 2	,−−R	1RR00011	3	0	[,−−R]	1RR10011	6	0
Constant Offset From PC	8 Bit Offset	n, PC	1xx01100	1	1	[n, PC]	1xx11100	4	1
(2's Complement Offsets)	16 Bit Offset	n, PC	1xx01101	5	2	[n, PC]	1xx11101	8	2
Extended Indirect	16 Bit Address	—	—	—	—	[n]	10011111	5	2

R = X, Y, U or S
x = Don't Care

RR:
00 = X
01 = Y
10 = U
11 = S

$\overset{+}{\sim}$ and $\overset{+}{\#}$ indicate the number of additional cycles and bytes for the particular variation.

Index